®

References for the Rest of Us! ®

COMPUTER BOOK SERIES FROM IDG

Are you intimidated and confused by computers? Do you find that traditional manuals are overloaded with technical details you'll never use? Do your friends and family always call you to fix simple problems on their PCs? Then the *...For Dummies* ® computer book series from IDG Books Worldwide is for you.

...For Dummies books are written for those frustrated computer users who know they aren't really dumb but find that PC hardware, software, and indeed the unique vocabulary of computing make them feel helpless. *...For Dummies* books use a lighthearted approach, a down-to-earth style, and even cartoons and humorous icons to diffuse computer novices' fears and build their confidence. Lighthearted but not lightweight, these books are a perfect survival guide for anyone forced to use a computer.

Already, hundreds of thousands of satisfied readers agree. They have made *...For Dummies* books the #1 introductory level computer book series and have written asking for more. So, if you're looking for the most fun and easy way to learn about computers, look to *...For Dummies* books to give you a helping hand.

TM

IDG BOOKS WORLDWIDE

MORE
INTERNET
FOR
DUMMIES®
3RD EDITION

by John R. Levine
and Margaret Levine Young

Foreword by Ted Nelson

IDG Books Worldwide, Inc.
An International Data Group Company

Foster City, CA ♦ Chicago, IL ♦ Indianapolis, IN ♦ Southlake, TX

MORE Internet For Dummies®, 3rd Edition

Published by

IDG Books Worldwide, Inc.
An International Data Group Company
919 E. Hillsdale Blvd.
Suite 400
Foster City, CA 94404
`http://www.idgbooks.com` (IDG Books Worldwide Web site)
`http://www.dummies.com` (Dummies Press Web site)

Library of Congress Catalog Card No.: 97-70735

ISBN: 0-7645-0135-6

Printed in the United States of America

10 9 8 7 6 5 4 3 2 1

1B/RT/QV/ZX/IN

Distributed in the United States by IDG Books Worldwide, Inc.

Distributed by Macmillan Canada for Canada; by Transworld Publishers Limited in the United Kingdom and Europe; by WoodsLane Pty. Ltd. for Australia; by WoodsLane Enterprises Ltd. for New Zealand; by Longman Singapore Publishers Ltd. for Singapore, Malaysia, Thailand, and Indonesia; by Simron Pty. Ltd. for South Africa; by Toppan Company Ltd. for Japan; by Distribuidora Cuspide for Argentina; by Livraria Cultura for Brazil; by Ediciencia S.A. for Ecuador; by Addison-Wesley Publishing Company for Korea; by Ediciones ZETA S.C.R. Ltda. for Peru; by WS Computer Publishing Company, Inc., for the Philippines; by Unalis Corporation for Taiwan; by Contemporanea de Ediciones for Venezuela. Authorized Sales Agent: Anthony Rudkin Associates for the Middle East and North Africa.

For general information on IDG Books Worldwide's books in the U.S., please call our Consumer Customer Service department at 800-762-2974. For reseller information, including discounts and premium sales, please call our Reseller Customer Service department at 800-434-3422.

For information on where to purchase IDG Books Worldwide's books outside the U.S., please contact our International Sales department at 415-655-3023 or fax 415-655-3299.

For information on foreign language translations, please contact our Foreign & Subsidiary Rights department at 415-655-3021 or fax 415-655-3281.

For sales inquiries and special prices for bulk quantities, please contact our Sales department at 415-655-3200 or write to the address above.

For information on using IDG Books Worldwide's books in the classroom or for ordering examination copies, please contact our Educational Sales department at 800-434-2086 or fax 817-251-8174.

For press review copies, author interviews, or other publicity information, please contact our Public Relations department at 415-655-3000 or fax 415-655-3299.

For authorization to photocopy items for corporate, personal, or educational use, please contact Copyright Clearance Center, 222 Rosewood Drive, Danvers, MA 01923, or fax 508-750-4470.

is a trademark under exclusive license to IDG Books Worldwide, Inc., from International Data Group, Inc.

About the Authors

John R. Levine was a member of a computer club in high school (before high school students, or even high schools, had computers) where he met Theodor H. Nelson, the author of *Computer Lib/Dream Machines* and the inventor of hypertext, who reminded us that computers should not be taken seriously and that everyone can and should understand and use computers.

John wrote his first program in 1967 on an IBM 1130 (a computer roughly as powerful as your typical modern digital wristwatch, only more difficult to use). He became an official system administrator of a networked computer at Yale in 1975. He began working part-time for a computer company, of course, in 1977 and has been in and out of the computer and network biz ever since. He got his company on Usenet (see Chapter 2) early enough that it appears in a 1982 *Byte* magazine article in a map of Usenet, which then was so small that the map fit on half a page.

John used to spend most of his time writing software, but now he mostly writes books (including *UNIX For Dummies, The Internet For Dummies,* and *Internet SECRETS,* all published by IDG Books Worldwide, Inc.) because it's more fun and he can do so at home in the tiny village of Trumansburg, New York, and play with his baby daughter when he's supposed to be writing. He also cohosts a weekly radio call-in show on the Internet (visit `http://iecc.com/radio` for local times) and does a fair amount of public speaking. He holds a B.A. and a Ph.D. in computer science from Yale University, but please don't hold that against him.

Unlike her peers in that 40-something bracket, **Margaret Levine Young** (`http://www.gurus.com/margy`) was exposed to computers at an early age. In high school, she got into a computer club known as the R.E.S.I.S.T.O.R.S., a group of kids who spent Saturdays in a barn fooling around with three antiquated computers. She stayed in the field throughout college against her better judgment and despite her brother John's presence as a graduate student in the computer science department. Margy graduated from Yale and went on to become one of the first microcomputer managers in the early 1980s at Columbia Pictures, where she rode the elevator with big stars whose names she wouldn't dream of dropping here.

Since then Margy has co-authored more than 16 computer books on the topics of the Internet, UNIX, WordPerfect, Microsoft Access, and (stab from the past) PC-File and Javelin, including *Dummies 101: The Internet For Windows 95, Dummies 101: Netscape Navigator, Internet FAQs: Answers to Frequently Asked Questions, UNIX For Dummies,* and *WordPerfect 7 For Windows 95 For Dummies* (all published by IDG Books Worldwide, Inc.). She met her future husband, Jordan, in the R.E.S.I.S.T.O.R.S., and her other passion is her children, Meg and Zac. She loves gardening, chickens, reading, and anything to do with eating and lives near Middlebury, Vermont.

ABOUT IDG BOOKS WORLDWIDE

Welcome to the world of IDG Books Worldwide.

IDG Books Worldwide, Inc., is a subsidiary of International Data Group, the world's largest publisher of computer-related information and the leading global provider of information services on information technology. IDG was founded more than 25 years ago and now employs more than 8,500 people worldwide. IDG publishes more than 275 computer publications in over 75 countries (see listing below). More than 60 million people read one or more IDG publications each month.

Launched in 1990, IDG Books Worldwide is today the #1 publisher of best-selling computer books in the United States. We are proud to have received eight awards from the Computer Press Association in recognition of editorial excellence and three from *Computer Currents'* First Annual Readers' Choice Awards. Our best-selling *...For Dummies*® series has more than 30 million copies in print with translations in 30 languages. IDG Books Worldwide, through a joint venture with IDG's Hi-Tech Beijing, became the first U.S. publisher to publish a computer book in the People's Republic of China. In record time, IDG Books Worldwide has become the first choice for millions of readers around the world who want to learn how to better manage their businesses.

Our mission is simple: Every one of our books is designed to bring extra value and skill-building instructions to the reader. Our books are written by experts who understand and care about our readers. The knowledge base of our editorial staff comes from years of experience in publishing, education, and journalism — experience we use to produce books for the '90s. In short, we care about books, so we attract the best people. We devote special attention to details such as audience, interior design, use of icons, and illustrations. And because we use an efficient process of authoring, editing, and desktop publishing our books electronically, we can spend more time ensuring superior content and spend less time on the technicalities of making books.

You can count on our commitment to deliver high-quality books at competitive prices on topics you want to read about. At IDG Books Worldwide, we continue in the IDG tradition of delivering quality for more than 25 years. You'll find no better book on a subject than one from IDG Books Worldwide.

John Kilcullen
CEO
IDG Books Worldwide, Inc.

Steven Berkowitz
President and Publisher
IDG Books Worldwide, Inc.

*Eighth Annual
Computer Press
Awards ≥1992*

*Ninth Annual
Computer Press
Awards ≥1993*

*Tenth Annual
Computer Press
Awards ≥1994*

*Eleventh Annual
Computer Press
Awards ≥1995*

IDG Books Worldwide, Inc., is a subsidiary of International Data Group, the world's largest publisher of computer-related information and the leading global provider of information services on information technology. International Data Group publishes over 275 computer publications in over 75 countries. Sixty million people read one or more International Data Group publications each month. International Data Group's publications include: **ARGENTINA:** Buyer's Guide, Computerworld Argentina, PC World Argentina; **AUSTRALIA:** Australian Macworld, Australian PC World, Australian Reseller News, Computerworld, IT Casebook, Network World, Publish, Webmaster; **AUSTRIA:** Computerwelt Osterreich, Networks Austria, PC Tip Austria; **BANGLADESH:** PC World Bangladesh; **BELARUS:** PC World Belarus; **BELGIUM:** Data News; **BRAZIL:** Annuário de Informática, Computerworld, Connections, Macworld, PC Player, PC World, Publish, Reseller News, Supergamepower; **BULGARIA:** Computerworld Bulgaria, Network World Bulgaria, PC & MacWorld Bulgaria; **CANADA:** CIO Canada, Client/Server World, ComputerWorld Canada, InfoWorld Canada, NetworkWorld Canada, WebWorld; **CHILE:** Computerworld Chile, PC World Chile; **COLOMBIA:** Computerworld Colombia, PC World Colombia; **COSTA RICA:** PC World Centro America; **THE CZECH AND SLOVAK REPUBLICS:** Computerworld Czechoslovakia, Macworld Czech Republic, PC World Czechoslovakia; **DENMARK:** Communications World Danmark, Computerworld Danmark, Macworld Danmark, PC World Danmark, Techworld Denmark; **DOMINICAN REPUBLIC:** PC World Republica Dominicana; **ECUADOR:** PC World Ecuador; **EGYPT:** Computerworld Middle East, PC World Middle East; **EL SALVADOR:** PC World Centro America; **FINLAND:** MikroPC, Tietoverkko, Tietoviikko; **FRANCE:** Distributique, Hebdo, Info PC, Le Monde Informatique, Macworld, Reseaux & Telecoms, WebMaster France; **GERMANY:** Computer Partner, Computerwoche, Computerwoche Extra, Computerwoche FOCUS, Global Online, Macwelt, PC Welt; **GREECE:** Amiga Computing, GamePro Greece, Multimedia World; **GUATEMALA:** PC World Centro America; **HONDURAS:** PC World Centro America; **HONG KONG:** Computerworld Hong Kong, PC World Hong Kong, Publish in Asia; **HUNGARY:** ABCD CD-ROM, Computerworld Szamitastechnika, Internetto online Magazine, PC World Hungary, PC-X Magazin Hungary; **ICELAND:** Tolvuheimur PC World Island; **INDIA:** Information Communications World, Information Systems Computerworld, PC World India, Publish in Asia; **INDONESIA:** InfoKomputer PC World, Komputek Computerworld, Publish in Asia; **IRELAND:** ComputerScope, PC Live!; **ISRAEL:** Macworld Israel, People & Computers/Computerworld; **ITALY:** Computerworld Italia, Macworld Italia, Networking Italia, PC World Italia; **JAPAN:** DTP World, Macworld Japan, Nikkei Personal Computing, OS/2 World Japan, SunWorld Japan, Windows NT World, Windows World Japan; **KENYA:** PC World East African; **KOREA:** Hi-Tech Information, Macworld Korea, PC World Korea; **MACEDONIA:** PC World Macedonia; **MALAYSIA:** Computerworld Malaysia, PC World Malaysia, Publish in Asia; **MALTA:** PC World Malta; **MEXICO:** Computerworld Mexico, PC World Mexico; **MYANMAR:** PC World Myanmar; **NETHERLANDS:** Computer! Totaal, LAN Internetworking Magazine, LAN World Buyers Guide, Macworld Netherlands, Net, WebWereld; **NEW ZEALAND:** Absolute Beginners Guide and Plain & Simple Series, Computer Buyer, Computer Industry Directory, Computerworld New Zealand, MTB, Network World, PC World New Zealand; **NICARAGUA:** PC World Centro America; **NORWAY:** Computerworld Norge, CW Rapport, Datamagasinet, Financial Rapport, Kursguide Norge, Macworld Norge, Multimediaworld Norge, PC World Ekspress Norge, PC World Nettverk, PC World Norge, PC World ProduktGuide Norge; **PAKISTAN:** Computerworld Pakistan; **PANAMA:** PC World Panama; **PEOPLE'S REPUBLIC OF CHINA:** China Computer Users, China Computerworld, China InfoWorld, China Telecom World Weekly, Computer & Communication, Electronic Design China, Electronics Today, Electronics Weekly, Game Software, PC World China, Popular Computer Week, Software Weekly, Software World, Telecom World; **PERU:** Computerworld Peru, PC World Profesional Peru, PC World SoHo Peru; **PHILIPPINES:** Click!, Computerworld Philippines, PC World Philippines, Publish in Asia; **POLAND:** Computerworld Poland, Computerworld Special Report Poland, Cyber, Macworld Poland, Networld Poland, PC World Komputer; **PORTUGAL:** Cerebro/PC World, Computerworld/Correio Informático, Dealer World Portugal, Mac*In/PC*In Portugal, Multimedia World; **PUERTO RICO:** PC World Puerto Rico; **ROMANIA:** Computerworld Romania, PC World Romania, Telecom Romania; **RUSSIA:** Computerworld Russia, Mir PK, Publish, Seti; **SINGAPORE:** Computerworld Singapore, PC World Singapore, Publish in Asia; **SLOVENIA:** Monitor; **SOUTH AFRICA:** Computing SA, Network World SA, Software World SA; **SPAIN:** Communicaciones World España, Computerworld España, Dealer World España, Macworld España, PC World España; **SRI LANKA:** Infolink PC World; **SWEDEN:** CAP&Design, Computer Sweden, Corporate Computing Sweden, Internetworld Sweden, it.branschen, Macworld Sweden, MaxiData Sweden, MikroDatorn, Natverk & Kommunikation, PC World Sweden, Windows World Sweden; **SWITZERLAND:** Computerworld Schweiz, Macworld Schweiz, PCtip; **TAIWAN:** Computerworld Taiwan, Macworld Taiwan, NEW ViSiON/Publish, PC World Taiwan, Windows World Taiwan; **THAILAND:** Publish in Asia, Thai Computerworld; **TURKEY:** Computerworld Turkiye, Macworld Turkiye, Network World Turkiye, PC World Turkiye; **UKRAINE:** Computerworld Kiev, Multimedia World Ukraine, PC World Ukraine; **UNITED KINGDOM:** Acorn User UK, Amiga Action UK, Amiga Computing UK, Apple Talk UK, Computing, Macworld, Parents and Computers UK, PC Advisor, PC Home, PSX Pro, The WEB; **UNITED STATES:** Cable in the Classroom, CIO Magazine, Computerworld, DOS World, Federal Computer Week, GamePro Magazine, InfoWorld, I-Way, Macworld, Network World, PC Games, PC World, Publish, Video Event, THE WEB Magazine, and WebMaster; online webzines: JavaWorld, NetscapeWorld, and SunWorld Online; **URUGUAY:** InfoWorld Uruguay; **VENEZUELA:** Computerworld Venezuela, PC World Venezuela; and **VIETNAM:** PC World Vietnam.
3/24/97

Dedication

Margy dedicates this book to Jordan, Meg, and Zac, for making life interesting.

John dedicates it to Tonia and Sarah Willow, not necessarily in that order.

Authors' Acknowledgments

Both authors thank Jordan Young, who wrote the chapter on Windows 95; Arnold Reinhold, who wrote the chapter on privacy; and Philippe LeRoux and Carol Baroudi, who wrote the chapter on business on the Net. This book is greatly enriched by their contributions.

We'd also like to thank our Internet providers: LightLink, in Ithaca, New York; the Finger Lakes Technologies Group, in Trumansburg, New York; The Internet Access Company, in Bedford, Massachusetts; and SoVerNet, in Bellows Falls, Vermont.

Becky Whitney was a joy to work with, as usual. (Not that we're taking you for granted, Becky!) Thanks also to the rest of the gang at IDG, especially those listed on the Publisher's Acknowledgments page.

Margy thanks Jordan, the Cornwall Elementary School, Suzy Way, Joyce Newton, and Diane Guertin, for keeping her kids busy long enough for her to revise this book. John likewise thanks Anne Bonnet, the only person other than Mom who can persuade Ms. Pook to go to sleep.

Finally, many thanks to all you smarties (not to say "wise-acres") who have sent e-mail to us here at Internet For Dummies Central. If you have ideas, comments, or complaints about this book, e-mail us at `moreint3@dummies.net`.

Also, visit our Web site at `http://net.dummies.net` for updates to this book.

Publisher's Acknowledgments

We're proud of this book; please send us your comments about it by using the IDG Books Worldwide Registration Card at the back of the book or by e-mailing us at feedback/dummies@idgbooks.com. Some of the people who helped bring this book to market include the following:

Acquisitions, Development, and Editorial

Project Editor: Rebecca Whitney

Acquisitions Editor: Gareth Hancock

Product Development Director: Mary Bednarek

Media Development Manager: Joyce Pepple

Associate Permissions Editor: Heather H. Dismore

Technical Editor: Bill Karow

Editorial Manager: Mary C. Corder

Editorial Assistant: Chris H. Collins

Production

Associate Project Coordinator: E. Shawn Aylsworth

Layout and Graphics: Brett Black, Angela F. Hunckler, Drew R. Moore, Mark C. Owens, Brent Savage

Proofreaders: Christine Sabooni, Nancy L. Reinhardt, Joel K. Draper, Dwight Ramsey, Robert Springer

Indexer: Liz Cunningham

Special Help

Suzanne Packer, Lead Copy Editor

General and Administrative

IDG Books Worldwide, Inc.: John Kilcullen, CEO; Steven Berkowitz, President and Publisher

IDG Books Technology Publishing: Brenda McLaughlin, Senior Vice President and Group Publisher

Dummies Technology Press and Dummies Editorial: Diane Graves Steele, Vice President and Associate Publisher; Judith A. Taylor, Brand Manager; Kristin A. Cocks, Editorial Director

Dummies Trade Press: Kathleen A. Welton, Vice President and Publisher; Stacy S. Collins, Brand Manager

IDG Books Production for Dummies Press: Beth Jenkins, Production Director; Cindy L. Phipps, Supervisor of Project Coordination, Production Proofreading, and Indexing; Kathie S. Schutte, Supervisor of Page Layout; Shelley Lea, Supervisor of Graphics and Design; Debbie J. Gates, Production Systems Specialist; Tony Augsburger, Supervisor of Reprints and Bluelines; Leslie Popplewell, Media Archive Coordinator

Dummies Packaging and Book Design: Patti Sandez, Packaging Specialist; Lance Kayser, Packaging Assistant; Kavish + Kavish, Cover Design

◆

The publisher would like to give special thanks to Patrick J. McGovern, without whom this book would not have been possible.

◆

Contents at a Glance

Cartoons at a Glance

By Rich Tennant • Fax: 508-546-7747 • E-mail: the5wave@tiac.net

page 129

page 31

page 237

page 311

page 7

page 277

Table of Contents

· ·

Foreword

• •

*G*eez, another edition already. Has it really been that long? *But so much has changed!* Everybody called 1995, two years ago, "the year of the Internet" — when the secret madness of computer people spread across the world like an exploding birthday cake. Now there are 25 million Internet users (some say 40 million) in America alone, and the expansion curve is going practically straight up.

The Internet, or Net, has changed radically. It went from black-and-white (originally with just keyboard commands) to a single unified hypertext system (called World Wide Web by its creator, Tim Berners-Lee, who has the nerve to tell me it was just a random name). Then the Internet went to Technicolor overnight under the mischievous pragmatic cobbling of young Marc Andreessen, who threw together the artful Mosaic program. Then, no longer welcome at the University of Illinois where he had achieved this wonder, he wandered west, fell in with good company, and wrought the Miracle of Netscape — a virtual coup d'état of the Internet, a company whose public offering shot into the billions.

Last year was the big change. To insiders, the era of personal computers was a replay. We went through the same old endless fascinations — programming tricks, business applications, operating systems, programs, languages, new chips, ho hum. But — bang — we're in a new new world.

"Internet machines," or network computers, will soon be available cheap, with none of the complications of personal computers that you've gotten to know and hate. Only a year ago it seemed astonishing that 2 million pages of text were on the Net; now that number seems small. And it looks like everyone really *will* have a home page.

But counter to myth, all information still won't be free; only some of it. And, there will still be information haves and have-notes — and copyright. Stay tuned.

Welcome to John and Margy's *MORE Internet For Dummies,* 3rd Edition, their fourth brother-and-sister book together. It is, of course, exactly the right thing to follow their excellent *UNIX For Dummies* and their phenomenally successful *The Internet For Dummies* (written with Carol Baroudi).

John is mischievous and clever and seems to know everything; Margy is clever and gentle and wise. Both are frighteningly competent. I'm terribly pleased to have the opportunity to write a foreword for them, because we've been friends for a very long time. I first met John and Margy in 1970, when they were members of the famous R.E.S.I.S.T.O.R.S. computer club of Princeton, New Jersey (Radically Emphatic Students Interested in Science, Technology and Other Research Studies). The group was playful, zany, and clever. They ranged from age 12 to 16, but were doing professional-level work in computer languages and programming. The Levine home in Princeton was one of the warmest homes I have ever seen. Bob and Ginny Levine, the kind, trusting, and astute parents of John and Margy, made it a kind of a clubhouse where everyone was welcome.

For me, the Levine household became a home away from home. My excuse for hanging out in Princeton was that I was learning so much from the kids, but in fact it was also a place where my work was appreciated, as it was not yet appreciated in the Official Computer World. John was the know-it-all patrician of the club; Margy was warm and clever and eager. Both of them seemed to understand everything, but John managed to turn his insights into a constant stream of wisecracks.

With his glasses and curly hair, John bears a curious and unplanned resemblance to the academic-looking cartoon figure of the ...*For Dummies* books, though the character preceded him in the series. (I had forgotten John had a Ph.D. till I looked over the previous volume — most Ph.D.-encumbered friends don't let you forget it.)

John is a Class A wag, but his one-liners generally take a moment to understand. His dry delivery enfolds a pithy wisecrack like a fortune cookie. You can't laugh quickly because you have to unpack it. He was always like that. When he was 16, I was driving a car full of R.E.S.I.S.T.O.R.S. around Princeton. Boisterously they called out contradictory driving instructions. "I demand triple redundancy in the directions!" I barked. It was John who replied laconically, "Right up ahead you turn right right away."

The coolest subject of our day

Now the Internet is today's cool subject. Everybody wants in on the Internet because they hear it's important, but most people don't know what it is. However, as you insiders already know from the first book, *The Internet For Dummies,* the Internet is just a bunch of computers talking to each other, kind of. The Internet is not a Thing any more than the highway system is a Thing. You connect to the highway system by building a stretch of road from your house to any other piece of road that's *already* connected to the highway system; that makes the highway include your piece of road as well. The Internet is like that. And like the highway, the Internet is there for the taking, awaiting your particular use. (Except that the asphalt is a data-sending procedure that makes sure that messages get back and forth.)

The hottest topics

Not only is the Internet a cool place, but all the hot topics are piling into it, like overheated people into a midsummer swimming pool. Everybody wants to get into interactive multimedia — ahem, the *correct* term is "hypermedia," which I coined thirty years ago — and everybody wants to produce interactive texts, movies, whatever, for the TV screen or computer screen (which will no longer be distinct from one another). The computer world is getting just like Hollywood, where everybody says he's a producer. As a matter of fact, the computer world isn't getting just *like* Hollywood, it's turning into Hollywood and vice versa — Hollywood itself is now treating hypermedia as its new frontier.

But the hypermedia are no longer just on disks that people buy. Till recently, many people have thought electronic media meant CD-ROM disks — but CD-ROM publishing isn't electronic publishing, it's publishing *plastic*. CD-ROM forces a pre-Columbian view of the world — when you get to the edge, you fall off. The limited size of the CD-ROM — 600 megabytes — means that much of the editorial effort is concerned with deciding what's in and what's out. And it's not connectable: Every CD-ROM is absolutely separate from every other CD-ROM.

Whereas with *true* electronic publishing — that is, publishing *electrons, over networks* — there are no boundaries, there is no limit on size, nothing has to be left out. The publisher can keep filling up more disks up to any size, all available online; and you the reader/viewer can keep sending for the stuff indefinitely.

(Note that when the preceding paragraph was written a couple of years ago, it was sheer speculation. Nobody was publishing big things on the network, and few could imagine it — except a few of us who expected a vast anarchic electronic publishing network. Indeed, the growth curve — and the timing — were exactly what I predicted for the explosive growth of xanadu in the 1990s. I got the events right, but the name wrong.)

So *true* electronic publishing has begun. The World Wide Web is already a wildly successful network hypermedia publishing system. We will see many more that will make available media of every kind, across the world, under many different schemes of copyright and royalty. (Each of us seems to think that he, she, or it has the answer to copyright. We shall see what works.)

But the politics of the Net have now assumed center stage. We computer crazies thought that the Net would be a place of new freedom, but now our challenge is that some Bad Guys may try to take it away from us. One challenge is freedom of privacy. Some in government circles champion a police-state approach to monitoring the Net, claiming that they have a God-given right to spy on all communications so that users can *think* that their communication is private — but the government can listen in at will.

But no actual criminal will submit to these restrictions; any high school kid can figure out a code that the government *can't* listen in on. What, then, is the point of some of these proposed cryptography laws? What the advocates of the Clipper chip seem really to want are the laws that the chip was sneakily designed to impose on us — enabling laws that will make it illegal to aid and abet cryptography, enabling laws that will allow search and confiscation of computers, enabling laws that will allow search and confiscation of any private information and data by those suspected of actually trying to hide things in a way that the government cannot read.

And now governments say that somebody else is under the bed. That latest bogeyman is the fear that children will — shhh! — be exposed to sexual materials on the Internet. Well, we let kids go to the *bathroom,* even though public restrooms may have sexual material scrawled on the walls. Some think that what the government is *really* trying to do is keep alternative sources of information from us.

Didn't a guy named Orwell talk about this quite a while ago? Welcome to the New Order. But we're getting smart about such things. This book is intended to help make you smart. New sources of information are what this book is about.

Wasting time

People ask me: Do you surf the Internet? Oh, sure — the *old* Internet.

If your idea of fun is gossip columns, want ads, card catalogs, and graffiti, then the Internet is for you. A lot of Internet enthusiasts are people who apparently have nothing better to do than send and receive electronic chitchat and Hot News and look at silly cartoons all day long.

But actually I'm talking sour grapes here: The problem really is that all that Internet stuff is too interesting. You can throw your every waking hour into it. Don't go near it unless you're good at Tearing Yourself Away. Everybody's uncle and pet ferret is putting up a page on the World Wide Web, and looking at them is like eating potato chips. Once the bag is open or the screen is on. . . .

And e-mail can eat you alive. At three minutes a message (my own average), e-mail consumes hours of prime time a week. But I sure feel more in touch than I ever did before — even though I'm now working in Japan.

So welcome back to the sequel

New kinds of moving data, winds of data, are sweeping across the world. Eddies and gusts of data, hurricanes, cyclones of data. Now, John and Margy guide you with their warmth and wit through this wild and windy world.

Ted Nelson
Sapporo HyperLab
Sapporo, Hokkaido, Japan
January 1996
Updated by John Levine, April 1997

Ted Nelson is best known for coining the terms hypertext *and* hypermedia *and for designing a worldwide network publishing system with automatic royalty in 1960, now called xanadu — soon, we hope, to become a reality.*

© 1996 Theodor Holm Nelson

Introduction

● ●

*M*ore about the Internet? We've written so much already! Are you sure that you want to know more?

We didn't have nearly enough space in our other books to tell you everything you might want to know. Also, so much has happened in the world of the Internet over the past year that we have lots of new, exciting things to report on. Getting connected to the Internet is easier than ever, more programs are available for downloading from the Net, new Web browser plug-ins let you experience sounds and video over the Net, and "push" programs even let you turn your computer into a news and stock ticker.

So welcome to *MORE Internet For Dummies*, 3rd Edition!

About This Book

This book covers lots of new stuff on the Internet, especially new things you can do on the Internet after you're connected. If you don't have an Internet connection yet, try reading Part II, "Getting Your PC a PPP Account," to decide how to proceed. If you already use the Internet and want to get more from it, skip directly to Part III, "More Ways to Waste Time Online," or Part V, "Online Odds and Ends." If you want to create your own pages on the World Wide Web, jump to Part IV, "Home Page, Ho!" If you're curious about the innards of the Net, we suggest that you browse Part VI, "Hideous Technical Details."

How to Read, or Not to Read, This Book

We think, of course, that this book is one of the finest ever written in the English language, so the most appropriate way to read it is to

- ✔ Set aside several uninterrupted hours.
- ✔ Find a comfy chair and a suitable beverage, such as (depending on your cultural background) a fine old Madeira, a double espresso, or a warm can of Diet Mr. Pibb.

> ✔ Savor each page of the book in turn.
>
> ✔ When you're done, rush out and tell all your friends to buy the book and read it the same way you did.

Unfortunately, in the hurly-burly of modern life, not everyone has the opportunity to read books in this manner, so you can also read this book in any order you want because the parts are largely independent of each other.

Conventions in This Book

When you have to type something, it looks like this: **Hello, Internet!** Type it just as you see it. In many cases, you must use the same capitalization we do. We tend to use small letters unless the program we're talking to insists on capitals. (CAPITAL LETTERS always sound to us like shouting.)

If you have to follow a complicated procedure, we spell it out step by step, with the stuff you have to do also highlighted in **boldface.** We then tell you what happens in response and what your options are.

When you have to choose commands from menus, we write File⇨Exit when we want you to choose the File command from the menu bar and then choose the Exit command from the menu that appears.

You see a great many *URLs* in this book, which are the addresses of Web pages or other information on the Internet. Chapter 2 tells you what to do with them — you can usually just type the URL in the Location box in your Web browser.

In some cases, we have much more to say about a topic than we can fit into this book. We have created a bunch of our own Web pages with more information about the Internet and the latest updates to the topics in this book. You can find them at this address:

```
http://net.dummies.net
```

(Hey, there's one of the URLs we were talking about!) In this book, when you can go to one of our Web pages for more information, you see the inimitable Whoosh icon in the margin.

Who Are We Talking To?

As we wrote this book, we assumed that

✔ You use the Internet or are interested in doing so and you don't want to turn into a nerd in the process.

✔ You have a copy of *The Internet For Dummies* lying around somewhere. This book builds on the first book, specifically the 4th Edition, and makes references to information that was fully covered there.

How This Book Is Organized

This book is split into six parts, each with its own theme. With few exceptions, each part stands on its own, so dip into the book as you see fit.

The following sections share what each part of the book contains.

Part I: We're Back!

Part I includes a refresher course on the Internet, including a round-up of the services it offers and a reminder about what to do with the URLs you see in this book, on the sides of soda cans, in car ads, and almost everywhere else.

Part II: Getting Your PC a PPP Account

In Part II, you find out how to connect your Windows PC directly to the Internet — not as a measly, lowly terminal but as a full-fledged Internet host computer. Having done so, you find out how to download, install, and use the most popular Windows Internet software for reading your mail, browsing through Usenet newsgroups, grabbing files, chatting, searching online databases, and reading the hypertext on the World Wide Web.

Part III: More Ways to Waste Time Online

In *The Internet For Dummies*, we concentrate on e-mail and the World Wide Web, the two most important Internet services. Part III of this book, however, describes lots of other ways in which the Internet can deliver you interesting information, including older Internet services that let you log on to computers and participate in online typing-based chats, and brand-new services that flash breaking news stories on your screen and let you use the Internet to talk with people in far-flung parts of the world.

Part IV: Home Page, Ho!

If you're dying to have your own home page on the World Wide Web or if you want to help your company, club, or church create Web pages, the chapters in Part IV take you through the entire process step by step.

Part V: Online Odds and Ends

Here are the interesting tidbits we've been saving for those diehard fans who are willing to read through both our volumes about the Internet. We describe how to keep your communications private on the Net, how to use the Internet effectively for business, and how to create your own domain name (such as dummies.net and greattapes.com).

Part VI: Hideous Technical Details

Part VI contains technical information for those who are so inclined. (Those who nod off at the thought of the innards of a network can just close this book and take a nap when they get to this part.)

Icons Used in This Book

This icon warns you that nerdy, technoid information is on the loose. Skip it if you don't like the looks of it.

When we describe a neat shortcut, timesaving step, or other cool little item, you see this icon.

Heads up! Watch for falling data!

When you see this icon, you find the address of some fascinating information on the Net.

Our Web pages (at http://net.dummies.net) have more fascinating information about this topic.

Talk to Us!

If you want to contact us with comments, questions, or complaints, send us e-mail at `moreint3@dummies.net`. In fact, if you just want to test whether your e-mail program works, drop us a line — our computer responds auto-magically and tells you your e-mail address. If you send a comment or question, we try to answer it. (Because we get an awful lot of e-mail, it can take a while.) Also, visit our Internet For Dummies Central Web site, at `http://net.dummies.net`, where we post information about and updates to all the *...For Dummies* books we've written.

Traditionalists can send snail mail (you know — regular old paper mail) by using the Registration Card in the back of this book. Although we read all the mail we get, we can't promise personal responses to every message.

If you want to see some information about other *...For Dummies* or *Dummies 101* books, check out the IDG Books *...For Dummies* Web site, at `http://www.dummies.com`, or write to IDG Books Worldwide, Inc., at `info@idgbooks.com`.

Part I
We're Back!

In this part . . .

*J*ust when you thought it was safe to surf the Internet, we're back with more information about the Net. This part of the book lets you dip a toe into the water by reminding you of what all those strange Internet terms (such as *Web* and *domain* and *URL*) mean. When you emerge, you'll be ready to tackle the rest of this book.

Chapter 1

Back into the Fray

*W*elcome to *MORE Internet For Dummies,* 3rd Edition, updated to include the latest stuff we could find about the Net! We crammed this book full of stuff that either is new since we wrote *The Internet For Dummies,* 4th Edition, or that we just couldn't fit in that book. In *The Internet For Dummies,* we helped you get connected to the Net and begin using e-mail, the World Wide Web, and a few other Internet services. In this book, you find out more about how to connect your computer to the Net, use advanced Web-browsing techniques, chat live on the Net, talk it up with Internet telephone programs, understand arcane technical details that you may rather skip, and more.

Naturally, you have read and memorized *The Internet For Dummies.* So, starting on page 31 in the discussion of V.32bis modems, we — ouch! What was that?

That was our editor slapping our wrists and pointing out that *MORE Internet For Dummies,* 3rd Edition, isn't one of those boring books for network weenies who enjoy memorizing TLAs (*t*hree-*l*etter-*a*bbreviations) — this book is for people who have a life and want to get something done. Oh, right — sorry.

What's New on the Net?

Instead, let's look at some new developments on the Internet. Here are the most exciting changes on the Net and what we have to say about them in this book:

✔ **Prices:** They continue to drop for Internet accounts and computers, and everyone and her mother are jumping on the Net. WebTV and similar devices make Internet access even easier. Face it — if you don't have an e-mail address, people are beginning to wonder what's wrong with you. The coolest accounts let you use Netscape, Internet Explorer, and other graphics-based programs. Part II of this book tells you how to get connected.

✔ **World Wide Web:** It has conquered the world, to hear the media talk about it. Web addresses ("URLs") appear everywhere, including on billboards, in television ads, and inside the caps of beer bottles. Chapter 2 talks about how to use and understand URLs, and Chapter 8 explains some tricks for effective Web surfing.

✔ **Winsock:** Microsoft Windows users have this standard way of creating cool Internet programs that run equally well no matter what brand of underlying Internet software you're using. As a result, lots of excellent new Windows Internet software is available, most notably Netscape and Internet Explorer, and we spend several chapters explaining how you can get Winsock loaded on your Windows PC. (Mac users have an equivalent standard, known as MacTCP.) Take a look at Chapters 6 and 7 to see how to get and install this cool software.

✔ **Home pages:** As the World Wide Web has swept the online world, everyone has to have a Web page containing overly personal information and pictures of their kids or their dog. (Even we do, at `http://net.dummies.net`. Although neither of us owns a dog, one of us has chickens.) We have included a few chapters (in Part IV) about how to make your very own home page.

✔ **New Internet applications:** They're arriving on the scene: VRML, Internet phone, push technology, and voice and video conferencing programs. *Push technology* turns your computer into a data receiver, by tuning you in to channels of information on the Net. VRML lets Web pages include 3-D images and animation, and Internet phone programs let you talk — really talk, with your mouth and vocal chords — to other people using the Net. After you have Winsock set up, you can try out VRML, Internet phone, and other applications available from the Net — see Chapters 8, 10, and 13.

The Internet has continued to grow faster than anyone expected, resulting in an explosion of new resources on the Net. You can find *long* books — we're talking 600 pages — that list only Internet mailing lists. Although *MORE Internet For Dummies,* 3rd Edition, isn't one of those books (the only thing more boring than reading a book full of mailing-list names is writing a book full of mailing-list names), we tell you where you can find lots of swell new stuff worth looking at.

A Brief Refresher Course

We cover the basics of Internetology in *The Internet For Dummies,* 4th Edition, and that's where you should look for the true introductory material, such as explanations of what e-mail, the World Wide Web, Usenet newsgroups, and FTP are. In case a friend borrowed your copy of that must-read book, this section is a short course in Internet Basics.

What is the Internet?

The short answer is that the Internet is a bunch of computer networks all connected together. Several million computers all over the world are connected to those networks, and if you have access to one network, you have access to all the others. (In reality, the number of computers that let you connect to them and then do anything interesting after you're connected is much smaller, but a small fraction of a million computers is still a large number of computers.)

Names and numbers

Computers on the Internet, known as *hosts* (which we suppose makes us users *parasites*) are identified by names and by numbers. The numbers are written in four parts, something like

```
205.238.207.92
```

The names are written in two or more parts, like

```
xuxa.iecc.com
```

Every machine on the Net has a number. Machines connected to more than one network, which is fairly common for large systems, have a number for each network they're connected to, although which of those numbers you use doesn't matter.

Serve that client

In business computer circles, client/server computing is considered to be really cool and totally advanced. On the Internet, we have been doing client/server computing for 25 years, only at first we didn't know that that's what it would be called. Whoop-de-doodle.

(continued)

(continued)

(Students of European literature may be reminded of the scene from Molière in which a character, newly apprised of literary styles such as poetry and prose, is astounded to discover that he has been speaking prose all his life.)

The idea of client/server computing is, in fact, simple. One computer (the server) has some resource available, such as a database. Another computer (the client) wants to use that resource, most likely because a human being wants to. Some sort of network connects the two computers.

The client sends a request to the server asking it to do something, and the server sends back the response. (If a human user is involved, the client generally presents the response to the user, perhaps after spiffing it up a little to make it look nice.) This dialogue is repeated until the client is done.

On the Internet, all the swell stuff you can do is provided by servers — Web pages by Web servers, file transfer by file-transfer servers, and so on. The program you run is considered the client, but it contacts the server automatically. In nearly all cases, the client/server business is either obvious (if you're logged in to some other machine, that machine is the server) or irrelevant. The main case in which the client/server distinction is notably evident is when the client machine is working and the server isn't. In that case, you tend to get not-very-helpful messages from the client program, along the lines of "No Route to Host," when it finds that it can't contact the server.

On some low-rent kinds of networks (if we were naming names, Novell is one of the names we would name), some computers are permanently anointed as servers and the rest are clients. On the Internet, because it's resolutely egalitarian, any computer can take either or both roles. If the computer runs server programs, it's a server; if it runs client programs, it's a client; if it runs both, as many do, it can be both.

The clienthood and serverdom are a little (to put it mildly) obscure in two cases: electronic mail and the X Windows system used on workstations to display stuff on-screen. In the case of electronic mail, when you send a message to someone, the recipient's machine is considered to be the server, the sender's machine is the client, and the service is that the server graciously agrees to accept mail from the client (sender). If you think about it for a while, this scenario makes sense — think of the server as a mailbox into which you can drop letters. In the case of X Windows, the machine with the screen on which X is displaying its windows is considered to be the server, and the program that's doing the work and telling it what to display is the client. If this scenario seems backward, that's because it is, but it's too late to do anything about it.

The Internet is a *peer-to-peer* network, which means that every computer on the Net (from a tiny laptop to a behemoth supercomputer) is, in principle, equal, and any computer can connect to any other computer. On a peer-to-peer network, any computer attached to the Net can offer services to anyone else, and many do. When you use an Internet service, the computer on the other end providing that service can be anything from a PC to a CM-5 supercomputer.

Deep down, the only thing the Internet does is to deliver data from one place to another. Interestingly, programs running on all the computers on the Net use that data delivery to provide useful (useful considering that computers are involved) services, such as electronic mail, remote file retrieval (FTP), and real-time networked versions of Dungeons and Dragons. In this book, we talk about the cool services available on the Internet. (For the extremely cool people who read *...For Dummies* books, only the coolest in computing will do.)

Most machines on the Net have a name, which is easier to remember than the numbers, unless you're blessed with a most unusual memory. Because the connection between names and numbers is quite flexible, a single host can have several names, and a single name can refer to several hosts (which is useful for a service with multiple machines and which of the machines you use doesn't matter). Much can be said about the structure of the names, but because you don't need to know anything about host names and numbers in order to use the Internet, we describe them in Chapter 21, where you can ignore the whole discussion.

Upper- and lowercase letters don't matter in host names, so `xuxa.iecc.com`, `XUXA.IECC.COM`, and `XuXa.IeCc.CoM` are all valid forms of the same name.

Essential Services

Here's a roundup of the basic services that Internet hosts support.

Electronic mail and mailing lists

Electronic mail remains the number-one service that people use on the Internet. All mail is sent to mail addresses, which look something like `moreint3@dummies.net` (that's us — drop us a line and tell us how you like the book). Each address has a name part that identifies the recipient, an at-sign (@), and a host part that identifies the host computer to which the message should be sent.

Although most addresses correspond to actual people, many of them are other things:

- **Mailing lists,** which send a message to a whole slew of people
- **Mail server robots,** which automatically send back a response
- **Gateways to other kinds of services,** such as Usenet (discussed in the section "Usenet newsgroups," later in this chapter)

Thousands of special-interest mailing lists are active on the Internet, and you can join them to exchange messages with people with interests similar to yours. The topics of lists can be quite specific — for example, one list is for dairy cattle, and a separate list is for beef cattle. See Chapter 2 for more information about mailing lists.

We discuss e-mail programs and e-mail addresses and how to send and receive e-mail in *The Internet For Dummies,* 4th Edition.

The World Wide Web (WWW or Web)

The Web is a huge collection of pages, each consisting of text, pictures, and other stuff. You can view these pages on your computer screen using a Web-browsing program such as Netscape or Internet Explorer. What makes Web pages cool is that they're linked together; when you click a link (usually underlined text) on one page, another page appears.

For example, you might start at a Web page with information about Vermont. On the listing of colleges in Vermont, you click the link for Middlebury College to see a page about the college. The page lists upcoming events, including one by Voices of the Caribbean. Clicking the link for that group takes you to the group's *home page* (the page about them on the Web). A few more clicks takes you to a page about the Dominican Republic or musical groups in the Northeast or any of a hundred other related topics. You would be amazed at what you can find on the Web!

Because the Web is so big, you may have to use a Web directory or search page to find what you want. We recommend Yahoo (at `http://www.yahoo.com`) and AltaVista (at `http://altavista.digital.com`). Chapter 2 explains what these cryptic addresses mean, and Chapter 8 has information for advanced Web surfers.

The Web supersedes Gopher, a menu-oriented way of presenting information on the Internet. It also largely replaces FTP (File Transfer Protocol) for downloading files to your computer. You may still have to use an FTP program to upload (send) files from your computer to another computer, as described in Chapter 6.

Usenet newsgroups

Usenet (or *netnews*) is a bulletin board system. Each item someone "posts" to netnews is passed from system to system until the message eventually goes to all the Usenet hosts in the world. The amount of news is enormous — close to a gigabyte per day and growing. To make sense of this flood, items are tagged with topics known as *newsgroups,* and users can look at only the newsgroups they're interested in, skipping the rest. Even within a single group, a great deal of traffic occurs, enough that spending every waking minute of your day reading news is easy to do. Tens of thousands of newsgroups exists, on every conceivable topic (and many inconceivable ones).

To read Usenet newsgroups, you need either a newsreader program or a Web browser that includes a newsreader (such as Netscape). We describe Usenet newsgroups in *The Internet For Dummies,* 4th Edition.

Live chat

Internet Relay Chat *(IRC)* lets Internet users all over the world enter into lively debates online. It's unfortunate that so much of the conversation on IRC brings new meaning to the word *banal*. See Chapter 9 to try it for yourself.

MUDs and MOOs, online worlds in which lots of people can participate at the same time, are another way to chat live on the Net and end up being much more interesting than IRC (in our humble opinions) — see Chapter 13.

Odds and Ends

A dozen other minor services are available on the Net. Most are useful only to computers and the weenies who love them — things such as a service to get the time-of-day clocks on two computers in sync or one that lets various computers on an Ethernet network check their network addresses.

Old, boring stuff

A few minor services are of use to humans:

- **Telnet** lets you to connect to a remote computer and then use that computer as though you were sitting at a plain character terminal (one that can display only text — no fancy graphics) directly connected to the remote host. Telnet used to be a very popular service but has faded in the past few years as people have moved to the much zoomier World Wide Web (see Chapter 11 if you want to try telnetting anyway).

- **Finger** lets you check on the status of a person or system, as described in Chapter 12.

- **Whois** looks up people in the official Internet directory. Whois would be a swell service except that the only people listed are the ones who run the various networks comprising the Internet. If you happen to be looking for one of those people (for example, the one of us who takes care of the computers is listed as JL7), whois is quite handy. The other 99.7 percent of the people on the Net are not listed.

- **Ping** checks to see whether a remote system is alive at all, as described in Chapter 12.

New stuff

Here's a list of some cool new services that are just coming into general use:

- ✔ **Netscape plug-ins** are programs that extend the capabilities of Netscape Navigator, the world's most popular Web browser. (Internet Explorer, the Microsoft browser, works with plug-ins too.) Plug-ins let your browser deal with new types of information on the Web, such as three-dimensional virtual worlds and interactive chats (see Chapter 13) and sound and video (see Chapter 10). Chapter 8 tells you how to find, download, and install plug-ins.

- ✔ **Internet phone programs** let you use your computer like a telephone, making long-distance calls over the Internet. You need speakers, a microphone, and an Internet phone program, which you can find out about in Chapter 10.

- ✔ **Channels** (aka push technology) are sources of information your computer can "tune in" to. Using a "tuner" program, such as Castanet (from Marimba), PointCast, or BackWeb, your computer can act like a news ticker, by displaying the latest news, weather, sports results, and stock quotes. You can also tune in to games, programs, and other information — see Chapter 8.

And now — on with the Internet!

Chapter 2

Resource, Resource, Who's Got the Resource?

● ●

In This Chapter

▶ A roundup of resource types and how to get to them

▶ Mysteries of mailing lists

▶ What about the Web?

▶ Reminders of news

▶ Facts about files

▶ Nibbling on Gopher

● ●

*H*ow many ways are available to get to Internet information, anyway? Roughly a zillion. Among the services are e-mail, the World Wide Web (WWW), Usenet newsgroups, IRC, telnet, FTP, and Gopher (we describe these services in Chapter 1). A few items arrive in other hard-to-characterize ways. What's more, a great deal of overlap occurs among the various services. You can do FTP (file transfer) using Web pages. You can use e-mail to retrieve Web pages. In this chapter, we summarize the ways to get to these different resource types, depending on which sort of hardware and software you have available. For each type, we list the ways in rough order of quality so that a fast and easy-to-use way is listed before a slow and painful one.

This chapter tells you exactly how each type of resource is described in technical Internet-ese, usually using things called URLs. You have to know this stuff in order to access the information we describe in the rest of this book.

Don't Hurl! It's Only an URL!

The World Wide Web brought us the extremely useful concept of *Uniform Resource Locators,* or *URLs.* (A big thank-you goes out to Tim Berners-Lee, the inventor of the World Wide Web, for thinking them up.) A URL, pronounced "url" or "U-R-L," is a simple and consistent way to name Internet resources. A URL consists of a resource type, a colon, and a location. The location is, in most cases, two slashes, the host name where the resource can be found, a slash, and a name on that host. Table 2-1 shows commonly used URL resource types.

Table 2-1	Types of URLs
Type	*Description*
http:	A HyperText Transfer Protocol document (something in native Web format — a Web page)
gopher:	A Gopher menu
ftp:	A directory or file on an FTP server
mailto:	An e-mail address
news:	A Usenet news item (not supported by every Web browser)
file:	A file on your own computer (useful when you create your own Web pages)

Some typical URLs are

```
http://net.dummies.net/countries
```

and

```
ftp://ftp.microsoft.com/dirmap.txt
```

The first URL is a World Wide Web page, which is accessible by HTTP (the standard scheme the Web uses). The host name is net.dummies.net, and the name on that site is countries. The second URL is a text file stored on the Microsoft FTP server.

Web-Walking Wisdom

The World Wide Web is by far the coolest thing mortal internauts can use. Unlike all the other programs we mention, Web browsers use URLs directly. What do you do if someone tells you the URL of a cool Web page or if you find a URL listed in this book? What you do varies a little depending on which Web program you use. Here are some hints for using Netscape and Internet Explorer, the most popular Web programs.

Telling Netscape about a URL

Using Netscape, simply type the URL in the Location box near the top of the Netscape window and then press Enter. Netscape shows you that URL. Easy!

Telling Internet Explorer about a URL

Because Internet Explorer grimly matches Netscape feature for feature, you won't be surprised to hear that you can type your URL in the Address box near the top of the Internet Explorer window.

Other ways to go to URLs

We often find URLs in Usenet messages we're reading. Lazy typists can find ways to avoid typing by copying the URL from the news message, which saves time and is more accurate than retyping the URL.

Here are two ways:

   ✔ Because some e-mail programs and newsreaders automatically recognize URLs, you only have to click (or maybe double-click) them to go there. You can tell when this method will work because the URL appears underlined, usually in blue type.

   ✔ If a URL appears in another program, you can use the Windows or Mac cut-and-paste feature to copy the URL into your Web browser. Select the URL with your mouse, and then press Ctrl+C to copy the URL to the Clipboard. Click in the Location or Address box of your Web browser and press Ctrl+V to paste the URL there.

You can use this same cut-and-paste method to include URLs in e-mail messages. If you want to tell your mother about a cool Web page you found, you can copy the URL of the Web page from the Location or Address box of your Web browser into an e-mail message to her. (And tell her hello from us.)

E-Mail — Not!

E-mail isn't an Internet resource. That is, e-mail isn't available to anyone except the person to whom the message is addressed. Most e-mail messages aren't archived anywhere for others to peruse. As a result, e-mail messages don't have URLs.

Put Me on the Mailing List

E-mail mailing lists are the oldest way — and still one of the most popular — for people of like interests to get together on the Net. You send and receive messages from a mailing list in the same way as you send and receive messages from individual correspondents. You can use mailing lists even if the only Internet service you have is e-mail (which is true for many people).

Because mailing lists consist of e-mail messages, the messages on mailing lists don't have URLs. Instead, to read the messages on a mailing list, you *subscribe* to the list.

The basic operation of a list is simple: Any messages sent to the list are relayed to all the list members. Other people usually reply, which creates a sequence of back-and-forth comments in a running discussion. Different lists have different characters. Some lists are sociable, and other lists are formal. Some lists have a great deal of traffic — dozens of messages per day — and other lists go for weeks or months without a message.

Immoderation and indigestion

Some mailing lists are moderated, and some lists are digests (many are both). In a *moderated* list, messages are not automatically relayed but are given to a human moderator who weeds out the irrelevant messages and forwards the approved messages. Different moderators have different styles — for some lists, practically everything is approved; for others, only a few messages are approved. Many lists are quite popular, and the moderator doesn't reject inappropriate messages but rather acts as an editor who chooses the best submissions to create a high-quality list.

Some people grumble that moderators are petty fascists who choose messages to serve their own whims. Well, we (yes, *we* — one of your authors moderates a list about a technical computer topic) do pick messages to serve our own whims, but users who grumble the most seem to be the ones whose messages need to be weeded out.

Some moderated lists are really one-way mail distributors. That is, the messages on the list come not from the subscribers but rather from some outside source. One list relays National Weather Service (NWS) hurricane announcements, for example, and all the messages on that list originate from the NWS. These announcement-only lists can be useful ways to get news by e-mail.

When a list sends out more than two or three messages a day, subscribers' mailboxes can fill quickly. A common way to lessen the mail overload is to collect all the day's messages in a single large message, known as a *digest,* which replaces the dozen little messages sent throughout the day. Some lists are available only in digest form, and other lists are available either way.

An open-and-shut case

Most mailing lists are *open,* which means that anyone can send in a message. Others are *closed,* which means that only people who subscribe to the list are allowed to send in messages. If you try to send a message to a closed list to which you don't subscribe, you get back an automatic response rejecting your message. Closed lists can sometimes be a pain: If the return address on your e-mail message doesn't exactly match your address as listed in the subscriber list, you can't send in a message. If your return address doesn't match your listed address (if your system manager changes the configuration, for example, and your address is improved from gw@musket.mtvernon.va.us to George.Washington@mtvernon.va.us), send a nice message to the person who manages the list and ask to have your new address added as one allowed to send in messages. (The next section has hints for finding the manager.)

A few lists are open to only qualified subscribers, who apply to belong to the list. A Usenet moderator's list is limited to people who moderate Usenet groups, for example. If you apply to a list with these types of restrictions, the list manager will probably ask you to show how you qualify.

Mailing-list wrangling

Be sure to remember the difference between the mailing list *administrative addresses* you write to in order to get on and off the list and the *list address* you write to in order to send messages to the list members. A common newbie mistake (and you certainly wouldn't want to be mistaken for a newbie) is to send an administrative message to the list itself. Everyone doesn't have to know that you want to subscribe or unsubscribe to the list, so send the message to the administrative address, not to the list address.

This type of mistake is particularly embarrassing because everyone on the list sees how you messed up. Don't make this mistake.

You get on and off mailing lists in three major ways. (You didn't think that getting off and on a mailing list would be simple, did you?) The way depends on whether the mailing list is run by the LISTSERV or Listproc program, the Majordomo program, or a human being. (You can tell by looking at the administrative address: See whether it's LISTSERV@something, majordomo@something, or something else.) Fortunately, they're all easy to deal with.

LISTSERV and Listproc

The most popular mailing-list maintenance software is LISTSERV, and Listproc works in almost the same way. LISTSERV and Listproc lists usually have such names as SAMPLE-L. Remember that all management-type messages, such as requests to subscribe and unsubscribe, should be addressed to listserv or listproc, not to the list address.

You can tell when you're dealing with a LISTSERV mailing list because the administrative address is LISTSERV@something. Listproc addresses look like listproc@something.

To subscribe to a LISTSERV or Listproc list, send a message to its administrative address with a single line containing the word *subscribe* or *sub,* the list name, and your name. For example, to subscribe to the sample-1 LISTSERV mailing list on the Internet host sample.org, send an e-mail message to listserv@sample.org that contains this line:

```
sub sample-1 George Washington
```

The line contains sub (short for *sub*scribe), the exact name of the mailing list you're talking about, and then your real, human name. Remember to substitute the list's real name and your name for George's in this example and send the message to the Internet LISTSERV host computer's real name. Be sure that the *subscribe* line appears in the text of your e-mail message, not in the subject line.

To get off the list, send to the same address a message containing this line:

```
signoff sample-1
```

(The command _unsubscribe_ works too.) If the list has optional digesting (urp!), you can switch between getting daily digests (see the section "Immoderation and indigestion," earlier in this chapter) and individual mail messages by sending one of the following messages to the LISTSERV address:

```
set sample-l digest
set sample-l mail
```

The `digest` message gets you the daily digest, and `mail` gets you individual mail messages.

If you have trouble getting on or off a LISTSERV list, you can contact the list manager at `OWNER-SAMPLE-L@sample.org` (which is the list name prefixed by `OWNER-`).

After you're on the list, send messages to subscribers by mailing to the list name, not to LISTSERV (`SAMPLE-L@sample.org`, for example).

Majordomo

Originally a LISTSERV wannabe, Majordomo is not the automatic mailing-list manager that everyone likes the best. Majordomo has escaped the annoying LISTSERV IBM-isms, however, such as the TENDENCY TO PUT EVERYTHING IN UPPERCASE LETTERS and the LISTSERV eight-character name limitation. To get on or off a Majordomo list, send a message to `majordomo@sample.org` (using the actual host name, of course, rather than `sample.org`).

You can tell when you're dealing with a Majordomo mailing list because the administrative address is `majordomo@something`.

To subscribe to a list, send the following message:

```
sub name-of-list
```

To unsubscribe, send this message:

```
unsub name-of-list
```

Unlike with LISTSERV, with Majordomo you _don't_ put your real name after the list name in the `sub` command. Majordomo regards whatever you type after the list name as the mailing address to use, not as the message's return address, which can come in handy if your mail system puts a bad return address on your outgoing mail.

To contact the human manager for a Majordomo list, send mail to `owner-name-of-list@sample.org`, the same way as you do with LISTSERV.

Manually maintained lists

A fair number of lists are still maintained manually by humans. To subscribe or unsubscribe to these lists, you send a polite message to the list maintainer asking to be added to or deleted from the list. For manual lists, you concoct the maintainer's address by adding `-request` to the list name; for a list named `sample`, for example, the maintainer's address is `sample-request@whatever.org`.

Humans, not being computers, sometimes leave their keyboards to eat, sleep, or otherwise have a life. (Hard to believe, isn't it?) For a manually maintained list, therefore, the maintainer can take a couple days to act on your message. We can tell you from experience that sending lots of extra messages to the maintainer doesn't get you attention any sooner, and any attention you *do* get is probably not the kind you want.

URLs for mailing lists

Unlike most of the other types of resources listed in this chapter, you can't get to a mailing list's contents via the World Wide Web. A useful URL for a mailing list doesn't exist. Many mailing lists have home pages on the Web, though, with information about the list. Some lists put archives of messages on the Web; if so, the welcome message you get when you subscribe to a list generally tells you.

For more information about mailing lists, see *The Internet For Dummies,* 4th Edition (IDG Books Worldwide, Inc.).

Usenet Newsgroups: The World's Biggest Bulletin Board

The largest volume of public information and misinformation comes flooding in through Usenet newsgroups, which currently run close to an astonishing gigabyte per day. Usenet is a system of thousands of distributed bulletin boards. You need a newsreading program, such as Free Agent, Netscape Messenger, or Microsoft Internet News on a PC; Newswatcher on a Mac; or `trn` or `nn` or `tin` on UNIX. (See *The Internet For Dummies,* 4th Edition, for information about reading Usenet newsgroups.)

Almost any system, except those that handle only mail, provides a newsreading program (or, if you're using a PC with SLIP or PPP, a news server you can use from a local news program). If you're unaccountably stuck in a newsfree environment and use a World Wide Web browser, visit `http://www.dejanews.com`, a Web site that lets you browse through the last year's Usenet messages.

Subscribing to a newsgroup

When you find out about an interesting newsgroup, tell your news program to present the newsgroup to you. To subscribe to a group you haven't read, follow the appropriate procedure in this list (we list instructions for users of each of the most common newsreading programs in use):

- **Free Agent:** Choose Group⇨Show⇨All Groups to see the complete list of groups, choose the group you want, and press Ctrl+S.

- **Netscape 4.0:** In the Message Center window, click the Add a Newsgroup icon (which looks like a little newspaper), and, in the pop-up window that appears, type the name of the group you want.

- **Netscape 3.0:** In the News window, choose Options⇨Show All Newsgroups to display the full tree of newsgroups. Scroll to the newsgroup you want, and click the box to the right of the newsgroup name so that it displays a check mark, indicating that you're subscribed.

- **Microsoft Internet News (Explorer 3.0):** Choose News⇨Newsgroups to open the newsgroup selection window. Scroll to the group you want, and double-click it to subscribe.

- **trn:** At the newsgroup selection level, press **g** and type the newsgroup name.

- **nn:** At the menu listing newsgroups, press **G** and type the newsgroup name.

- **tin:** At the screen showing newsgroups, press **g** and type the newsgroup name.

News by way of e-mail

A few Usenet groups are also available by e-mail in the form of mailing lists. The group `comp.dcom.telecom` is the same as the mailing list `telecom@eecs.nwu.edu`, and the group `comp.compilers` is the same as the mailing list `compil-l@american.edu`. Anything that appears in the group is mailed to the list and vice versa. Every few weeks, a message posted to the newsgroup `news.lists` contains a list of groups available by e-mail.

If a group doesn't have a specific parallel mailing list, there's no way to receive that group by mail.

URLs for newsgroups

Newsgroups use a URL that starts with `news:`. A newsgroup URL is useful if you want to use a Web browser to read newsgroup articles. The URL for a newsgroup looks like

```
news:news.group.name
```

For example, the `rec.gardens.orchids` newsgroup is called

```
news:rec.gardens.orchids
```

You can add URLs such as these to your Bookmark or Favorites list to give yourself a one-click shortcut to the groups you read most often. (You can't add them automatically — you have to edit the bookmarks window yourself.)

Individual news messages also have URLs, though they're nowhere nearly as useful. The URL is the message ID of the message, something like

```
news:m0vuVro-000I2vC@ivan.iecc.com
```

Your Web browser can fetch the message to which the URL corresponds only if the message is available on your Internet provider's news server. Because most messages are deleted after a week or so, these URLs are pretty evanescent.

FTP: Files Delivered to Your Door

FTP (File Transfer Protocol) is a way of sending files from one Internet host to another. A computer that stores files for transfer is called a *file server,* or *FTP server.* To get (download) files or send (upload) files, you run an *FTP client program.* If you use Winsock programs, you can use your Web browser or an FTP program. WS_FTP is a good shareware Winsock FTP client program. Most Internet software suites come with an FTP client program. Windows 95 and UNIX both come with FTP programs too (called, strangely enough, `ftp`), but you have to type a lot of commands to use them.

On many FTP servers, you don't need an account in order to grab their files. Instead, you can use *anonymous FTP,* in which you use the user name `anonymous` and your e-mail address as your password.

The Web meets FTP: URL that file

The World Wide Web has built-in features that make it a good way to get files from FTP servers. Any public FTP server has a Web URL that lets you look at the available directories and files. If the FTP server is called `sample.com` and the directory you want is `/pub/samplefiles`, the URL is

```
ftp://sample.com/pub/samplefiles
```

If you give this URL to your Web-browsing program (such as Netscape or Internet Explorer), the program automatically takes care of the details of logging in to the server, retrieving directories, and so on. Conversely, if someone gives you this URL and you don't have a Web browser, don't worry — you're not stuck. Fire up your FTP program, connect to `sample.com`, move to the `/pub` directory, and retrieve `samplefiles`.

FTP classic

You can also use a plain FTP program to retrieve files, which is often faster than cranking up an entire Web program. Here's how:

1. **Connect to the Internet.**

2. **Start your FTP program, by typing a command or clicking an icon (depending on the antiquatedness of your computer).**

   In Windows 95, for example, choose Start⇨Run, type **ftp** followed by a space and the name of the FTP server you want to connect to, and press Enter. You see an FTP window.

3. **Connect to the FTP server.**

   In our Windows 95 example, the FTP program connects for you without your having to type any other command. Other programs, such as WS_FTP, start up and *then* ask which FTP server to connect to.

4. **Log in by typing** anonymous **as your username and typing your e-mail address as the password.**

5. **Change to the directory that contains the files.**

6. **Set binary mode (unless it's a text file).**

7. **Get the file.**

For details about FTPing, see *The Internet For Dummies,* 4th Edition.

Hot Spots to Gossip with IRC

Internet Relay Chat (IRC) is one of the least organized parts of the already rather disorganized Internet. Scheduled chats happen on IRC all the time. Although there's no such thing as a URL for an IRC chat (yet), you can locate a chat using these three handy coordinates:

- The IRC network on which the chat is happening. Widely used networks include EFnet, Undernet, and DALnet, and lots of others are available.
- The name of the IRC channel, something like #dummies.
- The time that it's happening, such as 7:00 P.M. EST every Tuesday evening. IRC spans the globe along with the rest of the Internet, so when you get a time, be sure that you know what time zone it's relative to.

Readers of ...*For Dummies* and *Dummies 101* books, for example, could congregate on the #dummies channel every Thursday night at 8:00 p.m. EST on Undernet. (Go ahead — see whether anyone's there.)

See Chapter 9 for more info about IRC.

Telnet: The Next Best Thing to Being There

Telnet is the classic (that is, somewhat outdated) service that lets you log in to other computers on the Net. When you use a telnet program to log in to a computer, you have to know the name of the computer you want to connect to and the *port number* on that computer (the standard telnet port is number 23). The more interesting Telnet services are provided on nonstandard network ports. If you use a UNIX-based system, run telnet by giving the host name and, if it's nonstandard, the port number, as in this example:

```
telnet martini.eecs.umich.edu 3000
```

Windows 95 comes with a free telnet program, so you can choose Start⇨ Run and type the same thing. For more information about telnetting, see Chapter 11.

You occasionally see a telnet address written as a URL:

```
telnet://martini.eecs.umich.edu:3000/
```

You need a telnet address in this URL format if you want to use a World Wide Web browser program for telnetting. (Your browser doesn't do anything surprising — it just starts your telnet program for you, if you have one.)

Going for Gopher

Gopher is another system of organizing information about the Internet that predates the Web. (We describe Gopher in more detail in Chapter 12.) Lots of Gopher pages are still available partly because Gopher is a highly advanced information-retrieval system, but mostly because the Gopher server software is free and not difficult to set up.

To find a Gopher menu item, you have to know the name of the Gopher server and the menu choice, starting at the server's main menu.

Gopher meets the Web and gets the URL

Here's the URL for a typical Gopher item:

```
gopher://gopher.zilker.net:70/1bruces
```

This line tells you that the host is gopher.zilker.net, port 70 (the standard Gopher port, so you could have left out the port number), and that the host's pathname is 1bruces. Who knows exactly what 1bruces means? If you ask Netscape or Internet Explorer to show this URL to you, though, either one can find it.

You can also type a URL into a Gopher client program, but surgery on the name is required first. Although the host name and port number are perfectly okay, the path needs work. The problem is that Gopher items have types that are internally remembered as single digits and letters. Most notably, a Gopher menu is type 1, and a plain file is type 0. In a URL, the first character in the path part of the URL (the part after a single slash) is the item type (in this case, 1). Our earlier URL example, therefore, refers to a Gopher menu (the first 1) whose actual path is bruces (the rest of the path). You type **bruces** for your Gopher path.

You can usually get away with leaving out the path on Gopher URLs. In almost every case, an empty path gives you the main Gopher menu for the server, and you can more easily go through a few menus to find the item you want than you can unscramble the path by hand.

UNIX Gopher

If you use a UNIX-based Internet system, you can run the `gopher` program. Type **gopher** followed by the name of the Gopher server, like this:

```
gopher gopher.zilker.net
```

You can tell `gopher` which menu item you want to see. Type the `gopher` command followed by the path, host, and port. To start at the Gopher menu discussed in the preceding section, you type

```
gopher -p bruces gopher.zilker.net 70
```

Don't Take Our Word for It

Throughout this book, and especially in Chapter 14, you can find the URLs for information we find useful on the Net. The Internet is growing like crazy, however, and new resources appear literally every day. Existing resources move or get shut down. The Internet is a moving target.

Because we haven't yet figured out how to update this copy of this book after you have brought it home from the store, we have done the next best thing and put the updates on our Web server. Check it out at this Web page:

```
http://net.dummies.net/update
```

The Usenet group `comp.infosystems.announce` contains only announcements of new Internet resources, almost all of which are new Web pages or other resources, such as Gopher menus, that you can use by way of the Web. This group is strictly moderated so that no extraneous messages appear. Because messages are posted only once or twice a week, monitoring the group doesn't take much time, and all sorts of interesting new stuff appears there.

Two considerably busier newsgroups are `comp.infosystems.www.announce` and `comp.internet.net-happenings`, which have announcements of new Web sites and other online resources. Because new sites seem to appear about every 15 seconds, these groups have much to announce.

Another good idea is to use a Web index or search service, such as those listed in Chapter 14, to find the information you're looking for.

Part II
Getting Your PC a PPP Account

The 5th Wave   By Rich Tennant

©RICHTENNANT

"SINCE WE GOT IT, HE HASN'T MOVED FROM THAT SPOT FOR ELEVEN STRAIGHT DAYS. ODDLY ENOUGH THEY CALL THIS 'GETTING UP AND RUNNING' ON THE INTERNET."

In this part . . .

*1*f you use a PC and run Windows 3.1 or Windows 95, the Internet is a happening place. This part of the book talks about how to get your PC a PPP account, the type of account that makes your PC a full-fledged Internet host and lets you use cool software such as Netscape, Internet Explorer, and Eudora.

What's the best thing about the software you need to connect to and use PPP accounts? It's all freeware or shareware! You can download most of the programs you need from the Net itself or ask your Internet provider for a copy. Chapter 6 tells you how to find and download programs from the Internet, and Chapter 7 lists some programs you should consider downloading.

Chapter 3

The Coolest Way to Get Connected: Dial-up PPP Accounts

In This Chapter

▶ What are SLIP and PPP, and why do you care?

▶ What you need to connect to the Internet

▶ Finding an Internet provider

*T*he three ways to get your computer on the Net are

✔ **Sign up for an online service.** In *The Internet For Dummies,* 4th Edition, we describe how to sign up for and use America Online and CompuServe. Windows 95 users can sign up for Microsoft Network by double-clicking its icon on the desktop. Online services are easy to get started with but can be expensive if you use them for more than a few hours a month or if they don't have a local phone number in your area and don't offer access to all Internet services.

✔ **Sign up for a UNIX shell account with an Internet provider.** UNIX shell accounts are boring — you can't use all the new, snazzy graphical software, such as Netscape. (If your Internet provider runs TIA or SLIRP, your shell account can pretend to be a PPP account; see the sidebar "Shell users, don't despair," later in this chapter.) We don't explain in this book how to use shell accounts because they're declining in popularity; if you can get to the Web, though, you can read some information at this Web page:

```
http://net.dummies.com/shell
```

✔ **Sign up for a PPP account with an Internet provider.** This is the coolest way to connect to the Net over the phone. You can use all the latest programs to see pictures, hear sounds, watch video, and have little animations dance all over your screen (or not — your choice).

Getting connected, Mac style

Mac users, go ahead and read this chapter to find out the general principles of using PPP accounts and choosing an Internet provider. Don't worry about how to get connection software — you already have most of the software you need to connect to the Internet because System 7.5 comes with MacTCP. Upgrade to System 7.5 to get MacTCP, or ask your Internet provider to give it to you, or get a book about Macintoshes and the Internet that comes with a disk. You also need a PPP dial-up access program, such as FreePPP, included on the CD-ROM in *The Internet For Dummies*, Starter Kit Edition.

After your Mac is connected, skip to Chapter 7 to find out how to get e-mail programs, Web browsers, and other programs you will want to use. This chapter talks about Winsock programs, which follow a Windows standard for Internet software. Mac has a standard too; most Mac Internet software is designed to be compatible with MacTCP. Chapter 7 lists only Winsock- and MacTCP-compatible programs.

You can tell which type of account is our favorite: a PPP account. This chapter gives you general information about the steps you have to follow to get connected to one. Chapter 4 helps Windows 3.1 users get the necessary software (a shareware program called Trumpet Winsock), install it, and run it. Chapter 5 does the same for Windows 95 users. Mac users should check out the preceding sidebar, "Getting connected, Mac style."

What Are SLIP and PPP Again?

In case you take our advice and skip all that technical stuff in Part VI, we had better explain what PPP is. Here are the three incomprehensible acronyms you need to know:

- **SLIP (Serial Line Internet Protocol)** enables your PC to connect to the Internet, not as a terminal but as a full-fledged member of the Net, at least while your computer is on the phone to its Internet provider.

- **CSLIP (Compressed SLIP)** involves the same idea as SLIP, except that CSLIP is a little faster.

- **PPP (Point-to-Point Protocol)** is a newer system that does more or less the same thing as SLIP and CSLIP but is much easier to set up.

Because these three protocols are identical for your purposes, we refer to them all as PPP. (If you care about the differences, which you probably don't, see Chapter 21.) All three are versions of IP (Internet Protocol), the underlying part of TCP/IP (Transmission Control Protocol/Internet Protocol), which is the way that all computers on the Internet communicate with each other. All three protocols are cool because many network operations are much simpler when your own computer is on the Net instead of acting as a terminal to someone else's big computer — programs running on your own computer can do much nicer sound, graphics, and animation than a terminal can.

These days, any Internet provider that can give you a SLIP or CSLIP account can give you a PPP account, so ask for PPP. Henceforth, we assume that you're using PPP, and we skip the SLIP.

The really cool thing about running TCP/IP software on your PC is something called Winsock. *Winsock* (which stands for *Win*dows *sock*ets — don't you love the names they come up with?) is a standard way for Windows programs to work with PPP accounts. If your TCP/IP software does Winsock, you can run any Winsock application, including nice ones such as Eudora for reading e-mail, Free Agent for checking out newsgroups, and Netscape Navigator for browsing the World Wide Web. Remarkably, many of the best Winsock applications are available for free on the Net.

A bunch of different Winsock-compatible TCP/IP Internet connection packages are available for DOS and Windows. All packages support Winsock, and most support PPP. If your Windows computer is already set up with software that connects you to a PPP account, you're in luck. Luckily, all Winsock programs work the same no matter which connection software is running underneath. If you already have a Winsock-compatible PPP connection, skip the rest of this chapter and go to Chapter 6.

When you're online with your Internet PPP provider, your computer is *on* the Net. Conversely, when you hang up with your provider, your computer drops off the Internet. If someone wants to look at a Web page you store on your own computer and you're not on the phone, your page doesn't appear. Not staying online all the time isn't a big problem for most people — see Chapter 15 to find out where to store your Web pages.

Still with us? Right now may also be a good time to find a local Internet expert and ask for help in getting your TCP/IP software and PPP connection set up. Having in hand a plate of cookies, particularly freshly baked ones, when you ask for help is never a bad idea.

Ready to Be PPP

Okay, you're raring to go. What are the steps you have to follow? And what hardware and software will you need?

PPP and e-mail — a digression

When you use PPP to communicate with your Internet PPP provider, your lowly PC (or Mac) becomes a full-fledged node on the Internet. That is, your PC becomes a *host* computer. This elevated status may entitle your PC to a name. For one PC, for example, we chose the name of our favorite six-year-old, meg. The full network address of your PC is its host name, followed by the name of your Internet provider. For example, we use a local provider, TIAC (The Internet Access Company), whose Internet address is tiac.net. The address of the PC, therefore, is meg.tiac.net. Not all providers assign host names to PPP users, and some assign boring names, such as ppp247.gorgonzola.net, but your PPP account works just fine anyway.

The PC is not on the Net all the time, however — when the computer is turned off, for example, or when we aren't connected to the PPP provider. Incoming Internet mail is normally delivered directly to the recipient's computer (see Chapter 21 for the gory details). When our PC is not connected to the Net,

however, what happens to our incoming mail? Do you really have to keep your computer on the phone 24 hours a day just to get your mail?

A good question, and we're glad you asked. No, you don't. PPP Internet providers receive your mail for you and hold on to it until you next log in, at which point you can move your mail to your own computer. As long as your PPP provider's computer is connected all the time (and you have a pretty poor provider if it's not), mail flows unimpeded.

This arrangement means that, as far as the rest of the Internet can tell, your mailbox is on your Internet provider's computer, not on your own PC. Your e-mail address is usually your login name, followed by an at-sign (@), followed by your provider's address. We have a login called margy on TIAC, for example, whose address is tiac.net, so mail can come to margy@tiac.net. (Don't send us mail at that address, though; you get better results from moreint3@dummies.net, which connects you to Internet For Dummies Central — it's on the Net continuously.)

The big picture, PPP-wise

To get your computer set up for PPP:

1. **Arrange for a PPP account from a local provider.**

   In the section "Who Will Provide?" later in this chapter, we give you ideas about how to choose one.

2. **Get the basic TCP/IP software loaded into your computer somehow, either from a disk or over the phone.**

   Use the software your PPP provider gives you to get connected. If you don't get any software, think about switching providers.

3. Enter about a thousand setup parameters.

Don't worry — we tell you what they are.

4. Crank up your TCP/IP program and fiddle with it until it works.

After doing so, you can go on to load the swell applications described in Chapter 7.

Do you have what it takes?

Hardware- and software-wise, here's what you need to cruise the Net:

- ✔ **A modem that connects your computer to a phone line:** The faster the modem, the better. Try to get a modem that talks at 28.8 Kbps (bits per second) or faster. Otherwise, things will be sluggish.

- ✔ **A phone line (you probably guessed that):** Make sure that your phone line doesn't have call-waiting. If it does, you have to type ***70** or **1170** at the beginning of your provider's phone number to tell your phone company to turn off call-waiting for this phone call.

- ✔ **TCP/IP software that handles PPP or one of its variants:** We tell you how to get this software in Chapter 4 (for Windows 3.1) and Chapter 5 (for Windows 95). Mac users need FreePPP or something like it.

- ✔ **Software for getting your mail, reading newsgroups, and so on:** We talk about these things in Chapter 7.

- ✔ **A PPP account with an Internet provider and a bunch of technical information about the account (described in the next section).**

If your PC is on a local-area network, things get confusing. You have to talk to your network administrator to find out how to get connected to the Internet, with or without PPP. Rather than connect your individual PC, your network may use a gateway to connect the entire local-area network to the Internet.

Who Will Provide?

To use Winsock software, you need a PPP account. (You may actually be able to use a UNIX shell account; see the nearby sidebar "Shell users, don't despair: TIA is here." Some online services can work with Winsock too, such as America Online, CompuServe, and Prodigy Internet.) Dozens of national Internet providers have phone numbers all over the United States, and hundreds — probably thousands, by now — of regional and local providers have phone numbers in limited areas. Be sure to find a provider that

- Offers PPP accounts
- Has a phone number that's an untimed local call for you so that you don't have to pay long-distance phone charges
- Has reasonable phone support
- You can afford (otherwise, you never use it!)

Where to look for a provider

To find an Internet provider:

- Look in your local newspaper, especially in the business pages.
- Ask friends which providers they use.
- Ask the reference library at the local public library.

- Find someone who has an online account, and go to the following World Wide Web site, which contains a huge listing of Internet providers by area code:

```
http://thelist.com/
```

When you open your account, ask your Internet provider whether it has software you can use. Many providers give you a disk containing a nice set of freeware and shareware software for connecting to the Net, along with instructions.

Can online services do it?

Some online services let you use Winsock software. If you already have an online account, consider using it for running Netscape, Agent, and that other cool Winsock stuff. Here's the rundown on the major online services:

- **America Online** works with most Winsock software. Be sure that you have Version 3.0 (or later) of the America Online connection software. We describe how to use America Online with Winsock software in *The Internet For Dummies,* 4th Edition.

- **CompuServe** works with most Winsock software. You have to use Version 3.0 or later of its software. We describe how to use CompuServe with Winsock software in *The Internet For Dummies,* 4th Edition, too.

- **Microsoft Network** (MSN) works with Winsock software.

- **Prodigy Internet** can work with Winsock software, although Prodigy Classic can't.

Shell users, don't despair: TIA is here

If you have a UNIX shell account, you may be able to get it to act like a PPP account. Talk to your Internet provider's support folks and find out whether they can run TIA, The Internet Adapter. TIA makes a shell account pretend to be a PPP account so that you can use all the neat Winsock software we talk about in Chapter 7.

If your Internet provider has never heard of TIA, tell it to e-mail InterMind, at this address:

`tia-host-pricing@marketplace.com`

Another package called SLIRP does much the same thing as TIA, so if your provider supports that package, you can also do PPP.

Ask your provider

Before you can use a TCP/IP program to connect to your PPP account, you need a bunch of scary-looking technical information. Ask your Internet provider for this information, and write it down in Table 3-1.

Table 3-1	Information about Your PPP Connection	
Information	*Description*	*Example*
Your own numeric Internet (IP) address	Your PC's own numeric Internet address. You get this number from your Internet provider. Some providers issue you a number every time you call, in which case they don't give you a permanent number, which works okay too.	`123.45.67.89`
Your Internet provider's domain name server (DNS) address	The numeric Internet address of the computer that can translate between regular Internet addresses and their numeric equivalents (between `dummies.net` and `205.238.207.82`, for example). Your Internet provider should give you this address.	`123.45.67.99`

(continued)

Table 3-1 *(continued)*

Information	Description	Example
Your domain name (aka domain suffix)	The name of your Internet provider's domain. It looks like the last part of an Internet address and usually ends with .net or .com (in the United States, anyway).	dummies.net
Interface type	The exact type of interface the provider uses. The three choices are SLIP, CSLIP, and PPP. Most packages handle all three. If your software and provider handle PPP, use it; the next best choice is CSLIP; the worst (but still okay) choice is SLIP.	PPP
Your communications port	The communications port on your own computer to which your modem is attached, usually COM1 or COM2. Even if your modem lives inside your computer and doesn't look as though it's connected to a port, it is.	COM1
Your modem speed	The fastest speed that both your modem and your Internet provider's modem can go. If your modem can go at 9600 or 14.4 Kbps, for example, but your Internet provider can handle only 9600 bps, choose 9600 bps. Conversely, if your modem can do only 2400 bps (which seems really slow when you get connected), choose 2400 bps.	28.8 Kbps
User name	The name on your account with your Internet provider, also called a login name.	myoung
User password	The password for your account.	poultry4u

Information	*Description*	*Example*
Phone number	The number you call to connect to your Internet provider, exactly as you would dial it by hand. If it's long-distance, include the 1 and the area code at the beginning. If you have to dial 9 and pause a few seconds to get an outside line, include 9,, at the beginning (each comma tells your modem to pause for about a second, so stick in extra commas as necessary to get the timing right).	1-802-555-1234
Your modem	The type of modem you have. Winsock programs are only dimly aware of the details of different types of modems. A regular PC-type modem is probably similar enough to a Hayes model to fool the programs we're using here. If you have an unusual type of modem, you may have to tell your Winsock program which commands initialize your modem, tell it to dial, and tell it to hang up.	Hayes
Start-up command	The command your Internet provider should run when you call in. Your provider can tell you this command. If your provider starts PPP right away when you log in, you may not need a start-up command, so you may be able to leave this entry blank when the time comes to type it.	PPP

The Programs You Need

You need four types of programs to get useful work done on the Internet:

> ✔ **TCP/IP connection:** Talks to the Internet in the Internet's own language (Internet Protocol, the IP part of TCP/IP).

 ✔ **FTP:** Can be used for transferring other programs from the Internet. Your Internet provider may give you an FTP program, or you may receive a Web browser (such as Netscape Navigator or Internet Explorer), which can do FTP. Any FTP program will do. (*The Internet For Dummies,* 3rd Edition, describes how FTP works.)

 ✔ **Ping:** Tests your Internet connection. Although this little program isn't absolutely necessary, it's very useful when you're getting your PPP account set up.

 ✔ **Web browser, e-mail, and others:** The programs you use every day for reading your mail, browsing the Web, and doing other stuff on the Internet, as described in Chapter 7.

A Home for Your Programs

Before you begin filling your computer's disk with network software, you have to make a *folder* (also called a *directory*) in which to put these new programs. You can use this folder for the programs you download in this chapter and useful little programs you find on the Net. In the rest of this book, we call the folder C:\Internet. Here's how to create the folder:

 ✔ **Windows 3.1:** In Windows File Manager, move to the directory in which you want to create the new folder (probably the root, or C:\) and choose File⇨Create Directory.

 ✔ **Windows 95:** In Windows Explorer or My Computer, move to the folder in which you want to create the new folder (probably C:\) and choose File⇨New⇨Folder.

 ✔ **Macintosh:** In the Finder, open the folder in which you want to create the new folder and choose File⇨New Folder (or press Command-N).

If you don't already have a folder for storing things temporarily, you should create one. You need a temporary folder when you're installing many programs. We recommend calling the folder something like C:\Temp.

The Next Step

You have the concepts, you're psyched, and you're ready for the next step. Windows 3.1 folks should go to Chapter 4 to find out how to install the connection software they need, and Windows 95 folks should skip to Chapter 5 to find out how to use the connection software that comes with Windows 95.

Tip for Mac users

When you download a program by using your Web browser, you usually end up with three files: a .hqx file (the program in Binhex format), a .sit file (the compressed archive file), and an installer. Although you can trash the first two files after you install the program, you might want to hang on to the installer in a temporary folder in case you have to reinstall stuff.

A handy tip is to make still another folder and put aliases of all your Internet applications in it. You can then use this folder as a launcher for all the Internet applications. (Double-clicking the alias works the same as double-clicking the original icon.) To make an alias, select the application program icon in the Finder by clicking on it once, choose File⇨ Make Alias, and then drag the newly created alias to the alias folder you made.

(Thanks to Arnold Reinhold for this tip.)

Chapter 4
The Ways of Windows 3.1

*U*nlike Windows 95, Windows 3.1 doesn't come with Internet software. Bummer! When Windows 3.1 was invented, the Internet was still used, of course, only by geeks like us. Luckily, lots of good, free Internet software is available for Windows 3.1. You just have to get it and install it.

In this chapter, we explain how to connect your Windows 3.1 computer to a SLIP or PPP account using the wildly popular Trumpet Winsock shareware TCP/IP package. We chose Trumpet Winsock because it's widely available shareware (we thought that you would like that) — in fact, most Internet providers give new users a disk with Trumpet Winsock on it, along with a Web-browsing program, such as Netscape Navigator or Internet Explorer. After you're connected, we tell you (in Chapter 6) how to use the Web browser to get software from the Internet; Chapter 7 describes other nifty Windows-based software your SLIP or PPP connection enables you to use, including programs for reading your mail, reading newsgroups, and browsing the Web.

Read Chapter 3 first so that you understand how SLIP (and PPP) accounts work, what information you need to get from your Internet provider, and what kinds of programs you need. As you may recall, you need a TCP/IP program to communicate with your SLIP account, a Web browser (or FTP program) that can download files from the Net, and (optionally) a ping program to test your connection.

Matching up your Winsocks

You may have available full or sampler versions of commercial Windows TCP/IP packages from vendors such as Chameleon (from NetManage) or SuperTCP (from Frontier). Or you may have bought Netscape Navigator; the retail version of this program comes with a TCP/IP program. If you have one of these products available, you may as well use that package rather than Trumpet Winsock because the commercial versions tend to be somewhat better supported and sometimes faster. Part of the charm of Winsock is that it's an actual standard: No matter which TCP/IP program you have, you can install and run the other Winsock applications we describe.

Where Does All This Software Come From?

You can find Trumpet Winsock and a Web browser in several places:

- **Your Internet provider may offer the program on a disk.** That's certainly the easiest way to get it. Most Internet providers give you the connection software you need, and some give you an e-mail program and a Web browser too. If your Internet provider gives you software, use it. That way, when you call for help, your provider knows what to do (one hopes!). Note that the software your provider gives you is probably shareware — which means that you're honor-bound to send a donation to the author if you use it unless your provider is one of the few that preregisters the shareware it hands out (see Chapter 7).

- **Your Internet provider may make the programs available from a shell account.** You use Windows Terminal (or a better terminal program, such as Procomm, if you have it) to download it. Follow your Internet provider's instructions for downloading the program.

- **You can get Trumpet Winsock from a book.** If all else fails, get *The Internet For Dummies,* Starter Kit Edition, by us, Carol Baroudi, and Hy Bender. The CD-ROM in the back has all the software you need to get connected.

Version 3.0 of the Trumpet Winsock program comes in one file, named TWSK30D.EXE. It's about 500K in size. This file also includes Trumpet Ping, which is a handy way to test whether your connection is working. The Trumpet Winsock program takes about 1MB of disk space (tiny, in this age of bloated programs).

What if I'm already on a network?

If your PC is already connected to a network via a modem, you can still use Trumpet Winsock to communicate by way of SLIP. Just be sure that no other program is trying to use your modem at the same time as Trumpet Winsock does.

Configuring Trumpet Winsock to use a real Ethernet network rather than a modem is also possible, but the instructions for doing so are, unfortunately, way beyond what we can print here. The details depend on the type of network, the particular brand and model of network card installed in your computer, and what (if any) other network software is already installed.

Whoever runs your existing network is the right person to talk to, to find out whether also installing Trumpet Winsock makes sense. Information about using Trumpet Winsock over a network is included in the README.TXT file that appears when you uncompress the Trumpet Winsock distribution file (follow Steps 1 through 3 in the following section, "Installing Trumpet Winsock," and then double-click the README.TXT filename.

Microsoft offers for free a program called Microsoft TCP/IP-32 for WfWG 3.11, for use with networks running Windows for Workgroups 3.11. Go to the Microsoft Web site (at `http://www.microsoft.com`) and look for it.

If you have trouble finding Trumpet Winsock and a Web browser or if you want a program for which you can get telephone support, you can buy Netscape Communicator at any software store. This popular Web browser comes with TCP/IP connection software and complete installation instructions.

Installing Trumpet Winsock

If you received Trumpet Winsock from your Internet provider and it came with instructions, follow those instructions. If you got a lone disk with no instructions, this section gives you some. These steps describe how to install Trumpet Winsock Version 3.0 on your Windows 3.1 computer. You end up with an icon for the program in Windows Program Manager.

If your Internet provider gave you an older version of Trumpet Winsock, these instructions may not work. Ask your Internet provider for Version 3.0 or later.

1. Exit any programs you're running and run Windows File Manager.

Because you restart Windows later in this procedure, you may as well save your work and exit any other programs you're using.

2. **In File Manager, move the Trumpet Winsock files into your C:\TEMP folder or wherever you have decided to store files to be deleted later.**

   That is, move the files if they aren't already in that folder. Trumpet creates a bunch of temporary files during its installation. You can delete these files when you're done installing the program.

3. **Still in File Manager, double-click the filename for the Trumpet Winsock program, which is usually TWSK30D.EXE.**

   The file automagically self-extracts, which means that the compressed files contained in the file pop out.

4. **Press F5 to tell File Manager to update the list of files in the current folder (directory).**

   Wow! Look at all those files that have appeared! One of them, INSTALL.EXE, is the installation program.

5. **Double-click the INSTALL.EXE file to run the installation program.**

   You see the Trumpet Winsock installation program.

6. **Click Install to proceed.**

   The installation program may warn you that any old Trumpet Winsock files will be overwritten. If so, click OK.

   If you have any files named WINSOCK.DLL on your computer (the part of the program that works with Winsock-compatible programs), the installation program asks whether it can rename them; click Yes.

   Then the installation program asks for the name of the folder in which it should install the program and suggests C:\TRUMPET.

7. **Change the folder name, if you want to install the program somewhere else (such as in your C:\INTERNET folder), and then click OK.**

   Installing the program in C:\TRUMPET is usually a fine place.

   The installation program makes a program group in Windows Program Manager in which the Trumpet Winsock icons appear and asks what you want to name this program group. It suggests Trumpet Winsock, a reasonable name.

8. **Click OK.**

   The installation program installs the program and then tells you that it's planning to add the name of the Trumpet Winsock program folder (the one you specified in Step 7) to the DOS PATH statement in your AUTOEXEC.BAT file. This arcane technical move tells Windows where to find Trumpet Winsock when it's looking for programs.

9. **Click OK.**

   Next you see two windows, showing your existing AUTOEXEC.BAT file and the one with the addition the installation program is about to make. Yikes!

10. Click Save to save the changes the installation needs to make.

Your old AUTOEXEC.BAT file is saved too, as AUTOEXEC.000.

Now the installation program has to restart your computer so that the changes in your AUTOEXEC.BAT take effect. A message reminds you to remove any disk from your disk drive.

11. Click OK.

You're ready to restart the computer.

12. Click Restart.

If your computer doesn't restart by itself, exit from Windows, restart your computer, and rerun Windows. In Windows Program Manager, you see a new program group named Trumpet Winsock with a whole slew of icons in it, as shown in Figure 4-1.

If the Trumpet Winsock program group is huge, you can make it smaller by dragging the edges around with your mouse.

Figure 4-1:
The Trumpet Winsock program group.

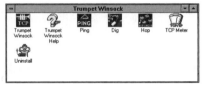

Cool! The icons in the Trumpet Winsock program group include the Trumpet Winsock program, Trumpet Winsock Help, a Ping program for testing your connection, and an Uninstall icon for getting rid of the program if you decide not to use it.

Telling Trumpet Winsock about Your Internet Provider

Now you can fill in the fields in the Trumpet Winsock Setup dialog box based on information from your SLIP provider; refer to the notes you made next to Table 3-1 in Chapter 3. Here's how to tell Trumpet Winsock about your particular Internet provider and who you are:

1. **Double-click the Trumpet Winsock icon to run the program.**

   You see a message explaining that you have to register the program if you want to use it for more than 30 days. Fair enough — this is shareware, after all, not freeware.

2. **Assuming that it's okay with you to pay a modest sum to use all this neat software (Trumpet Winsock and its Ping program), click Accept.**

   You see the Trumpet Winsock Setup dialog box, as shown in Figure 4-2. Although it's a scary-looking box, the setup process doesn't take long.

Figure 4-2:
Tell
Trumpet
Winsock
how to
connect to
your
Internet
provider.

3. **In the IP address box, type your own numeric Internet (IP) address, if your Internet provider gave you one.**

   If not, leave this box with its original contents, 0.0.0.0. The IP address is always in the form of four numbers (each between 0 and 255) separated by dots.

4. **In the DNS server(s) box, type your Internet provider's domain name server (DNS) address.**

   This IP address also consists of four numbers connected by dots. Each number is between 0 and 255 (inclusive).

5. **In the Domain suffix box, type your Internet provider's domain name, such as** `dummies.net`.

   This domain name is usually the same one that appears after the @ in your e-mail address.

6. **In the Driver section of the box, click either SLIP or PPP.**

   If you have a CSLIP account, click SLIP.

7. **Click the Dialler Settings button to tell Trumpet Winsock how to call your Internet provider.**

   "Dialler" isn't misspelled — the author's from Australia. You see the Trumpet Winsock Dialler Settings dialog box, as shown in Figure 4-3.

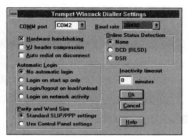

Figure 4-3: Trumpet Winsock needs to know about your modem too.

8. **Click in the COMM port box and choose your modem's communication port from the list that appears.**

   That is, choose the port on the back of your computer to which your modem is connected. If you have an internal modem (one that lives inside your computer), choose the port the modem uses.

9. **Click in the Baud rate box and choose your modem's speed.**

   Enter **38400** if you have a 28.2 Kbps modem or **19200** if you have a 14.4 Kbps modem.

10. **Leave the Hardware handshaking box checked, unless you have a really crummy old modem that doesn't properly signal the computer when the remote end connects.**

11. **In the Online Status Detection box, choose the method your modem uses to indicate when your Internet provider picks up the phone.**

    Select DCD unless you have a crummy old modem.

12. **If you have a CSLIP account, click the VJ header compression box so that it contains a check.**

    Van Jacobson compression is what makes the difference between SLIP and CSLIP, so you want this option turned on.

13. **Recheck all those settings to be sure that they're right, and then click Ok.**

    The Trumpet Winsock Dialler Settings window disappears, leaving you looking at the Trumpet Winsock Setup window.

14. **Recheck your entries here too, and then click Ok again.**

You may see an error message saying that Trumpet Winsock couldn't open your modem. Remain calm — Trumpet Winsock doesn't digest the information you just entered until you exit the program and restart it. If you see an error message, click OK.

The regular Trumpet Winsock window appears.

15. **Choose File⇨Exit to leave Trumpet Winsock and then double-click its icon in Program Manager to restart it (cognizant of all the swell things you've told it).**

You see the Trumpet Winsock window again, as shown in Figure 4-4.

```
                        Trumpet Winsock                        ▾ ▴
File  Edit  Special  Trace  Dialler  Help
Trumpet Winsock Version 3.0 Revision D
Copyright © 1996 distributed by
Trumpet Software International Pty Ltd.
A.C.N. 070 065 860
Under Licence from the Copyright owners.
All Rights Reserved.
THIS IS AN UNREGISTERED COPY FOR EVALUATION ONLY (29 DAYS LEFT).

Use of this copy for more than 30 days requires the copy to
be registered - select the "Special/Register" option from the program menu.

License terms and conditions apply to your use of this software - select the
"Special/license" option from the program menu.

This program incorporates a time lock feature and will cease to operate if
not registered within 30 days.  Trumpet Software International encourages
you to register your evaluation copy early and well within the 30 day
evaluation period.

This software may not be distributed or otherwise made available to the
public except in accordance with the license conditions stated in menu
option "Help/Distribution".

PPP ENABLED
PPP driver COM2 Baud rate = 38400 Hardware handshaking
IP buffers = 32 Packet buffers = 16
My IP = 0.0.0.0 netmask = 0.0.0.0 gateway = 0.0.0.0
```

Figure 4-4: Trumpet Winsock isn't pretty, but it does the job of connecting you to the Internet.

If you have to go back and change any of the information you just entered, you can get back to the Trumpet Winsock Setup dialog box by choosing File⇨Setup from the Trumpet Winsock menu.

Actually Making an Actual SLIP or PPP Connection

Thought this moment would never come, eh? Well, it's about time. You can tell Trumpet Winsock to dial and make a connection in two ways (one way would be too simple — computers are involved here): the manual way and the automatic way. The manual way is extremely manual: You type commands directly to your modem to make the connection and start the SLIP, CSLIP, or PPP session and then tell Trumpet Winsock to go ahead. The automatic way involves a *login script* that tells Trumpet Winsock what to send to the modem, what to expect from your Internet provider's computer, what to type next, and so on until the connection is made. The manual way works perfectly well if you don't mind doing the typing every time, although we find that setting up the automatic way is worth the effort. Your Internet provider may have a Trumpet Winsock script for you to use — just ask them.

Dial ho!

"All right, already," you're doubtless saying. "Let's cut to the chase." Okay:

1. **If Trumpet Winsock isn't running, run it by double-clicking its icon in Program Manager.**

   You see the Trumpet Winsock window, shown back in Figure 4-4.

2. **Choose Dialler⇨Login from the menu.**

   Trumpet Winsock uses its sample login script, which may well work for your account. You see the Login Profile dialog box, as shown in Figure 4-5.

Figure 4-5:
Tell
Trumpet
Winsock
how to dial
in to your
account.

3. **In the Username box, type your username (account name).**

   Refer to Table 3-1 in Chapter 3, where you wrote this stuff down.

4. **In the Password box, type your password.**

   Only asterisks appear, in case a malefactor (or a nosy teenager) is looking over your shoulder.

5. **In the Phone box, type the phone number you dial to connect to your Internet provider.**

   Enter dashes in the phone number or not — your modem ignores them.

6. **Click Ok to see whether this sample login script works for your Internet provider.**

   You see the Trumpet Winsock Dialler Status window, which shows you how the connection process is going. The Trumpet Winsock window shows you the conversation the program is having with your Internet provider.

   If this step works, Trumpet Winsock dials up, connects, and displays the message SCRIPT COMPLETED. You're ready to use the Net! Skip to the section "Testing Your Connection by Pinging," later in this chapter.

   If the script doesn't work, you see the message SCRIPT ABORTED. Drat. Don't panic — you may be able to salvage the situation by changing your server profile (the prompts that Trumpet Winsock expects your Internet provider to display while you're logging in). Follow the steps in the next section to connect to your Internet provider manually, noting how your Internet provider prompts you for your username and password. Then continue with the section "Fixing your server profile."

You can change the username, password, and phone number later by choosing Dialler⇨Profile from the menu.

Dialing your Internet provider manually

To dial manually, follow these steps:

1. **If Trumpet Winsock isn't running, run it by double-clicking its icon in Program Manager.**

   You see the Trumpet Winsock window, shown back in Figure 4-4.

2. **Choose Dialler⇨Manual login from the menu.**

   Trumpet Winsock says something like

   ```
   AFTER LOGGING IN, TYPE THE <ESC> KEY TO RETURN TO NORMAL
           SLIP/PPP PROCESSING.
   SLIP (or PPP) DISABLED
   ```

   Not being clairvoyant, you may not be able to guess that this message is the Trumpet Winsock way of telling you to begin typing.

3. **Type whatever command your modem needs to get it ready to dial the phone. Try typing** AT&B1&H1 **and pressing Enter.**

   For most modems, you get its attention by typing AT and then a command that tells it always to use the port-connection speed (&B1) (regardless of the connection speed at the other end) and to use hardware modem flow control (&H1).

Sorry to say, modem command settings are among the least well-standardized features in the PC biz. You can probably get by with whatever settings your modem comes with. Failing that, try AT&B1&H1, which usually works for us, or, gasp, see whether the modem manual makes any suggestions. The modem says OK.

If you're not sure which commands get your modem in the mood, skip this step.

4. **Tell the modem "Ahoy there, dial the telephone!" and give it your provider's phone number. For example, type** ATDT555-2368 **and press Enter**.

Your modem dials the phone and, when it makes the connection, says something like

```
CONNECT 28800/ARQ/V34/LAPM/V42BIS
Welcome to SoVerNet
Vermont's Sovereign Internet Connection
granite.sover.net.login:
```

Holy digital data stream, Batperson! You're connected. Your provider greets you and asks you to type your login name and password. (No, we're not going to tell you our password. We're not totally stupid. Almost, but not totally.)

5. **Type your login name and password when your Internet provider prompts you, pressing Enter after each one. Make a note of *exactly* what your Internet provider displayed to prompt you.**

Your Internet provider displays a message, similar to

```
PPP session from (206.25.66.20) to 206.25.66.125
        beginning. . . .
```

followed by a bunch of garbage. Hey, how about that? PPP started (or CSLIP or SLIP, depending on what kind of account you have).

6. **Now tell Trumpet Winsock that the connection has started by pressing Esc.**

You see a message like

```
PPP ENABLED
```

or

```
My IP address = 206.25.66.120
```

That's it — you're connected. That you're now on the Internet is not obvious. The best way to check is by using the Trumpet Ping program, described later in this chapter.

If you want to take a stab at telling Trumpet Winsock how to connect to your Internet provider automatically, continue with the next section or come back to it later.

Fixing your server profile

If the sample login script fails to connect, you have two choices: Settle for manual dialing so that you have to type a series of commands every time you connect to the Internet (boring!), or fix the login script to work with your Internet provider. When you have manual dialing working, try changing the text that Trumpet Winsock expects to see when your Internet provider prompts for your username and password.

Trumpet Winsock normally expects to see the characters sername: (a set of characters that matches either Username: or username:) to prompt for your username. Then it expects ssword: (which matches either Password: or password:). If your Internet provider asks for your username by displaying login: or Type your username here:, Trumpet Winsock never recognizes the prompt.

This problem is, luckily, easy to fix:

1. **Choose Dialler⇨Profile from the menu.**

   You see the Login Profile dialog box, shown back in Figure 4-5.

2. **Click the Server Settings button.**

   You see the Server Profile dialog box, as shown in Figure 4-6.

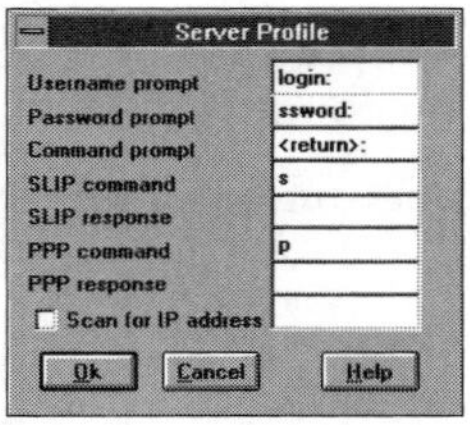

Figure 4-6:
What does
your
Internet
provider say
when you're
logging in?

3. **Change the text in the Username prompt box to match what your Internet provider says when it asks for your username.**

   Type carefully, and use the same capitalization your Internet provider uses.

4. **Change the text in the Password prompt box to match what your Internet provider says when it asks for your password.**

   Leave the rest of the entries alone.

5. **Click Ok, and then click Ok again in the Login Profile dialog box.**

6. **Choose Dialler⇨Login to try an automated login again.**

If you still can't connect, you can stick with manual dialing or consider making a login script that works, as described in the section "More about Connections," later in this chapter.

Testing Your Connection by Pinging

Before you merrily start installing Internet programs to check your mail and browse the Web, you may want to make sure that the connection works. You can use a program called Trumpet Ping, a little program that "pings" remote hosts to make sure that you can in fact reach them (your computer says "ping" and the other computer says "pong"). When you installed Trumpet Winsock, Trumpet Ping came along for the ride.

1. **In Program Manager, double-click the icon for Trumpet Ping.**

   You see the Trumpet Ping window, as shown in Figure 4-7.

Figure 4-7:
Trumpet
Ping is
ready to
test your
Internet
connection.

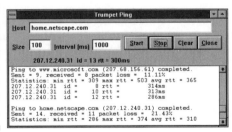

2. **In the Host box, type either the name of your provider's server computer or a well-known system, such as** `www.microsoft.com`, `home.netscape.com`, **or** `rs.internic.net`.

3. **Click the Start button.**

   Trumpet Ping starts sending a series of "ping" messages to the other computer. If it works, you should see responses (right below the Host box) like

   ```
   205.238.207.65 id = 56 rtt = 394ms
   ```

The `rtt` number is the Round Trip Time for the ping to travel from your host to the other one and back (we bet that you expected this number to be more obscure). The round-trip time is reported in milliseconds ($^1/_{1000}$ second), so a round-trip time of 219 is $^{219}/_{1000}$ seconds, or about a fifth of a second. This amount is a reasonable round-trip time for a SLIP message; if the time is consistently more than 350, you probably have a setup problem.

4. **Click the S̲top button to stop pinging.**

   Ping displays some statistics about all that pinging.

5. **Exit from Trumpet Ping by clicking the C̲lose button.**

Now you know that you're on the Internet.

Hanging Up

One last important detail: How do you hang up? Fortunately, it's pretty easy:

1. **In Trumpet Winsock, choose D̲ialler⇨B̲ye to hang up the phone.**

   You don't have to exit from the Winsock programs you're using, such as Eudora or Netscape. You see a box which tells you that the program is disconnecting.

2. **If you don't plan to connect to the Internet again for a while, choose F̲ile⇨E̲xit to exit.**

Don't just tell Trumpet Winsock to exit, because it will, without hanging up the phone. Be sure to hang up explicitly before you leave Trumpet Winsock.

More about Connections

If the Trumpet Winsock sample login script works for you or if you're satisfied with manual dialing, you can skip the rest of this chapter and go to Chapter 6, in which we tell you how to set up a bunch of other useful Internet software. Or you can skip the rest of this chapter for now and come back when you get tired of typing the commands all the time.

You can tell Trumpet Winsock how to call up and log in to your Internet provider so that you don't have to type the dialing command, your login name, and your password. This section describes how to create a *login script* that tells Trumpet Winsock what to do.

Don't forget to register

Trumpet Winsock is shareware — and pretty darned good shareware at that. If you use Trumpet Winsock regularly, please choose Special⇨Register, which includes the registration instructions, including the address in Australia to which you send the form and check. You can even register right over the Internet. It's not expensive ($25 at the time this book was written), you feel great, and you're supporting Mr. Trumpet (whose name is really Peter) so that he can keep improving it.

Later, after you have your Web browser working, look at the Trumpet Winsock home page, at this URL:

http://www.trumpet.com

Some other programs you downloaded are shareware too. If the programs are worth using, they're worth registering.

A sample conversation

For our example, here's what you have to type to log in to another regional provider, ClarkNet (what we typed is in boldface):

```
atz
OK
at&c1&b1
OK
ATDT5551212
CONNECT 14400/ARQ Annex Command Line Interpreter * Copy-
         right 1991 Xylogics, Inc. Checking authoriza-
         tion, Please wait. . .
Connecting to port 37 using AT&T Paradyne V.32bis/V.42bis
         modem
Welcome to ClarkNet! Log in as "guest" for ClarkNet info
         and registration.
ClarkNet Username: dummies
ClarkNet Password: *******
Permission granted
     * ClarkNet's Menu
   Now using Class B network address.
   1) Enter clarknet host (UUCP users only)
   2) Enter explorer host (All users and guest)
   3) SLIP (SLIP users only)
   4) PPP (PPP users only)
   5) Hosts? (All users)
```

(continued)

(continued)

```
    6) Who? (All users)
    7) Telnet (IP users only)
    8) Exit (All users)
Enter Number (1-8): 3
Switching to SLIP.
Annex address is 168.143.0.4. Your address is 168.143.1.87.
```

Your provider may have made a login script for use with Trumpet Winsock. Before going to great effort to make your own script, call and ask whether someone there can send it to you on a disk or e-mail it to you.

It's all in the script

Scripts are not altogether unlike the script for a play. The script describes what you (or the computer, on your behalf) type, what the modem or remote computer responds with, what your computer types next, what the next response should be, and so on. In the preceding example, the computer types a couple of modem commands, and the modem replies OK after each one. Then the computer dials the phone, and the modem says CONNECTED and some other junk. The remote system prompts you with Username, the computer types the login name, the remote system prompts you with Password, and the computer types the password. Next is a long menu from the remote, ending with a request to enter the number to choose, and the computer types 3. The script automates all that typing.

Trumpet Winsock uses two scripts that are stored in files: LOGIN.CMD, which logs you in, and BYE.CMD, which hangs up the modem, and it comes with sample versions of both. Because the way you hang up a modem is, fortunately, now standardized well enough that the bye script always works, we concentrate on the login script.

Editing your script

To edit a script, you use a text editor, such as Windows Notepad. A script consists of a bunch of lines of text that Trumpet Winsock follows to hold up its end of the conversation with your Internet provider. Choose Dialler⇨Edit Scripts from the menu, and then double-click LOGIN.CMD to start Windows Notepad working on that script.

You see the existing LOGIN.CMD script that comes with Trumpet Winsock. Your job is to modify this script to work with your Internet provider's computer. When you see lines you don't understand, leave them alone.

Here's the script to log in to ClarkNet, the Internet provider in the preceding example (we go through it bit by bit afterward):

```
#
# initialize modem
#
output atz\r
input 10 OK\n
#
# set modem to indicate DCD
#
output at&c1&b1\r
input 10 OK\n
#
# send phone number
#
output atdt5552368\r
#
# now we are connected.
#
input 30 CONNECT
#
# wait till it's safe to send because some modems hang up
# if you transmit during the connection phase
#
wait 30 dcd
#
# wait for the username prompt
#
input 30 name:
output dummies\r
#
# and the password
#
input 30 word:
output hahaha\r
#
# we are now logged in
# so start SLIP
input 30 (1-8):
output 3\r display \n
display Connected. \n
#
#
# now we are finished.
#
online
```

Script lines that begin with a sharp sign (#) are comments. The computer disregards these lines because they're present for the benefit of humans who have to read the script.

This script begins by sending initialization commands to the modem. The `output` command tells Trumpet Winsock to send a message to your modem or your Internet provider and is followed by the text you want to send. The \r is the Enter key, which used to be known as Carriage Return. This `output` command resets the modem (Hayes-compatible modems use AT as the "attention" command and Z as the reset command):

```
output atz\r
```

The `input` command is followed by a maximum number of seconds to wait and the message to wait for the modem or your Internet provider to send:

```
input 10 OK\n
```

This `input` command waits for the modem to respond "OK." The \n means that the "OK" is followed by a newline character.

The next `output` command advises the modem about how it can tell when the Internet provider has answered:

```
output at&c1&b1\r
```

Don't worry about why it's this particular collection of characters — if you insist on knowing, refer to your modem's manual.

Again, you wait for the modem to respond "OK":

```
input 10 OK\n
```

The `ATDT` modem command tells the modem to dial the phone, followed by the phone number:

```
output atdt5552368\r
```

It can take as long as 30 seconds until the modem responds with a `CONNECT` message:

```
input 30 CONNECT
```

The wait command says to wait as long as 30 seconds for the modem to turn on the DCD signal, which means that the modem is indeed connected to your Internet provider:

```
wait 30 dcd
```

After the modem is connected, your Internet provider eventually prompts you to enter a username:

```
input 30 name:
```

(The input line doesn't have to specify everything your Internet provider will send — just enough of it for the computer to figure out when it's time to send the next message.)

In response, the script types your username (dummies, in our example) followed by a Carriage Return.

```
output dummies\r
```

More waiting is required for the Password prompt:

```
input 30 word:
output hahaha\r
```

Notice that, as lazy typists, we waited for only the tail end of it (word:) before sending the password. No, that's still not our real password.

ClarkNet displays a long menu, ending with a prompt that ends with (1-8):. After yet more waiting for that prompt, select the entry you want, in this case by pressing 3:

```
input 30 (1-8):
output 3\r
```

The display command displays a message merely for the benefit of a user (you) sitting and watching Trumpet Winsock:

```
display Connected. \n
```

A final online command tells Trumpet Winsock that the connection is made and the script is finished:

```
online
```

Your LOGIN.CMD script is a variation of this script. Make notes of what your Internet provider says and what your computer has to type, and write alternating input and output lines. The modem-dialing lines (other than the phone number) and the display and output at the end should work as is (as are?).

Using your login script

After you have made a stab at creating a login script, save it by choosing File⇨Save from the menu, leave Notepad, and try running the script by choosing Dialler⇨Login from the Trumpet Winsock menu. If it works, your script should dial the phone, log you in, and display Connected, ending with Trumpet Winsock saying PPP ENABLED or SLIP ENABLED. Unless you're incredibly lucky, however, your script won't work on the first try. Look to see where the script messed up. Then go back into Notepad by way of Dialler⇨Edit Scripts and fix the lines starting at the place the script messed up. For all except the most horrible dialing situations, you should be able to get the script to work on the second or third try. For more hints about dialing scripts, see the Trumpet Winsock Help file.

After your script works to your satisfaction, choose Dialler⇨Options, select Automatic login on start up only, and then click Ok. This step says that, in the future, whenever you start up Trumpet Winsock from the Program Manager, run the login script immediately so that you get connected right away.

Installing a Browser

After you're on the Net, install the Web browser program you got from your Internet provider. You use this program to download the other software you need for the Internet and to browse the Web.

Both Netscape Communicator and Internet Explorer come on CD-ROMs from many Internet providers, as part of the software you get when you sign up for your account, and both come with easy-to-use installation programs. Both programs are excellent, so use whichever one you get. You can always download, install, and try out the other one later.

What Next?

We haven't told you how to download programs from the Net — a major omission. Not to worry; Chapter 6 covers this subject in gory detail!

Chapter 5

Tricking Windows 95 into Letting You Connect to the Net

● ●

(Contributed by Jordan M. Young II)

In This Chapter
▶ Telling Windows 95 that you have a modem
▶ Telling Windows 95 that you want to connect to the Internet
▶ Telling Windows 95 about your Internet provider

● ●

Suppose that you have a zoomy PPP Internet account so that you can run Netscape and those other slick Internet programs. You have just upgraded to Windows 95, and you have heard that it comes with Internet software. "Great!" you think. "I'll just dial in and start surfing!"

Everyone expected Windows 95 to make connecting your computer to the Internet easy. After some fits and starts, it probably did. If you're lucky, you will find the Internet Setup Wizard (aka the Internet Jumpstart Kit — it has gone by a couple of different aliases over the years) on your computer. With the wizard, connecting to the Internet is easy. If you don't have the wizard, we tell you where you might be able to find it. If you can't find it, it turns out that Microsoft did sort of a good job of getting you on the Net anyway — you can find in and around Windows 95 all the pieces you need to get on the Net. If you can't find the wizard, don't worry. In this chapter, we give you all the clues you need to put the jigsaw puzzle together.

To give you the general idea, here are the steps you have to follow:

1. Figure out whether you're already connected to the Internet.

2. If you're not connected, we help you determine whether you have the wizard. If so, we give you some tips on how to speak to the wizard effectively. If you don't have the wizard, we take you through the following six steps — the ones that the wizard otherwise would guide you through.

3. Tell Windows 95 that you have a modem, if it didn't already find one.

4. Figure out whether you really want to be connected directly to the Internet anyway.

5. Tell Windows 95 that you want to dial in to a network, if it didn't already figure that out.

6. Tell Windows 95 who your Internet provider is.

7. Connect to your Internet provider.

8. Do some nitty-gritty stuff you should ignore if at all possible.

9. Get some software so that you can get useful work done.

This chapter describes each of these steps in detail. Chapter 3 describes how to find an Internet provider, if you don't already have an account. Be sure to read the section "What Are SLIP and PPP Again?" in Chapter 3 so that you know which type of account to get.

It's much easier to get Windows 95 to connect to a PPP account than to a SLIP or CSLIP account. When you open your Internet account with your service provider, ask for a PPP account to save yourself some trouble. If you already have a SLIP or CSLIP account, ask your provider to switch it to a PPP account.

Maybe You're Already Connected

Start with the easy way out: You may already be connected to the Internet. That's a likely scenario if you're using your computer at work or school and are connected to a *local-area network,* or *LAN.* That LAN may be connected directly to the Internet. A direct connection has several advantages: It's usually fast, and it's usually free to you. It does, however, have the disadvantage that if you're at work, your supervisors probably expect you to get some work done. (Because some companies have fairly strict policies about what you're allowed to do on their computers and on their time, before you go surfing the Internet from work, you might want to make some discreet inquiries.) If you're a student, these constraints don't apply, of course.

Another advantage of being connected to the Internet from work is that you usually don't have to set it up on your computer — the higher-ups pay network wizards to do that for you. If you're connected to a LAN at work and you think that it's prudent to surf the Net from there, you still need some software to be able to see what's going on out there in Netland. See Chapter 6 for software you may want to download and use.

Stop! Maybe Professor Marvel Can Get You Connected!

You probably have noticed that Microsoft is big into *wizards* nowadays. The Microsoft idea is to take all the steps, such as the ones we outline in this section for connecting to the Internet, and program them into your computer. The wizard asks questions when it needs to make a choice about what you want to do.

Two wizards of this type exist for connecting your computer running Windows 95 to the Internet. Why, you ask, don't we just tell you about one wizard or the other and let either one of them explain it all? Because, like all wizards, they're not particularly predictable, especially about when they show up and where you're likely to find them.

We know that you can get the Internet Setup Wizard (or the Internet Jumpstart Kit) by purchasing Microsoft PLUS!, a product containing features that many of us think should have been included in Windows 95 in the first place. Instead, after almost giving away Windows 95, Microsoft is charging $45 or more for the "rest" of the operating system. You may already have Microsoft PLUS! and not even know it. At least one new computer system we know of came with the PLUS! CD, but, unlike the rest of the software that shipped with the system, PLUS! wasn't installed. Buy PLUS! if you don't have it, or install it if you do. You definitely get the wizard that way.

If you know someone who's already connected to the Internet, ask your friend to download a copy of Internet Explorer (the Microsoft Web browser). Sometimes, when you install Internet Explorer, the wizard comes along for the ride. Or else you can look around on your computer and see whether you have a file named Inetwiz.exe. (You can check by opening Windows Explorer and choosing Tools⇨Find⇨Files or Folders. Look in My Computer for a file named Inetwiz.exe.) If you find it, that's the wizard — drag it to the desktop for easy access. You may also find that you have on your desktop an icon that looks like the one shown in Figure 5-1.

Figure 5-1:
The Internet
Wizard
icon.

The express route to the Internet

The Internet Connection Wizard (not to be confused with the Internet Setup Wizard or the Internet Jumpstart Kit) is the fastest way to get connected to the Internet. Its main limitation is that you have to use one of the Internet service providers that have made a deal with Microsoft to get promoted on their "referral service." That list includes many of the national service providers, but not many of the smaller regional ones (and none of the four that offers local access from our area, for example).

As usual, it's not entirely clear how you get the Internet Connection Wizard. The best way we know to get it is to download a copy of the Microsoft Internet browser, called Internet Explorer, that comes with the Internet Connection Wizard. (If you could download it from the Net, of course, then you wouldn't be reading this chapter, would you?) It may have come preinstalled on your computer, though, so it's worth looking for.

If you start up the wizard and it displays a screen that says Internet Connection Wizard, you're in the right place. Leave the Automatic option selected. If Windows 95 hasn't already found out about your modem, it asks you. Take a detour over to Step 9 in the section "Hey, Windows 95 — I Have a Modem!," later in this chapter. That section takes you through the steps of introducing your modem to Windows 95.

After the wizard gets your modem straightened out (if necessary), the Internet Connection Wizard asks you for your area code and the first three digits of your phone number. It then calls the Microsoft 800 number and, based on your area code and phone number, figures out which Internet provider it thinks you should use. After a delay, you see a screen that lists its suggestions. You can read about the provider by clicking the document icon to the right of its name, or you can decide to sign up with one by clicking the check mark to the right of

its name. Some of these providers have slicker procedures than others for signing up. Whatever they decide to do, you basically give the provider a bunch of information about yourself, including your billing information (we're talking credit card here), and it signs you up. *Make sure that you write down all the relevant information about your Internet provider, especially its technical-support telephone number!* Because the Internet Connection Wizard does everything for you, you don't have quite as much information about your Internet account as you otherwise might have. You have to call your Internet provider to straighten out any snags.

The Internet Connection Wizard then takes care of all the geeky stuff that Windows 95 needs to know about to connect you to your Internet service provider. It also takes care of remembering your user name and password at your new Internet service provider. This automation is a mixed blessing. If everything works right and never breaks and if you never want to use your Internet connection from a different computer — no problem. If you want to know who you are and how to sign on, however, you're in a pickle. You can figure out your user name by following the procedure in the section "At Last — Connecting to Your Internet Provider," later in this chapter. As for finding out what your password is, you'll be glad that you copied your provider's technical-support number. Only they can help you on that one. Still, when it's all over, you should be able to click the Internet icon on your desktop and be on the Internet. If you were that lucky, go directly to Chapter 6 to get the rest of the software you need to surf the Net.

Maybe you were adventurous and selected the Manual option on the Internet Connection Wizard's opening screen. You just spurned the Internet Connection Wizard and all her charms. In that case, read the following section.

You may find that you have a Get on the Internet command on your Start menu, specifically, if you click Programs➪Accessories➪Internet Tools➪Get on the Internet. That's a whole different wizard; see the following sidebar, "The express route to the Internet."

If you can't find the Internet Wizard, skip ahead to the section "It's a beautiful day in the neighborhood," later in this chapter.

The Internet Wizard Does Her Thing

What good is the Internet Connection Wizard? It takes you through the following steps (click the Next button to proceed from step to step):

1. **Double-click the Internet Wizard icon.**

   After the obligatory welcome, the wizard asks you some optional questions, depending on what she finds on your computer. Optional question one: "Do you want to access the Internet through your phone line or through your LAN?" If you get asked this question, choose the phone-line option. If you're connecting through your LAN, you have to get your local LAN guru to help you out.

   Optional question two: You need a modem! If Windows 95 hasn't found your modem, you have to tell it about the modem now. Head on down to Step 9 in the section "Hey, Windows 95 — I Have a Modem!" When you're done, come back here.

   Finally, no matter what, Ms. Wizard asks whether you want to access the Internet via Microsoft Network or an Internet service provider. Because Microsoft Network can be installed and configured with Windows 95, that option is an easier way of installing it. If that's what you want to do, don't bother with Ms. Wizard here.

2. **Tell the wizard that you have an account with a different provider.**

   You do, right?

3. **Choose whether to install Microsoft Exchange.**

   Next, the Internet Wizard asks about Internet Mail and Microsoft Exchange. Microsoft Exchange was an interesting idea gone wrong. At the very least, it lacks some necessary features, such as signature lines and message sorting. Others have more heated things to say about it. Our advice is to forget about it.

   The wizard asks whether you're ready for Ms. Wizard to install some files.

4. Choose <u>N</u>ext to continue with the installation.

Make sure that you have your Windows 95 distribution media handy — the CD-ROM it came on, your 13 disks, or the disks you created when you got Windows 95 preloaded on your system.

After much whirring and clicking and installing of disks (if you went that route), you're asked for the name of your Internet provider. The wizard needs this information in order to create a dial-up connection named after your provider.

5. Type the name of your Internet provider.

Then you're asked for the telephone number you dial to contact the Internet.

6. Type the access phone number for your Internet account.

It's important that you include the area code because Windows 95 uses the area code when it's figuring out how to dial the phone (whether to dial an area code).

Next, Ms. Wizard needs your user name and password so that she can try to sign on.

7. Type the user name and password for your account on your Internet provider.

Here we get to the geeky stuff. Your Internet provider may have given you an address for your computer. These addresses are called IP (Internet Protocol) addresses and are numbers in the form 123.245.167.189, though you may not have three digits between each set of periods. Look at the section "Some Nitty-Gritty Stuff You Should Ignore If at All Possible," later in this chapter, for more information.

8. If you were issued an IP address, select the option called <u>A</u>lways use the following, and enter your IP address and your subnet mask (a number such as 255.255.255.0).

The next step is more geeky stuff, also explained in the "Nitty-Gritty" section. If you know these numbers, type them in the box. If you don't, try leaving them blank.

9. Type the other IP addresses the Internet Wizard asks for, if you know them.

If you were misguided enough to tell Ms. Wizard that you want to use Microsoft Exchange for your Internet mail, she wants to know your e-mail address and your mail server (where it should send your mail).

10. Type your e-mail address and the name of your mail server.

Your mail server is the name of the computer on which you send and receive mail. It's usually a computer at your Internet service provider, something like `postoffice.oz.net`. Your e-mail address is something like `dorothy@oz.net`.

You're done! Click the Finish button (as though you have any choice!).

Windows 95 may take this moment to restart your computer. Let it; you can't get on the Internet if you don't. When you come back, you have on your desktop (we hope) an icon like the one shown in Figure 5-2.

Figure 5-2:
The Internet
desktop
icon.

Double-click that icon and see what happens. With any luck, you see the Internet Explorer window. As soon as you type the address of a Web page (such as `http://net.dummies.net`), you may really be online!

Using the Internet Wizard lets you skip lots of unpleasant dialog boxes and menus. In fact, to see about getting some real software, you can skip all the way down near the end of this chapter, to the section "You Wanted to Get Some Useful Work Done on the Internet?" You may want to take a look at the step-by-step portions of this chapter anyway, in case Ms. Wizard didn't get everything exactly right or in case something changes in your setup.

Hey, Windows 95 — I Have a Modem!

Okay, your computer isn't on the Internet already, and the wizards have let you down. That's okay — take it one step at a time, and you'll get yourself on the Internet anyway. To access the Internet, whether you do it via an Internet provider, an online service, or the Microsoft Network (MSN), you have to tell Windows 95 that you have a modem. (You do have a modem, right? If you have gotten this far and you're not sure, you haven't been paying attention!)

You probably never had this problem — DOS and Windows 3.1 didn't know and didn't care whether you had a modem. Because Windows 95 wants to be in charge of everything, however, it really wants to know. Fortunately, Windows 95 tells you all about what it believes is inside your computer. Here's how to see what it thinks:

1. **Click the Start button on the taskbar and choose Settings⇨Control Panel.**

You see one of the folders that should be familiar to you now that you're working in Windows 95. The last (or almost last) entry in this folder is labeled System.

2. **Double-click the System folder.**

Windows 95 displays your system properties. This dialog box has four tabs in it, one of which is the Device Manager.

3. **Click the Device Manager tab.**

You see a Modem entry on your list of devices.

4. **Click the + (plus sign) beside the modem entry.**

Your modem should be listed in the System Properties window, which looks like Figure 5-3.

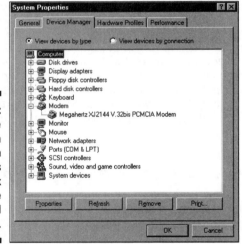

Figure 5-3:
The Device
Manager in
the System
Properties
dialog box
in the
Control
Panel.

5. **If your modem is listed, you're done. Skip the rest of these steps.**

If you see your modem listed here, you may congratulate Windows 95 — it found your modem (and you were luckier than we were). If Windows 95 didn't find your modem, you can tell it about your modem specifically. Windows 95 has, in fact, a cute little wizard that guides you through the modem-installation process. Continue to the next step to find this wizard.

6. **Click the Cancel button to close the System Properties dialog box, and double-click Add New Hardware, which should be one of the first items listed in the Control Panel.**

After this wizard introduces itself, the first question it asks you is whether it should look for the new hardware itself or let you tell it about the hardware. If Windows 95 hasn't already figured out that you have a modem, you have to tell it.

7. **Click No and save some time, especially if you know the make and model of your modem, and skip to Step 9.**

   If you choose to let Windows 95 look for your modem, you see a dialog box telling you whether it found anything.

8. **Click Details to see exactly what it found.**

   You should see a modem mentioned in this list. If you see other things too, don't worry about them; you have the opportunity to cancel out of the various wizard programs before they wreak any mayhem on your system. Just keep clicking the Cancel button until the Install New Modem Wizard appears.

   If you choose to tell Windows 95 about your modem specifically, you see a listing of hardware components similar to the one you looked at earlier.

9. **Double-click Modem.**

   No matter how you got here, you're looking at the Install New Modem Wizard's window. The wizard tells you that it plans to look around your computer for a modem.

10. **Click Next because this process gives Windows 95 a chance to see whether it can talk to your modem.**

    You see the Verify Modem dialog box, as shown in Figure 5-4.

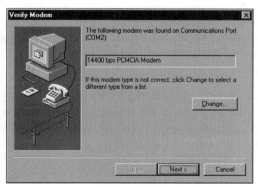

Figure 5-4: The Install New Modem Wizard guesses what kind of modem you have.

11. **Click the Change button in this dialog box so that you can tell Windows 95 specifically about your modem.**

12. **Select your modem manufacturer from the list on the left and the specific model of your modem from the list on the right.**

    If your modem isn't on the list, choose something that you know works — Standard Modems at the top of the list is a good choice if nothing else looks right. If a Windows 95 installation disk came with your modem, you can try inserting the disk in your disk drive and clicking the Have Disk button to see whether Windows 95 can find the installation information on the disk.

13. **Either way, you're ready to let Windows 95 have a go at the modem; click OK and move on to complete the installation.**

    You have to do one more thing to get your modem ready to dial: Windows 95, in its ceaseless quest to tailor itself to the way you work, wants to know where you're dialing from and how you place your telephone calls. It has a good reason for this task — well, sort of a good reason. What you dial to make a phone call depends on where you are. If Windows 95 knows where you are, it knows whether to dial 9 for an outside line, whether your Internet service provider is in one area code and you're in another, and the like. If you have a desktop computer, you don't have to think about this process much — just set it up one time, and you're done. If you have a portable computer you take from place to place (home and office, for example, and perhaps home and office are in different area codes), setting up two locations (call them Home and Office) and switching between them is a handy option.

    The way you set up a location initially and later switch to a different location is by using the Modems icon in the Control Panel. If you didn't have a Modems icon before, you have one now — it appears when you tell the Add New Hardware Wizard that you have a modem.

14. **Double-click Modems.**

    You see a dialog box with a button labeled Dialing Properties. In this dialog box, you tell Windows 95 about where you are. (Microsoft could have called the button Locations, but that would have been too obvious.)

15 **Click Dialing Properties.**

    You see the Dialing Properties dialog box, like the one shown in Figure 5-5.

    The Dialing Properties dialog box contains everything Windows 95 wants to know about where you are. Because you have to be some-where, Windows 95 decides that you're at your Default Location.

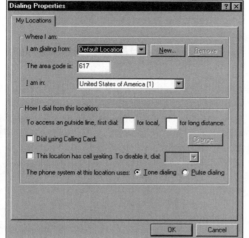

Figure 5-5:
Telling
Windows 95
where you
are and
how to dial
the phone.

16. **If this is the only place you expect to be using this computer, just change the settings appropriately.**

    If you expect to be using your computer in a number of places (places with different phone numbers, that is), you may want to use the New button to create a location for each of those places. Then, whenever you're in a new place, you tell Windows 95, and it knows whether it has to dial any extra codes before it dials a phone number. If you're in a different country, for example, Windows 95 may have to dial the area code and country code. If you're dialing from inside an office, you may have to dial 9 for an outside line or perhaps something else, such as 98 for a long-distance outside line. You can enter this stuff in the area of the dialog box labeled How I dial from this location.

    Use the New button to define as many locations as you think you're likely to need. When the time comes to dial the phone, Windows 95 gives you a chance to choose which location you're in.

17. **When you're done, click OK.**

Congratulations: It's a modem. If you want to check whether it's really working and communicating with Windows 95, click the Diagnostics tab in the Modem Properties dialog box (the one you were just looking at to define your locations) and select your modem from the list that appears. Click the More info button to encourage Windows 95 to try to communicate with your modem. If it succeeds, you see a dialog box full of incomprehensible and irrelevant stuff. If it doesn't succeed, you see a message such as Unable to communicate with Modem — in which case you should go find an expert. Click the OK buttons until the Modem Properties dialog box goes away, and then close the Control Panel. Job well done!

TIP

Using a telephone calling card

Getting Windows 95 to dial a telephone calling-card number for you is possible but not easy. If you use a calling card for long-distance calls, you can enter the calling-card number as well. In the Dialing Properties dialog box (which you display by double-clicking the Modems icon on the Control Panel), click the Dial using Calling Card check box, and you see the Change Calling Card window. Although Windows 95 has thoughtfully provided a number of predefined calling-card formats for you to use, you can't use them quite the way you might expect. You want to be able to type your calling-card number in that little gray box labeled Calling Card Number, but you can't. What you can do is use the Windows 95 list of calling cards to create your own personalized calling cards.

To use a telephone calling card with Windows 95, click the New button to create a new personalized card, and enter the name for that card. Notice that you still can't enter the thing you want to enter — your calling-card number. Click the Advanced button to see the Dialing Rules dialog box. Click the Copy From button to choose the type of long-distance calling card you use — with luck, your type appears on the list. Click OK to select the type of calling card you use, and click Close to close the Dialing Rules dialog box. Presto! — you can type your credit card number.

If you want to go back and try to understand or change the dialing formula, click Advanced again. Click the question mark on the title bar, and point to one of the dialing formulas. You get some hint about what these things mean.

Do You Really Want to Be Connected Directly to the Internet?

So you have a modem. If you're reading this chapter, you clearly want to be connected to *somebody* out there. The question is "Do you want to be connected directly to the Internet?"

You do have an alternative. You may have already discovered that Windows 95 comes complete with software for using Microsoft's own network, called the *Microsoft Network,* or MSN, for short. That's what the MSN icon is doing on your Windows 95 desktop. If you're not already connected to the Internet, you may want to use MSN as your gateway to the Internet. Microsoft certainly wants you to. If you decide to use MSN, check out *The Microsoft Network For Dummies,* 2nd Edition, by Doug Lowe (IDG Books Worldwide, Inc.).

You've decided not to use MSN? That's okay — Microsoft graciously permits you to access your Internet provider from Windows 95 anyway.

Gimme a Real Network

To use a real Internet account, you have to tell Windows 95 that you want to dial in to a network and then (of course) tell it all kinds of gory technical details about itself. Yes, we know that Windows 95 was supposed to let you skip that type of thing, but think again!

It's a beautiful day in the neighborhood

The first thing you have to do is tell Windows 95 that you want to talk on the phone. If you have any type of network installed on your computer, a Network Neighborhood icon appears on your Windows 95 desktop. It also appears if you told Windows 95 during installation that you want to talk on the phone or if the Windows 95 install program just decided (for reasons known only to itself) to put it there. If you don't have Network Neighborhood, don't panic (yet) — we get you into the neighborhood anyway. You need that Network Neighborhood icon in order to set up your Internet connection.

I've got the icon!

If you *do* have a Network Neighborhood icon, you're not out of the woods yet. *Right*-click (click using the right mouse button) the Network Neighborhood icon to see what happens. You get a pop-up menu that has a selection labeled Properties. Choose Properties, and you see a dialog box showing you what Windows 95 thinks that you use to connect to another computer. Figure 5-6 shows you a sample network configuration that appears on the Configuration tab in the Network window.

Does your Network Neighborhood contain entries for Dial-Up Adapter? It should contain *at least* the following entries:

- Dial-Up Adapter
- TCP/IP⇔Dial-Up Adapter

In the example in Figure 5-6, *lots* of things connect this computer to other computers. If everything has been working so far, don't worry about any stuff in there you don't understand. As long as you have the two Dial-Up Adapter entries, you can connect to the Internet. Skip down to the section "Welcome to the neighborhood," later in this chapter.

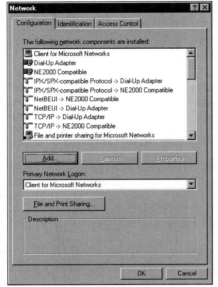

Figure 5-6:
Here's what
Windows 95
thinks
about our
Network
Neigh-
borhood.

Moving into the neighborhood

If you do *not* have a Network Neighborhood icon, here's what to do:

1. **Go to the taskbar and choose Start⇨Settings⇨Control Panel to begin messing with the guts of Windows 95.**

   You still have one more chance to get lucky. In the Control Panel window, you *may* see an icon labeled Network. If you do, you can double-click it. If you see the Dial-Up Adapter and TCP/IP⇨Dial-Up Adapter, you're all set. Skip the rest of this section.

   Otherwise, you had better see an icon labeled Add/Remove Programs, usually in the upper left corner. If you don't, you're in deeper than you want to be — call your local guru for help.

2. **Double-click the Add/Remove Programs icon.**

   You see a dialog box with three tabs at the top. The middle tab is labeled Windows Setup.

3. **Click the Windows Setup tab.**

   You see the Add/Remove Programs Properties window, as shown in Figure 5-7.

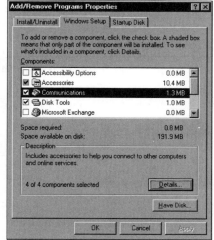

Figure 5-7:
The
Windows
Setup tab of
the Add/
Remove
Programs
dialog box
in the
Control
Panel.

4. Make sure that the Communications option is checked.

Do *not* uncheck anything that's already checked — otherwise, you're telling Windows 95 to remove parts of itself from your computer! Checking the Communications options tells Windows 95 to add four items to your configuration: Dial-Up Networking (which is what you're after here), Direct Cable Connection (useful for connecting computers that are physically near each other), HyperTerminal (a simple communications program), and Phone Dialer (which might be useful to see whether you have everything else set up correctly).

5. Click OK.

Windows 95 asks where it can find the CD or disks on which Windows 95 was supplied. It also asks to reboot your computer. After it does, you see a Network Neighborhood icon on your desktop.

Welcome to the neighborhood

Great! You have a Network Neighborhood icon you can use to configure your connection to an Internet account. Now all you have to do is make sure that Windows 95 knows that your PC should be talking on the telephone:

1. *Right*-click (click using the right mouse button) the Network Neighborhood icon.

You see a pop-up menu that includes Properties.

2. **Choose Properties.**

   The Network dialog box shows you what Windows 95 thinks that you use to connect to another computer. Refer to Figure 5-6 to see a sample network configuration. If your configuration contains the Dial-Up Adapter and TCP/IP⇨Dial-Up Adapter, you're all set — skip the rest of these steps.

3. **If you don't have a Dial-Up Adapter and TCP/IP⇨Dial-Up Adapter, click the Add button.**

   You see the Select Network Components dialog box.

4. **Select Adapter and click the new Add button.**

   You see the Select Network Adapters dialog box.

5. **Scroll down the list of manufacturers to Microsoft and click it. In the box on the right, click Dial-Up Adapter.**

   (We know — Microsoft didn't make your modem, but the folks there did write the software that will let your modem talk on the phone.) Figure 5-8 illustrates this series of steps.

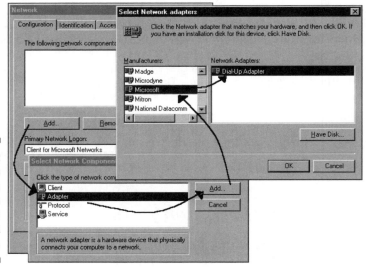

Figure 5-8: The series of steps you follow to add some network hardware.

6. **Click OK to finish.**

7. **Repeat Steps 3 through 6 to add the TCP/IP protocol the Internet uses: Click the Add button, select Protocol, and click the new Add button. Scroll down the list of manufacturers to Microsoft again and click it. In the box on the right, click TCP/IP. Click OK to finish.**

8. Click OK to close the Network Properties dialog box.

Windows 95 may ask you to restart your computer (again).

Closer and closer, nearer and nearer — but not there yet.

Meet My Internet Provider

You may have noticed that Windows 95 does not yet know a couple of things about you and your Internet provider (hard to believe, but true). These facts include the telephone number you use to dial your Internet provider, your user name, and your password. Some of the less obvious stuff includes your domain name servers and the like. Here's what you should have handy:

✔ Your Internet service provider's telephone number

✔ Your user name

✔ Your password

Making the connection

To type the phone number you're going to dial

1. Choose Start➪Programs➪Accessories➪Dial-Up Networking from the taskbar.

You see the Dial-Up Networking window, as shown in Figure 5-9, with a line that says Make New Connection.

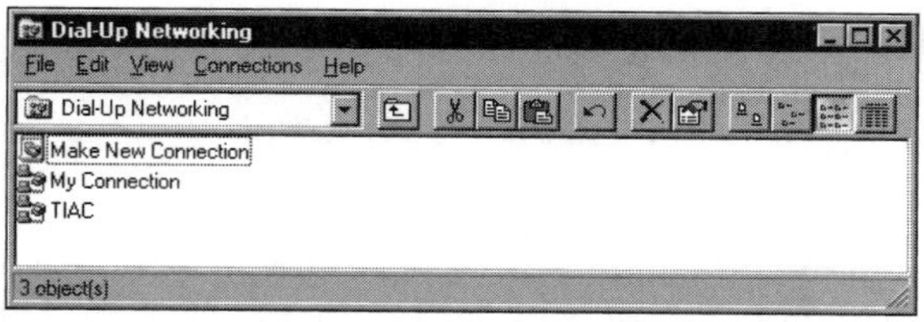

Figure 5-9:
The Dial-Up
Networking
window.

2. Double-click the Make New Connection line.

You see another of the cute Windows 95 wizards, the Make New Connection Wizard. This one asks you three questions to find out about your connection.

3. **Give your connection a name.**

   What's it called? Because our Internet service provider is named The Internet Access Company, we call ours *TIAC* — creative, huh?

4. **What modem will you use?**

   You see the description of your modem in a choice box. If you have only one modem, you're all set with this step. Otherwise, choose the modem you want this connection to use.

5. **Click Next to proceed to the next step in the wizard.**

6. **What's the phone number?**

   Enter the telephone number of your Internet provider. Notice the choice boxes for your area code and for your country. Windows 95 wants to know where your Internet provider is so that it can figure out what to do with those dialing rules we discuss earlier in this chapter, in the section "Hey, Windows 95 — I Have a Modem!"

7. **Click Next to proceed to the next step in the wizard.**

8. **Click Finish.**

   Your connection is added to the list of available connections, and you're done.

Sort of. Accounts at Internet providers come in a couple of flavors. Vanilla is a PPP account with a dynamic IP address. (Impress your friends: When they ask you whether you use the Internet, don't just say, "Yes," say, "I like my PPP account, even though it has a dynamic IP address.") If you have a PPP account, you're all set — skip down to the section "At Last — Connecting to Your Internet Provider," later in this chapter. If you have a SLIP account, you had better read on.

SLIP-sliding away

Windows 95 really wants to use a PPP account to talk to other computers on the Internet. If you have an older SLIP or CSLIP account, Windows 95 can be coaxed into talking to it using a program called DSCRIPT on your Windows 95 CD-ROM. (If you don't have Windows 95 on CD-ROM, you're out of luck.) DSCRIPT is in the \Admin\Apptools folder on the CD-ROM, and you can run it by double-clicking its filename in Windows Explorer or My Computer.

If you have a SLIP or CSLIP account, call your Internet provider. Almost all providers can turn your SLIP or CSLIP account into a PPP account with a single phone call (we did, with TIAC, our Internet provider in Massachusetts).

At Last — Connecting to Your Internet Provider

After only hours of agony, you're ready to call up your Internet account:

1. **If you have closed the Dial-Up Networking dialog box, you have to open it again by choosing Start⇨Programs⇨Accessories⇨Dial-Up Networking from the taskbar.**

2. **Double-click the connection name you just created (in the "Making the connection" section, earlier in this chapter).**

   Windows 95 suggests My Connection for the name.

   You see a Connect To dialog box, as shown in Figure 5-10. Windows 95 may or may not suggest a user name, depending on whether you have other networking set up. Make sure that the right user name is in the box, and remember that cApiTaliZaTioN matters!

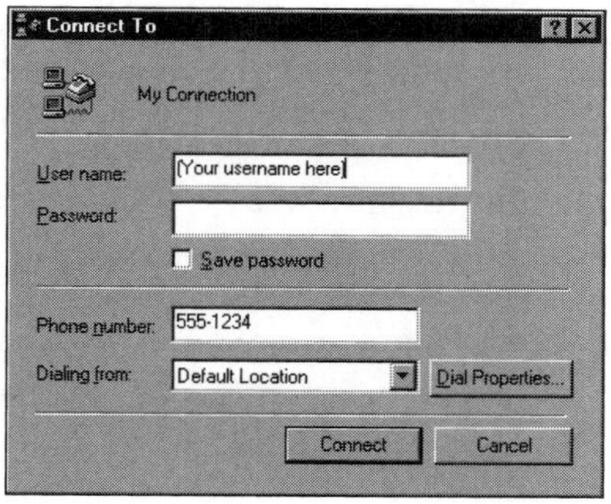

Figure 5-10: The Windows 95 Connect To dialog box dials the phone and makes the connection.

3. **Enter your password in the Password box.**

4. **Decide whether to check the Save password check box so that you don't have to enter your password again.**

   Advantage: You don't have to type your password every time you want to call the Internet. Disadvantage: Anyone can walk up to your PC and sign on to the Internet as you.

5. **Fill in the Phone number and Dialing from boxes.**

   The phone number should be familiar from the Make New Connection Wizard. You can type a new telephone number here, although you probably don't want to — you're better off modifying the telephone number permanently (see the section "Some Nitty-Gritty Stuff You Should Ignore If at All Possible," just ahead in this chapter) or creating a new connection.

The Dialing from box contains the name of the location where Windows 95 thinks that you are right now. This box should be familiar if you read the section "Hey, Windows 95 — I Have a Modem!" way back at the beginning of this chapter. See how all the pieces are beginning to fit together?

6. **Click the Connect button.**

   If you're using a PPP account, you see a series of messages beginning with `Initializing` and ending with `Connected`. Skip to Step 8.

   If you're using SLIP, you see `Initializing`, `Dialing`, and then a terminal window.

7. **If you use SLIP, sign on to your Internet provider and do whatever you have to do to get your IP address.**

   (Ask your Internet provider if you don't know.) In many cases, your provider issues you an IP address after you type your password.

8. **Then click Continue on the terminal screen.**

   Windows 95 asks you for your SLIP Connection IP address.

9. **Type the address you read off the screen and click OK.**

   You see the Connected box.

10. **Celebrate — you're finally connected to the Internet!**

    The Connected box stays on your desktop until you disconnect. You may want to minimize it so that it appears only on the taskbar — we usually do.

11. **When you're ready to disconnect, click the Disconnect button.**

    The dialog box automatically goes away.

Congratulations: You're on the Internet!

Some Nitty-Gritty Stuff You Should Ignore If at All Possible

When you call your Internet provider, you're connecting your computer to the Internet. Think for a second about what this means: Several million computers worldwide may need to be able to find your computer and talk to it. Furthermore, they want to be able to talk to your computer more or less instantaneously. Therefore, that somebody out there needs to know something about your computer should come as no surprise.

To enable the rest of the computers on the Internet to find your own computer, you have to enter some additional information. You may also have received one or more of the following pieces of information from your Internet provider:

- **A permanent IP address:** This number, which is in the form 123.45.67.89, is your real address on the Internet. If you didn't get one, your Internet service provider invents one for you every time you call up.

- **One domain name server (DNS) address or more:** These addresses, which use the same kind of numbers as your IP address, are for the computers your computer can ask for directions to find other computers.

- **A domain name:** This name indicates which family of computers your computer is a member of. It's usually a name related to your Internet service provider. Because one of our Internet providers is TIAC, for example, one of our domain names is tiac.net.

- **A host name:** This is the name by which your computer is known on the Net. You don't use the host name unless you do some really geeky stuff.

You can tell Windows 95 about this stuff like this:

1. **From the Dial-Up Networking browser (refer to Figure 5-9), *right*-click your connection name.**

   You see a pop-up menu that includes Properties.

2. **Choose Properties.**

   You see general information about this connection.

3. **Click the Server Type button.**

   You see the Server Types dialog box.

4. **Click the TCP/IP Settings button.**

   You see the TCP/IP Settings dialog box, as shown in Figure 5-11.

   This dialog box is the place to type your permanent IP address and your domain name server IP addresses, if you know them. In many cases, neither Windows 95 nor your Internet service provider cares if you don't bother.

5. **If your Internet provider gave you this information, type it in the box. If your Internet provider didn't tell you a permanent address, click Server Assigned IP address.**

6. **Click OK until you're back at the Dial-Up Networking window.**

When you're looking at the properties for a connection, you can click the Server Type button. Notice that the Server Types dialog box has check

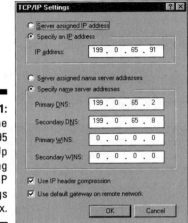

Figure 5-11:
The
Windows 95
Dial-Up
Networking
TCP/IP
Settings
dialog box.

boxes for N̲etBEUI and I̲PX/SPX Compatible. You can clear these check boxes and speed up your network communications a little.

You Wanted to Get Some Useful Work Done on the Internet?

Congratulations — you're on the Internet, and you're ready to download all sorts of interesting software.

Chapter 6 tells you the general procedures for downloading and installing software from the Internet, and Chapter 7 lists programs that are worth downloading.

Chapter 6

Grabbing Software over the Net

● ●

In This Chapter

▶ Getting files using your Web-browsing program
▶ Uncompressing compressed files with WinZip
▶ Checking software for viruses
▶ Installing software

● ●

*O*kay — you've installed Trumpet Winsock or something similar (if you use Windows 3.1) or you have gotten the Windows 95 Dial-Up Networking system to work. Mac folks have MacTCP and FreePPP or some other program running. You have some type of Web browser too; Windows 3.1 and Mac users got it from the same place they got Trumpet Winsock or MacTCP, and Windows 95 comes with Internet Explorer. Yes, you're ready to grab software right off the Internet. All the programs described in Chapter 7 are, in fact, available as freeware or shareware from the Net.

Luckily, if you followed the instructions in Chapters 3 and 4, you already have a nice Web browser capable of *FTP (File Transfer Protocol)*, a way to download files. You have to know a few things, however, about downloading and running software from the Net, and this chapter tells you about them. You need a few well-chosen software tools, including a program to uncompress compressed files. These useful little programs are usually called *utilities*.

This chapter describes how to use your Web browser to download and install programs.

Instructions in this part of the book assume that you're using a PC running DOS and Windows 3.1 or Windows 95. If you're using a Macintosh, you use different unzipping software. The concepts, however, are the same.

The Big Picture

Lots of software is out on the Net, usually stored on an *FTP server* (a computer that responds to requests for files from FTP programs and most Web browsers). Here are the steps for getting software from the Internet running on your own computer:

1. Find it.

In Chapter 7, we tell you good places to go hunting for programs.

2. Download it.

When you use a Web browser to download files, this step is as easy as clicking a link on a Web page, usually a link that says Download. Or you may be given the URL (Internet address) of the file on the FTP server. FTP URLs look like this:

```
ftp://hostname/pathname/filename
```

For example, the following line is the URL of a file on the Microsoft FTP server:

```
ftp://ftp.microsoft.com/Bussys/readme.txt
```

3. Unzip it, if it's zipped.

Most files on FTP servers are zipped (compressed) so that they download more quickly. Zipped files have the extension ZIP. One ZIP file can contain a bunch of compressed files. To uncompress the file, use WinZip or another decompression program. (Mac folks can use StuffIt Expander.) Unless you have retrieved the software directly from its home Web site, or even if you have, this wouldn't be a bad time to run a virus checker, just in case. See the section "Scanning for Viruses," later in this chapter.

4. Install it.

Different programs install differently, to our annoyance. To figure out how to install a program, you may have to read a text file that comes with it (if any) or follow the directions on the Web page from which you downloaded the file.

Some downloaded files are executable, with the filename extension EXE or COM. To run these files, just double-click them in the Windows 95 Windows Explorer or the Windows 3.1 File Manager. Mac users can just double-click the filename in its folder.

If you unzipped a ZIP file, at least one of the files is probably an EXE file. If one is named Install.exe, run it.

Some programs come with installation instructions in a Readme.txt or other suggestively named file. Be sure to read these files using your word processor or Windows Notepad.

The first program you should download, unless you already have it, is WinZip (or StuffIt Expander for Mac users) so that you're ready to unzip the other files you download.

Using Your Web Browser to Download Files

In the bad old days (two years ago), you needed a special FTP program to do your downloading; now, however, Web browsers can handle FTP too. You can use Netscape, Internet Explorer, or most other modern Web browsers to grab files from the Net.

When you click a link on a Web page that downloads a file or when you type an FTP URL (ooh — doncha love that technical talk?), you see a Save As window, which means that your Web browser wants to know where to put the file you're downloading. You choose a folder on your hard disk in which to store the file. Then you see a window that shows you the progress of your download. Although different browsers display different-looking windows, they all tell you how it's going and how much time is left (more or less, usually using a thermometer-like window that crawls across your screen painfully slowly). When the progress window disappears, your download is done!

Downloading a good unzipping program

Many files from the Internet are *zipped* (compressed) so that they transfer more quickly. After you have downloaded a ZIP file, you can do exactly nothing with them because they're in ZIP format (that's what the ZIP on the end stands for). The Connecticut shareware author Nico Mak has, fortunately, written a program called WinZip that decompresses those files, and he's willing to let you try it out for free.

Follow these steps to get the WinZip program:

1. Run your browser.

   To run your browser, double-click its icon. Just below the toolbar, most browsers have a box labeled Location or Address that shows the URL (Web address) of the current page.

2. **In the Location or Address box, type** www.winzip.com **and press Enter.**

   You go to the WinZip home page.

3. **Follow the instructions to download the latest version of WinZip for your system.**

   The WinZip home page changes from time to time as Nico Mak updates his material. It probably has a link you can click — it may be labeled Download Evaluation — to start the download. Then the Save As dialog box asks where you want to store the WinZip installation file.

4. **Using the dialog box, move to your temporary folder (remember that it's the one in Chapter 3 we tell you to create) and click Save.**

   If you have minded your Ps and Qs (well, your quotes and slashes), your browser begins downloading the file, and you see a window telling you how the download is progressing. Depending on the speed of your modem, downloading a program may take anywhere from a few minutes to more than an hour. The progress window should give you some idea. When the download is done, the dialog box disappears.

5. **Leave your browser running because you probably will want to do a little Web browsing before you're through.**

You have downloaded a file with a name such as Winzip95.exe, and you're ready to install WinZip. Now you know how easy it is to download files from the Net.

Now would be a good time to disconnect from your Internet provider, especially if it charges by the hour. If you don't disconnect yourself, it may hang up on you, which is okay too.

FTP won't speak to me!

FTP servers are sometimes broken or often too busy to talk to you. If you have a problem connecting to the FTP server, messages appear in your browser window. For example, rtfm.mit.edu is frequently overloaded and doesn't let you log on. Most FTP servers, however, send helpful messages about other FTP sites that may have the information you want.

Getting Ready to Decompress with WinZip

You need an unzipping program to deal with compressed files, specifically the ones with the file extension ZIP (these files are called, amazingly, *ZIP files*). Programs with names such as PKZIP, PKUNZIP, and UNZIP have been around for years. These programs are especially useful on the Internet because compressed files take up less space on FTP servers and take less time to download.

Although PKUNZIP, UNZIP, and their brethren work fine, most of them are DOS programs and not convenient to use from Windows. Using the MS-DOS icon every time you want to run one is annoying. Luckily, if you followed the steps in the preceding section of this chapter, you're ready to install a nice little Windows program called WinZip that can both unzip and zip things for you.

Installing WinZip

Now you can install WinZip from the file you downloaded. To uncompress and install WinZip, follow these steps (if you're installing a version later than WinZip 6.2, follow the instructions on-screen if they differ from these steps):

1. **In the Windows 3.1 File Manager or the Windows 95 My Computer, double-click the name of the file you just downloaded.**

   A dialog box asks whether you want to go ahead and set up WinZip.

2. **Click the Setup button.**

   The setup program asks in which directory you want to put the program. The program suggests C:\Winzip, but you can change the directory if you want to put the file somewhere else.

3. **Click OK.**

   WinZip displays information about the program.

4. **Click Next.**

   WinZip asks you to agree to its license agreement, which is only fair.

5. **Click Yes to agree.**

   The installation program asks whether you want the newfangled WinZip Wizard or the time-honored WinZip Classic. We favor the latter because we find it easier to use.

6. **Click Start with WinZip Classic and then click Next.**

   WinZip asks whether you want the Express or Custom setup.

7. **Click Next to go with the Express setup.**

   Things happen, and WinZip is installed.

8. **Click Finish.**

   WinZip runs automatically so that you can try it out.

WinZip is ready for use. Windows 3.1 users see a new program group in Program Manager, and Windows 95 users see a new folder on their desktop (as shown in Figure 6-1) and new commands on the Start⇨Programs menu.

Figure 6-1:
WinZip
installs
these icons
on your
computer.

Running WinZip

Give it a try! Double-click that icon, if WinZip isn't already running.

The first time you run the program, WinZip may display a bunch of helpful messages, including a question about your intention to register your copy. (We talk about this subject at the end of Chapter 7.)

Looking at the WinZip window

After WinZip is finished with its configuration questions, a window similar to the one shown in Figure 6-2 appears.

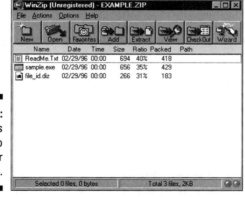

Figure 6-2:
WinZip is
ready to
unzip your
files.

To open a ZIP file (which the WinZip folks call an *archive*), click the Open button and choose the directory and filename for the ZIP file. Poof! WinZip displays a list of the files in the archive, with their dates and sizes.

WinZip remembers the last four ZIP files you opened and lists them at the bottom of the File menu. Thanks to this feature, reopening a ZIP file you used recently is easy.

Unzip it!

Sounds suggestive, we know, but it's not as much fun as it sounds. If you want to use a file in a ZIP file, you have to *extract* that file after you have opened the ZIP file: You ask WinZip to uncompress the file you want to use and to store it in a new file, not as part of the ZIP file.

To extract a file:

1. **Choose from the list of files the file you want to extract.**

   You can choose files listed together by clicking the first file and then Shift+clicking the last one. To select an additional file, Ctrl+click it.

2. **Click the Extract button.**

   A dialog box asks in which directory you want to put the file and whether you want to extract all files in the archive or just the file you selected.

3. **Select the directory in which to store the unzipped files.**

4. **Click OK.**

   WinZip unzips the file. The ZIP file is unchanged, and now you also have the uncompressed file (or files).

Zip it!

To add a file to a ZIP file:

1. **Open the ZIP file by clicking the Open button.**

   Or make a new ZIP file by clicking the New button.

2. **Click the Add button.**

   You see the Add dialog box, as shown in Figure 6-3.

Figure 6-3:
Adding a
file to a
ZIP file.

3. **Use the Directories/Drives box to select the directory that contains the file (or files) you want to add.**

   Select the files you want from the Select Files list.

4. **Choose a setting for the Action box.**

   Decide whether you want WinZip to compress the files into the ZIP file, leaving the original files untouched (Add), or delete the original files after they have been added (Move).

5. **Click the Add (or Move) button to do the deed.**

When you choose files, you can select a group of files listed together by clicking the first one and then Shift+clicking the last one. To select or unselect an individual file, Ctrl+click it.

Zipped out?

When you're all finished zipping and unzipping, quit WinZip by choosing File⇨Exit.

WinZip is close friends with Windows Explorer and Windows File Manager. If you drag a ZIP file from Windows Explorer or File Manager to the WinZip window, WinZip automatically opens the file. If you drag another type of file or a group of files to WinZip, they're added to the current archive. (If a current archive doesn't exist, WinZip starts a new one and asks you what to call it.)

Now that you know how to unzip software you get from the Internet, you're ready for the next topic: safe software.

Scanning for Viruses

We all know that you practice safe software: You check every new program to make sure that no hidden software viruses, which might display obnoxious messages or trash your hard disk, are lurking around. If doing so is true of you, you can skip this section.

For the rest of you, using a virus-scanning program is a good idea. Otherwise, you never know what naughty piece of code you might unwittingly FTP to your defenseless computer.

If you use Windows 3.1 and MS-DOS 6.2 (or later)

DOS 6.2 and Windows 3.1 come with a virus checker built right into the Windows File Manager. It's not a particularly good virus checker, but it's much better than nothing. Here's how to use it:

1. **Run File Manager.**

2. **Choose Tools⇨Antivirus.**

   You see the Microsoft Anti-Virus window, as shown in Figure 6-4.

3. **Choose a disk drive, by clicking it in the Drives box.**

4. **Click the Detect and Clean button.**

   If you're scanning a large hard disk for viruses, this step can take several minutes.

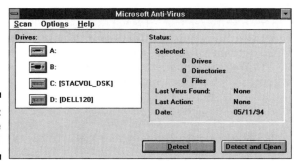

Figure 6-4:
Evict those
viruses!

Running Anti-Virus after obtaining new software is a good idea. Although the FTP servers on the Internet make every effort to keep their software archives virus-free, nobody is perfect. Don't get caught by some prankster's idea of a joke!

Much better virus checkers are available than the built-in one, including both commercial checkers and several shareware checkers you can download from the software archives we mention in Chapter 7.

If you use Windows 3.1 and an earlier version of MS-DOS

Upgrading from DOS 6.0 or 6.1 to 6.2 costs about $10, so we suggest that you do so. DOS 6.2 has lots of nice little features and installs easily and quickly.

If you don't want to upgrade, many virus checkers are available on the Net. Use your FTP program to connect to oak.oakland.edu, and go to the /pub/msdos/virus directory. Follow the instructions in the section "Netting a Program," later in this chapter.

If you use Windows 95

Strangely, Windows 95 doesn't come with virus-checking software. You may want to download one from the Net. Take a look at Chapter 7 to find one.

Netting a Program

Now you're ready to grab software from the Net, unzip it as necessary, make little icons for the software, and check it all over for diseases. This section gives you general instructions for getting a program off the Internet and installing it on your PC. We're assuming that you know which program you want and that you know which FTP server has the program.

Luckily, in Chapter 7, when we mention a program you can download, we tell you on which Web pages or FTP servers you can find it. Programs you can download include mail readers, newsreaders, and Web browsers.

Getting hold of the program

To copy the file from a Web site to your own computer:

1. **If you want to make a separate directory for the program, do so.**

   Otherwise, you can store the program in your \Internet directory.

2. **Connect to the Internet.**

3. **Run your Web browser program.**

4. **Go to the Web page that has the program you want.**

   We tell you which Web page to go to for each program in Chapter 7.

5. **Click the link to download the file.**

6. **Disconnect from the Internet to save connect-time charges.**

   If you don't pay for the Internet by the hour, this step is optional.

Unzipping the program files

If the program isn't in a ZIP file, skip this section.

1. **In Windows File Manager or Windows Explorer, double-click the ZIP file.**

   This step runs WinZip and opens the ZIP file. WinZip shows you the files the ZIP file contains.

2. **Click the Extract button.**

   You see the Extract dialog box, as shown in Figure 6-5.

Figure 6-5:
To get the compressed files from a ZIP file, just add water!

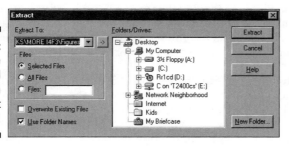

3. **In the Extract To box, type the full pathname of the directory in which you want the files to be stored.**

   Alternatively, you can use the directory box to its right to choose the directory.

4. **Choose All files so that you extract all the files in the ZIP file.**

5. **Click Extract.**

   WinZip begins copying and uncompressing the files from the ZIP file into their new home. As long as WinZip is uncompressing files, the little light in the lower right corner of the WinZip window remains red. When WinZip finishes copying files, the light turns green. Is this cute, or what?

6. **To leave WinZip, choose File⇨Exit.**

7. **Now that you have uncompressed the files in the ZIP file, you can delete the ZIP file if you need the space on your disk.**

   Another good idea is to copy the ZIP file to a disk to add to your software archive. This disk is invaluable if you have to reinstall the program later, install the program on another computer, or give the program to a friend.

If the ZIP file contains any files named Read.me or Readme.txt or anything else with a TXT or DOC extension, read those files by using Windows Notepad or your word-processing program. The files may contain instructions for installing and configuring the program that are more accurate than what we are about to tell you.

Installing the program

Now the program is ready to install. A few housekeeping tasks remain.

If the program comes with a file named Setup.exe or Install.exe, run it by double-clicking the filename in File Manager or Windows Explorer or the Mac folder. Then skip the steps in this section because the installation program performs these tasks for you — go directly to the section "Configuring the program," a little later in this chapter.

To make an icon for the program in Windows 95, simply drag the filename of the program to the desktop or to an open folder on the desktop. Windows 95 creates a shortcut icon for the program.

To make an icon for the program in Windows 3.1:

1. **Open both Program Manager and File Manager and arrange your screen so that you can see the program group in which you want to put the icon (in Program Manager) and the program name (in File Manager).**

2. **Drag the program name from the File Manager into the Program Manager, and place it in the program group where you want it.**

   You see a new icon in your new program group.

WS_FTP, for serious downloaders

For downloading a file or two, using your Web browser is fine. If you have to download a bunch of files or upload more than one or two files, however, you need a serious FTP program. Our favorite is WS_FTP, which comes with versions for Windows 95 and Windows 3.1. You can get WS_FTP from most of the software sources listed in Chapter 7. Mac users can get Fetch, another excellent FTP program.

After you have installed WS_FTP, you can use it to copy files from FTP servers on the Internet to your own computer:

1. **Run WS_FTP.**

   You see the Session Profile window, asking for information about the FTP server from which you want to get files.

2. **Type the name of the FTP server (such as** ftp.microsoft.com **or** ftp.winzip.com) **in the Host Name box.**

3. **Type your user name and password on the FTP server into the User ID and Password boxes.**

   If you don't have an account on the FTP server, type **anonymous** as the user name and your e-mail address as the password.

4. **Click the Ok button to connect.**

   Little messages from the FTP server appear at the bottom of the WS_FTP window. When you're connected, information about the files on your computer (the "local" computer) appears on the left side

of the window, and information about the files on the FTP server (the "remote" computer) appears on the right side of the window.

5. **Tell WS_FTP which file you want from the FTP server.**

   Use the right side of the WS_FTP window (the "remote" side) to move to the directory on the FTP server that contains the file or files you want.

6. **Tell WS_FTP where to put the file.**

   Use the left side of the WS_FTP window (the "local" side) to move to the folder where you want to put the downloaded file on your hard disk.

7. **Tell WS_FTP whether the file is ASCII (plain, unformatted text) or binary (anything else).**

   Click the ASCII or Binary button.

8. **Start the transfer by clicking the left-pointing arrow between the Remote and Local sides of the window.**

   You may want to step out for coffee at this point, if the file is large.

9. **Disconnect from the FTP server and exit from WS_FTP by clicking the Exit button.**

While you're connected to the FTP server, you can transfer more than one file. You can even transfer a file from your computer to the FTP server, but you had better be sure that you have permission to put it there!

Associating the program with data files

If the program uses files as input, associate those files with the appropriate file extension. These programs include editors, word processors, drawing programs, and other programs that store their data in files. For programs that don't work on input files or for programs that automatically register their file types, skip these steps.

Here's what to do in Windows 3.1:

1. **In Windows File Manager, choose File⇨Associate from the menu.**

   You see the Associate dialog box.

2. **In the File̲s with Extension box, type the filename extension of the files your new program works with.**

   If you just installed a graphics program that displays GIF files, for example, type **GIF**.

   The A̲ssociate With box shows the program associated with that type of file. If you see (None), no program is assigned to that type of file.

3. **Click the B̲rowse button, select the filename of the program you just installed, and click OK.**

4. **Click OK to make the Associate dialog box go away.**

Now File Manager knows which program to run when you double-click files with that extension. Because WinZip automatically associates itself with the ZIP extension, for example, when you double-click a ZIP file in File Manager, WinZip runs and displays the contents of the ZIP file.

In Windows 95, do the following:

1. **In Windows Explorer, choose V̲iew⇨O̲ptions.**

   You see the Options window.

2. **Select the File Types tab.**

   You see a list of registered file types (file types for which Windows 95 knows which program to run). As you select each file type on the list, you see details about the file type, including the filename extension and the program associated with it.

3. **Click the N̲ew Type button.**

   You see the Add New File Type dialog box.

4. **In the first two boxes, type the description of the file type and the filename extension.**

5. **Click the New button.**

   If a program is already associated with that filename extension, Windows tells you about it. If not, you see the New Action window.

6. **In the Action box, make up a description of what double-clicking a file of this type will do.**

   If double-clicking a graphics file will display the file, for example, type something like **Display the graphics file.**

7. **Click the Browse button, select the program you just installed, and click Open.**

8. **Click OK in the New Action dialog box.**

   You return to the Add new File Type window. (Windows 95 sure has enough windows — far more than 95!)

9. **Click the Close button.**

   You return to the Options window, and the new file type appears on the list of registered file types.

10. **Click the Close button.**

Now Windows 95 understands what your new program is good for. Double-clicking files of the type you specified now runs your new program automagically.

Configuring the program

Now you can run the program by double-clicking its icon. Hooray!

You may have to tell the program, however, about your Internet address or your computer or who knows what before it can do its job. Refer to the text files, if any, that came with the program or choose Help from the program's menu bar to get more information about how to configure and run your new program.

So Where Are All the Programs?

You're raring to download and install a program — you know all the moves! Chapter 7 has scads of Winsock and MacTCP programs you can download and run.

Chapter 7
Cool Winsock and Mac Software

- -

In This Chapter

▶ How to find Winsock software on the Internet for use with Windows 3.1 or Windows 95

▶ How to find MacTCP software on the Internet for use with the Macintosh

▶ Elegant e-mail programs

▶ Beautiful Web browsers

▶ Fabulous FTP programs

▶ Nifty newsreaders

▶ And more!

- -

*I*f you have read Chapter 6, you know how to download a program from the Internet using a Web browser, install the program using Windows 3.1 or Windows 95 or the Mac, and run it. So what programs might you want to download and install? This chapter tells all.

Before you can use any program described in this chapter, you must be up and running with an Internet SLIP or PPP account, as described in Chapters 3, 4, and 5, or with an online service that supports Winsock and MacTCP programs. You also need some blank space on your disk, usually no more than 5MB per program (and sometimes much less).

Super Sources of Software

Several internauts have created Web pages that list (and rate) hundreds of useful Winsock programs, including what they do, how well they work, and where you can find them.

TUCOWS

The Ultimate Collection Of Winsock Software (or *TUCOWS*) is our current favorite Web site for finding software. This Web site, started in 1994 by Scott Swedorski and maintained by ComputerLink Online, Inc., is at

```
http://www.tucows.com
```

Because this Web site is so popular, the TUCOWS folks have arranged for dozens of *mirror sites* (identical Web sites) so that you don't get the Internet equivalent of a busy signal (a "server is not responding" message) when you try to connect. TUCOWS can be a godsend when you want to download a popular program, such as a new version of Netscape that just became available yesterday.

On the TUCOWS home page, follow the instructions to find a mirror site that's geographically near you. Then click the Windows 95/NT, Windows 3.*x*, or Macintosh link to see a page that lists the categories of programs TUCOWS offers, as shown in Figure 7-1.

When you click a category of program, you see a listing of the programs of that type. Figure 7-2 shows some of the programs in the Text Chat category (programs for participating in Internet Relay Chat, as described in Chapter 9). To download the program, click its name. Chapter 6 tells you how to download and install programs.

Figure 7-1:
TUCOWS
includes all
types of
Internet
programs
for both
Windows
and the
Mac.

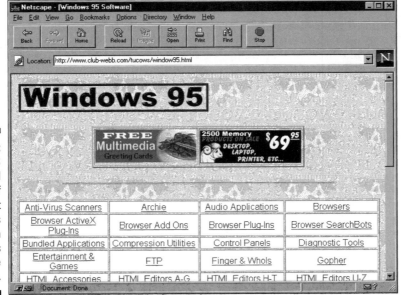

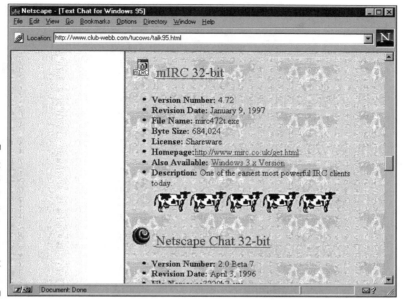

Figure 7-2:
TUCOWS
lists some
programs
for partici-
pating in
"text chats"
(Internet
Relay Chat).

Many programs also have home pages on the Web, and TUCOWS includes a link to the home page.

Forrest Stroud's Consummate Winsock Apps List

The first Web page, and still one of the best, about Winsock programs is the Consummate Winsock Apps List, created by Texas undergraduate Forrest Stroud. Go to either of these sites:

```
http://www.stroud.com
http://cws.iworld.com
```

and click either 16-bit Apps (for use with Windows 3.1) or 32-bit Apps (for use with Windows 95) — this site doesn't have Mac programs. Then scroll down to see the main menu of Winsock applications, and click the type of program you want. You see a Web page that lists programs of that type. Figure 7-3 shows part of the listing of virus-checking programs.

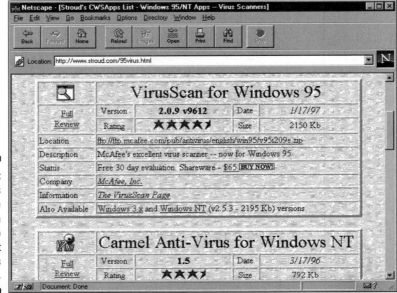

Figure 7-3:
Here's
some
information
about two
excellent
antivirus
programs.

Many entries on the Consummate Winsock Apps List contain links to a home page for the program so that you can get full details about the program. Entries also contain a link to an FTP server from which the program can be downloaded. To download the program, click the Location link and tell your Web browser where to save the program file. (Then refer to Chapter 6 for more information about installing software.)

Forrest updates the list continually, adding new programs and changing the listing to refer to new program versions. Browsing the pages from time to time to see what's new (or clicking the Newest Apps link on the main page) is well worth the effort.

Download.com

Download.com is a Web site with all types of downloadable software, including Internet software. It's at

```
http://www.download.com
```

In the Categories list, click Internet and then choose the subcategory you want. You see a list of program titles — just click a title to see a whole Web page about that program. If you want the program, click the big Click Here to Download button.

Dave Central

Who's Dave? We're not sure, but he sure has put together a great collection of Internet software.

```
http://davecentral.com
```

Extreme Mac Software

Joel Mueller maintains a Web site with lots of information about the Macintosh, at

```
http://www.extreme-mac.com
```

To find Joel's list of downloadable programs, click the Software link.

WinSite

WinSite is a huge repository of freeware and shareware programs for Windows 3.1 and Windows 95, including Winsock programs, at

```
http://www.winsite.com
```

WinSite is partially supported by America Online, which is making an effort to give back to the Internet in return for all the free stuff AOL users get from the Net. As you may have guessed, no Mac software is included. Although WinSite doesn't have much information about each program, it does have a broad variety of programs.

To look around for software by category, click the Browse icon, then the link for the type of computer you use, and then the category of programs in which you're interested.

The Papa FTP server

If you don't have access to the World Wide Web, you can download Winsock programs from many FTP servers, including the one at `papa.indstate.edu`. Go to the winsock-l directory and look around.

Your online service can do it too

What if you have an account with America Online or CompuServe or Prodigy? Can you use all this cool Winsock software? The answer depends on the service.

✔ America Online Version 3.0 or later lets you use all Winsock software except for e-mail programs.

✔ CompuServe Version 3.0 or later lets you use most Winsock software too.

✔ Prodigy Classic doesn't support Winsock programs. Prodigy Internet is actually just another Internet PPP provider and supports all Winsock and MacTCP programs.

✔ The Microsoft Network (MSN) can act as a SLIP or PPP account, so you can use Winsock software with it.

Yahoo!

Unless Yahoo has reorganized its pages again since this book went to press, here's how to get to its list of pages with information about Internet programs. Start at the Yahoo page:

```
http://www.yahoo.com
```

Click Computers and Internet, then click Software, and then click Internet. For listings of Winsock software, start at the Yahoo home page; then click Computers and Internet, then Software, then Protocols, then Winsock, and then Software Archives.

Elegant E-Mail

A good e-mail program makes sending, reading, forwarding, replying to, and saving mail messages easy. Ideally, the program should be capable of sorting incoming messages in folders based on what's in the headers. Luckily, several excellent e-mail programs are available as shareware or freeware.

Pegasus Mail

Pegasus Mail is an excellent freeware e-mail program. Its author, David Harris, lives in New Zealand and doesn't sell a commercial version of the program. He just gives it away over the Internet and supports the project by

selling the manuals. Don't think that because it's free, it's not good —
Pegasus rivals the good commercial programs! If you feel like supporting Mr.
Harris's Pegasus project or if you plan to use Pegasus extensively, you can
order a set of Pegasus manuals from him.

Pegasus is also available for DOS, the Mac, and a few other systems. It
handles both Internet mail and Novell network mail and can be configured to
work in about a dozen different languages. Amazing, for a free program!

Getting Pegasus Mail

You can find information about Pegasus and about downloading the latest
version or ordering a set of manuals at

```
http://www.pegasus.usa.com
```

Installing Pegasus Mail

Pegasus arrives as an executable installation file with a name such as
W32-242.exe. Here's how to install it:

1. **Double-click the filename of the Pegasus file you downloaded.**

   The Pegasus installation file comes with the WinZip self-extractor built
   right in, so it can unzip itself. (Strange things, these programs!)

2. **Click OK to let Pegasus unzip its files into the current folder.**

   Pegasus suggests a place to put the temporary files created during the
   installation process. It usually suggests the C:\Windows\Temp folder,
   which works fine. Don't change any other settings.

3. **Click Unzip.**

   The WinZip self-extractor program creates the temporary files the
   Pegasus installation program needs.

4. **Click OK to continue with the setup.**

   Now you see the Pegasus Mail Setup window.

5. **Click the Continue Installation button.**

   Pegasus asks whether you want the Netware version. If you're using a
   regular Internet account rather than a Netware local-area network in an
   office, you don't want Netware support.

6. **Click the No Netware Support button.**

   Pegasus asks where to install the program and suggests C:\Pmail. You
   can change this path if you want; Pegasus creates a folder if you type
   the name of a folder that doesn't exist.

7. **Change the folder name if you want Pegasus in a different folder, and then click the OK button.**

   The installation program displays one last window summarizing your choices to this point so that you can make sure that it knows what you want.

8. **Click the Install Pegasus Mail button.**

   Pegasus installs itself and creates a folder on your Windows 95 desktop or a program group in your Windows 3.1 Program Manager.

9. **Click the Exit button.**

You're ready to run Pegasus for the first time using the lovely little flying-horse icon.

Configuring Pegasus Mail

The first time you run Pegasus Mail, it asks for the information it needs to send and receive your mail.

1. **Run Pegasus by double-clicking the Pegasus Mail icon.**

   You see the Setting up mailboxes dialog box. Pegasus wants to know how many people plan to use this program on this computer.

2. **Click the choice appropriate for you.**

   If it's just li'l ol' you using your computer and you have just one li'l ol' Internet account, take the first choice.

   Pegasus asks where you want to put your e-mail directory and suggests C:\PMAIL\MAIL. You can change the location if you want your e-mail messages stored elsewhere.

3. **Click OK to tell Pegasus to make you a mail directory.**

   Depending on which version of Pegasus you're installing, you may see a troubleshooting message; take note of it and click OK if you do.

   Pegasus searches your computer for a file named Winsock.dll, which is part of Trumpet Winsock (or whatever software you use to connect to the Internet). When Pegasus finds the file, it asks whether it should use the file to connect to the Internet. (Well, what else would you use Winsock.dll for? A virtual paperweight?)

4. **Click Yes.**

   You see the big, scary Configuration for Built-in Internet Mailer dialog box, as shown in Figure 7-4.

5. **For the POP3 host, enter the name of your mail server (your Internet provider's host computer that stores your incoming mail until you're ready to pick it up).**

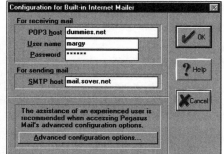

Figure 7-4:
You have to
tell Pegasus
how to get
and send
your e-mail.

This computer name is usually the same as the part of your
e-mail address after the at-sign (@). If your e-mail address is
elvis@presley.com, for example, enter presley.com.

6. For Username, enter your username.

Your username is the part of your e-mail address that comes before the
at-sign.

7. Type your password in the Password box.

On-screen, you see asterisks.

**8. For the SMTP host, enter the name of your mail gateway (your
Internet provider's host computer that accepts your outgoing mail
and sends it along to the Internet).**

If you don't know the name of the machine, try typing the same thing
you typed in the POP3 host box. If that doesn't work (later, when you
try to get your mail), call your Internet provider and ask.

9. Click OK.

You see the Pegasus Mail window, as shown in Figure 7-5, and Pegasus
tries to get your mail (it won't work if you're not online with your
Internet provider).

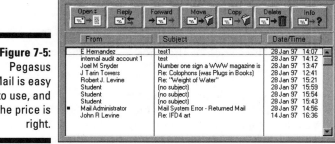

Figure 7-5:
Pegasus
Mail is easy
to use, and
the price is
right.

After you see the Pegasus Mail window, you're up and running.

Using Pegasus Mail

Here are some things you can do with Pegasus:

- ✔ To create a new message, choose File⇨New Message, press Ctrl+N, or click the Compose a new message button on the toolbar (the leftmost button).

- ✔ To see your new messages, choose File⇨Read New Mail, press Ctrl+W, or click the Read new mail button on the toolbar (the second button from the left).

- ✔ To read a message, double-click the message in your New mail folder or other folder.

- ✔ To delete a message after you have read it, click the Delete (trash can) button on the toolbar.

- ✔ To get your incoming messages from your Internet provider and send outgoing messages you have composed, choose File⇨Check and send mail or click the button labeled Both check and send mail in one operation (how's that for a long button name?), the third one from the right on the toolbar.

Eudora

Our favorite e-mail program is Eudora, by Qualcomm. A freeware version called Eudora Light is available free on the Net. If you like Eudora Light, for less than $70 you can trade up to the commercial version, Eudora Pro, which is even better than the shareware one. If you have questions about Eudora Pro, you can send e-mail to eudora-sales@qualcomm.com or call 800-2EUDORA. (Hmm. If you could send e-mail, you probably wouldn't have to ask the question.)

Getting Eudora Light

The freeware version of Eudora is available from

    http://www.eudora.com

It's also on lots of other Web sites, such as the ones listed earlier in this chapter.

Qualcomm has also written lots of documentation for Eudora Light that you can download from the Eudora Web site. The documentation is in PDF format (aka Adobe Acrobat format); see the "Literary Acrobatics" section, later in this chapter, to find out how to download a program that can display the documentation file.

Installing Eudora

The Eudora Light installation file is named something like Eudor30.exe (the number depends on the version you're getting). To install the program, simply double-click its filename in Windows 95 Windows Explorer (or My Computer), Windows 3.1 File Manager, or the Mac folder in which the file is located. Eudora Light installs itself, and you end up with an icon for it on your Windows 95 desktop or in Windows 3.1 Program Manager.

Before you can use Eudora Light, you have to tell it (her?) about yourself:

1. **Double-click the Eudora icon (the mailbox).**

   You see the Eudora Light window. We don't show a picture of it here because it's blank except for the menu bar at the top.

2. **If the Options window doesn't appear, choose Tools⇨Options from the menu.**

   You see the Getting Started section of the Options dialog box, as shown in Figure 7-6.

Figure 7-6:
Telling
Eudora your
life's story.

3. **In the POP account box, enter your e-mail address.**

   This entry doesn't have to be an address on your Internet provider's computer — it's wherever your mail comes.

4. **In the Real name box, enter your real name as you want it to appear in parentheses after your e-mail address.**

5. **Leave everything else as it is (for now).**

   You may want to change some settings later, but these settings should do for now.

6. **Click OK to save these settings.**

So who is Eudora, anyway?

According to the Eudora manual, the program's author was reading the Eudora Welty short story *Why I Live at the P.O.,* and he got inspired. It's nice to know that even nerds read some real books from time to time.

Eusing Eudora

Here's a quick list of things you can do in Eudora:

- ✔ To create a new message, choose Message➪New, press Ctrl+N, or click the New Message button on the toolbar.

- ✔ To see the messages in your Inbox, choose Mailbox➪In or press Ctrl+I.

- ✔ To read a message, double-click the message in your Inbox or other folder.

- ✔ To delete a message after you have read it, choose Message➪Delete, press Ctrl+D, or click the Delete (trash can) button on the toolbar.

- ✔ To get your incoming messages from your Internet provider, choose File➪Check Mail, click the Check Mail button on the toolbar, or press Ctrl+M.

- ✔ To send your outgoing messages to the Internet, choose File➪Send Queued Messages or press Ctrl+T.

See *The Internet For Dummies,* 4th Edition (IDG Books Worldwide, Inc.), for a complete description of how to use Eudora.

Other programs

Other e-mail programs include

- ✔ **Netscape Messenger or Netscape Navigator 3.0:** Netscape Messenger (which is part of Netscape Communicator 4.0), as shown in Figure 7-7, is the e-mail program that comes with recent versions of the famous Netscape Web browser. If you have Netscape Navigator Version 2.0 or 3.0, choose Window➪Netscape Mail.

- ✔ **Internet Mail:** This program, from Microsoft, comes with recent versions of Internet Explorer, or you can download it separately from the Internet software sites listed at the beginning of this chapter.

✓ Microsoft Exchange: Exchange comes with Windows 95 and can handle mail from Microsoft Network or your SLIP or PPP Internet account.

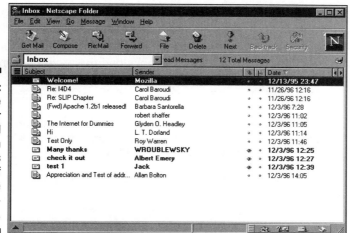

Figure 7-7:
Netscape
Messenger
is the e-mail
program
that comes
as part of
Netscape
Communi-
cator.

Most Usenet newsreaders can send e-mail messages because you often want to send an e-mail comment or question to the author of a message you just read.

Beautiful Browsers

A good Web browser can handle lots of different types of information, such as graphics, sound, and movies. It should have a good bookmark list, hot list, or other method of saving the URLs of pages you use often. It should display all types of Web pages, including those specifically designed to work with Netscape or Internet Explorer or that use HTML 2.0 (a version of the language in which Web pages are written).

Netscape

The star of Web browsers is, of course, Netscape Navigator, which is now part of the Netscape Communicator package. Netscape Communications, the company that makes Netscape Navigator, went public in 1995, and its stock price went through the roof. Because most people who use Netscape Navigator download it for free from the Net, of course, it remains to be seen how profitable the company will turn out to be. (It's doing surprisingly well selling boxed versions and server software.) Netscape is letting people download and use beta test versions of the program and asking folks to pay for the final versions — the registration fee is less than $50. Netscape Navigator and Netscape Communicator are available for Windows 95, Windows 3.1, the Mac, and several flavors of UNIX.

Getting Netscape

Netscape Navigator is part of the Netscape Communicator package, so we just call it Netscape, for short. You can download the program from

```
http://home.netscape.com
```

Because the file is large (at least 6MB), it takes a while to arrive, even with a fast modem. Be sure to save the file to a temporary directory, such as C:\Temp, not to the Netscape program directory.

If you use Windows 3.1, download the 16-bit version, even if you have installed the Win32s package, which supports some 32-bit programs. Windows 95 and NT users should download the 32-bit version.

Installing Netscape

When you download Netscape Navigator or Communicator, you get a self-extracting ZIP file with a name such as N32e40b.exe — the name is an unpronounceable bunch of characters which mean that it's the Netscape 32-bit version (for Windows 95), Version 4.0, beta test release. To install it:

1. **Create a temporary directory and move the file you downloaded into the new directory.**

   Don't put the file you downloaded into the directory you want the Netscape program to end up in.

2. **Run the file by double-clicking its filename in File Manager or My Computer or Windows Explorer.**

   The file expands into a whole bunch of files.

3. **Double-click the filename Setup.exe in File Manager or Windows Explorer.**

   The Netscape Setup program runs. During the setup, it asks in which directory you want to install the program.

If you have a previous version of Netscape installed, you can install the new version in the same directory.

Using Netscape

To run Netscape Communicator or Navigator, double-click its icon. The first time Netscape starts up, it shows you a page of legal boilerplate. Click Accept, if you can deal with the conditions. You then see the Netscape browser window. The Netscape Navigator 4.0 window is shown in Figure 7-8 (showing the home page for Great Tapes for Kids, an online catalog of quality kids' videos). As with any Web browser, to follow a hyperlink (text that appears underlined in blue or pictures with blue borders), just click one. To go to a particular URL (Web page), type the URL in the Location box near the top of the Netscape Navigator window. Click the Back button on the toolbar to return to the preceding page, or choose Go from the menu to see a list of the pages you have visited recently.

Netscape Navigator 2.0 and 3.0 include an e-mail program: Choose Window⇨ Netscape Mail to see the Main window. Netscape Communicator 4.0 includes an e-mail program called Netscape Messenger: Choose Communicator⇨ Messenger Mailbox to see the Messenger Inbox window.

Netscape Navigator 2.0 and 3.0 also have a Usenet newsreader, which you can use by choosing Window⇨Netscape News. In Netscape Communicator 4.0, choose Communicator⇨Collabra Discussions to see its newsreader.

For more information about using Netscape, see *The Internet For Dummies,* 4th Edition, or *Dummies 101: Netscape Communicator,* both from IDG Books Worldwide, Inc.

Figure 7-8:
Netscape is the most famous Web browser, and it works pretty well. You can use it to order excellent children's audio tapes and videotapes.

This page is Netscape enhanced

Lots of pages on the Web are "Netscape enhanced," which means that they use Netscape features that not all other Web browsers can handle. For example, Netscape added ways to center text, let text flow around pictures, break up a page into frames, and other nice formatting touches. Because the commands that are required aren't standard, some other Web browsers ignore them.

Most Netscape-enhanced pages, in fact, look fine in other up-to-date browsers, such as Microsoft Internet Explorer.

Internet Explorer

When Microsoft decided back in 1995 that the Internet was important, it began developing its own Web browser to challenge Netscape. The result is Internet Explorer. When Windows 97 comes out, Internet Explorer will be an integral part of its operating system; until then, however, you can download it for free from the Microsoft Web site. An early version comes with Windows 95 too, but you should download a more recent version.

Internet Explorer is available for Windows 95, Windows 3.1, and the Mac.

Getting Internet Explorer

You can get Internet Explorer from any of the Internet software Web sites listed at the beginning of this chapter or from

```
http://www.microsoft.com
```

Click the button for Microsoft Internet Explorer, or follow the instructions on the Web page.

Installing Internet Explorer

When you download Internet Explorer from the Net, you get a file with a name such as Msie301.exe (for Version 3.01). Follow these steps to install it:

1. **Double-click the filename in File Manager, Windows Explorer, My Computer, or the folder on the Mac that contains the file.**

   The installation program asks whether you want to install Internet Explorer.

2. **Click Yes.**

   You see the license agreement for the program.

3. **Click the I Agree button (unless you don't agree).**

   The installation program begins sticking files in various places, mainly in your Windows program folders. Unlike most civilized programs, Internet Explorer installs itself wherever it pleases instead of asking for your opinion.

   The installer may tell you that you have to restart your computer for the new settings to take effect — how annoying!

4. **If you're running any other programs, save your work and exit from the programs.**

   If you're connected to your Internet account, disconnect and exit the TCP/IP program.

5. **Click Yes.**

   Your computer restarts.

Now you're ready to do some Internet Explorering.

Internet Explorerology

Everything we said about Netscape applies to Internet Explorer too — click links to move from page to page, or type URLs in the box just below the toolbar. (In Internet Explorer, this box is called the Address box rather than the Location box, but it works in the same way.)

Although Internet Explorer doesn't have built-in e-mail and newsreaders, it sometimes comes bundled with Internet Mail, the Microsoft Internet e-mail program, and Internet News, the Microsoft newsreader.

For more information about using Internet Explorer, see *The Internet For Dummies,* 4th Edition.

Other browsers

Other good browsers exist, although the huge rivalry between Netscape and Internet Explorer tends to drown out any publicity the other browsers may get. To see a list of other Web browsers, go to TUCOWS, described at the beginning of this chapter.

Priceless Plug-Ins

Netscape Navigator and Internet Explorer (the world's most widely used Web browsers, in case you haven't heard of them) can accept *plug-ins,* or programs that attach to the browser and extend its capabilities. For example, you can install plug-ins that let Netscape or Internet Explorer play audio clips, display video files, participate in interactive online games, and lots of other cool things. Plug-ins and where to get them are described in Chapter 8.

Fabulous FTP

An FTP program transfers files between your computer and an FTP server. A good FTP program lets you store the hostnames of FTP servers you use often, including the name of the directory from which you usually want to download. It also lets you see the messages the FTP server sends you (these messages sometimes tell you what other servers have files of interest or that the FTP server is moving or when the server will be down).

WS_FTP, from Ipswitch Software, is our favorite FTP program (see the sidebar about WS_FTP in Chapter 6). WS_FTP Pro is a commercial program, but WS_FTP LE ("Limited Edition") is free. You can get it from TUCOWS or from its home page, at

```
http://www.ipswitch.com/pd_wsftp.html
```

(Click the Downloads button to find out about WS_FTP LE.) If you want to try another one, check out CuteFTP, a shareware FTP program written by Alex Kunadze. Some people like CuteFTP as well as WS_FTP. CuteFTP is available from TUCOWS and Stroud's Consummate Winsock Apps page and from

```
http://www.cuteftp.com
```

Mac users should take a look at Fetch, an excellent FTP program by Jim Matthews at Dartmouth College. You can get Fetch from TUCOWS as well as from its home page, at

```
http://www.dartmouth.edu/pages/softdev/fetch.html
```

Other FTP programs are available too — check out the FTP pages at TUCOWS.

To download an occasional file, just use your Web browser, as described in Chapter 6.

Nifty Newsreaders

A Usenet newsgroup is a public bulletin board on which Internet users can discuss, complain, or exchange useful information (occasionally) about a particular topic. More than 10,000 newsgroups cover an amazing array of topics. *The Internet For Dummies,* 4th Edition (IDG Books Worldwide, Inc.), tells you all about how to read Usenet newsgroups and even post your own articles.

Free Agent

Our favorite Winsock newsreader is Free Agent, the freeware version of a commercial product called Agent. If you use Free Agent frequently, you may want to upgrade to Agent — it's not expensive, and it lets you read your mail and your news with the same program. You can find out about Free Agent at this Web page:

```
http://www.forteinc.com/agent
```

Getting Free Agent

You can download Free Agent (which is about 800K) from TUCOWS or from the Forte, Inc., Web page.

Installing Free Agent

When you download Free Agent, you get a file named something like Fa32-11.exe. To install Free Agent:

1. **In Windows 3.1 File Manager or Windows 95 My Computer or Windows Explorer, double-click the filename of the file you just downloaded.**

   The installation program starts running and asks whether you really want to install the program.

2. **Click OK.**

   You see a dialog box asking in which folder you want to install the program.

3. **Change the name of the folder if you don't like it, and then click OK.**

   The installation program installs Free Agent.

4. **If the installation program asks about creating shortcuts (for Windows 95) or a program group (in Windows 3.1), click Yes or OK.**

   When the installation is done, you see a message.

5. **Click OK.**

Now the program is ready to run.

Configuring Free Agent

You still have to tell Free Agent where to get your newsgroup articles in addition to some information about yourself. The first time you run the program, Free Agent asks you for configuration information. Intelligently, if you have been using another newsreader, it extracts most of this information from that newsreader's configuration files. (How nice!)

Follow these steps to run Free Agent for the first time:

1. **Double-click the Free agent icon.**

   You see the usual license agreement window.

2. **Click Accept if the license agreement is okay with you.**

   You see the Free agent Setup window.

3. **If you have already configured another newsreader, click the Use Information From Another Program button and skip the rest of these steps.**

4. **In the News (NNTP) Server box, type the name of your Internet provider's news server.**

   If you don't know the name, check the information your Internet provider gave you when you signed up, or call and ask. Or guess, and type **news** followed by a dot and then your Internet provider's domain name (if you use SoVerNet, with the domain name sover.net, for example, type **news.sover.net**).

5. **In the Mail (SMTP) Server box, type the name of your Internet provider's computer that accepts outgoing mail.**

   Free Agent has to know this information because if you post an article to a moderated newsgroup, the article travels by e-mail to the moderator. If you're not sure, type **mail** followed by a dot and then your Internet provider's domain name (for example, **mail.sover.net**).

6. **In the Email Address box, type your e-mail address.**

   When you post articles, Free Agent has to include your e-mail address.

7. In the Full Name box, type your name.

This name appears in articles you post, too.

8. Click OK.

Free Agent asks whether it can go online and get a list of available newsgroups, which can take a while.

9. Click Yes if you're connected to your Internet account and want to start using Free Agent right away.

Otherwise, you can click No and do this later.

If you clicked Yes, you see the Free Agent window, which looks like Figure 7-9 except with no newsgroups or articles listed. The status line at the bottom of the Free Agent window tells you how many newsgroup names Free Agent has found out about so far; 15,000 newsgroups is not an uncommon number for Internet providers to carry.

Figure 7-9:
Free Agent
lists the
newsgroups
you
subscribe
to, the
articles in
the selected
newsgroup,
and the text
of the
selected
article.

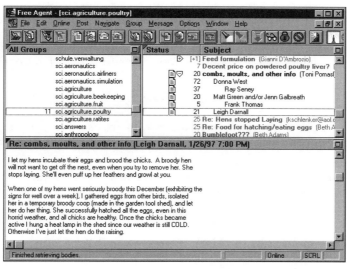

When Free Agent has retrieved the full list of newsgroups, you're ready to go!

Running Free Agent

The second time you run the program, it asks you for permission to register you as a user. Go ahead — this step doesn't cost anything. Registering is a good idea because it lets Forte, Inc., notify you about new releases.

You can customize Free Agent seven ways from Sunday. (It usually looks something like Figure 7-9.) The upper left *pane* (part of the window) lists newsgroups. The upper right part lists the articles in the newsgroup you select. The bottom half of the window shows the text of the article you select.

To see the articles in a newsgroup or to subscribe, double-click the newsgroup name in the list of newsgroups. Free Agent displays a window with buttons to see the subjects (headers) for a sampling of articles, to see all the message headers, or to subscribe to the group. After the headers appear in the upper right part of the Free Agent window, you can see the text of an article by double-clicking the article header.

Other newsreaders

Other newsreaders you may want to try include

- ✔ **Netscape Collabra:** Comes as part of the Netscape Communicator package. From Netscape Navigator 4.0, choose <u>C</u>ommunicator⇨ Collabra <u>D</u>iscussions to open the Netscape Message Center window, which includes a newsreader. You can get this program from TUCOWS or from

  ```
  http://home.netscape.com
  ```

- ✔ **Netscape Navigator 2.0 and 3.0:** A Web browser that comes with a built-in newsreader. Choose <u>W</u>indow⇨Netscape <u>N</u>ews to see it.

- ✔ **Internet News:** A newsreader from Microsoft that comes with some versions of Internet Explorer and is available for Windows 95, Windows 3.1, and the Mac (see Figure 7-10). You can get it from TUCOWS or from

  ```
  http://www.microsoft.com
  ```

- ✔ **Newswatcher (for the Mac), Internews, and Yet Another Newswatcher:** Three excellent newsreaders, all freeware or shareware and available from TUCOWS.

Lots of other good newsreaders are listed at TUCOWS, too.

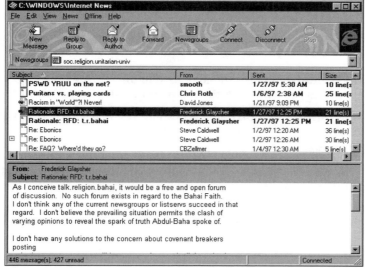

Figure 7-10:
Internet
News is the
Microsoft
newsreader.

Literary Acrobatics

In ancient days (about three years ago), programs came with instructions in plain old text files. Now, however, in the era of glitz, plain old text is just too boring and informative. The most popular way to pass around englitzed documents is Portable Document Format (PDF); the only way to read a PDF document on most computers is with the Adobe Acrobat reader, which, fortunately, is available for free. (The programs that create PDF documents cost money — the creators of Adobe aren't complete philanthropists.)

Because PDF is so popular, many Web browsers now come with a copy of the Acrobat reader. If yours doesn't, the next section tells you how to get it.

Downloading Acrobat Reader

Visit the Adobe home page, at `http://www.adobe.com`, and click the yellow Get Acrobat icon. This action takes you through a tedious but straightforward set of download pages. Although you're encouraged to register before you download, you don't have to. On the first download page, select the program you want (the most recent version of Acrobat Reader), the type of computer you have, and the language you prefer (English, most likely, if you're reading this book). Then follow the instructions to download a copy of Acrobat Reader.

Installing Acrobat Reader

When you download Acrobat Reader, you get a file named something like Ar32e30.exe. To install Acrobat Reader:

1. **In Windows 3.1 File Manager or Windows 95 My Computer or Windows Explorer, double-click the name of the file you just downloaded.**

   The installation program starts running and asks whether you really want to install the program.

2. **Click Yes.**

   The Acrobat Reader installer guides you through the installation process. Every time it asks you a question, it suggests an answer; the suggestions are all reasonable.

3. **You eventually get to a Setup Complete window. Click OK.**

   Setup is complete.

Acrobat Reader does a thorough job of installing itself. It creates program icons in the 3.1 Program Manager or on the Windows 95 Start menu, tells File Manager or Explorer that it's the program which handles PDF files, and hooks itself to Netscape or Explorer so that it runs automatically whenever your Web browser loads a PDF document.

Using Acrobat Reader

The Reader is basically a simple program. It shows you on your screen the contents of a PDF document. You can click the arrow buttons at the top of the window to page back and forth through the document or press the PgUp and PgDn keys. Although Acrobat has many fancy features with hyperlinks, sticky notes, and such (it has a severe case of browser wannabe), few PDF documents use them.

You can even (gasp!) print PDF documents by choosing File⇨Print.

Other Programs

For information about IRC (Internet Relay Chat) programs, see Chapter 9, which tells you all about IRC. Internet phone and conferencing programs are described in Chapter 10. Telnet, Gopher, and other programs are described in Chapter 12.

Doing Your Part

After you have used a new program for a while, perhaps a few weeks, you should begin to feel guilty. Someone has gone to enormous effort to make this wonderful piece of software, and you haven't even said thank you. It's time to Do Your Part.

Free versus not quite free

Software that comes from the Internet falls into three broad categories:

- **Freeware:** Given away for free. Restrictions may limit what you can do with the software — most freeware owners don't let you resell their programs, for example. Pegasus and WS_FTP are freeware.

- **Shareware:** Given away for a limited trial period. If you plan to continue using the program, you're honor-bound to pay for it. WinZip and Trumpet Winsock are shareware programs. When you register your shareware, you usually get a printed manual and a key that turns off any "please register me" screens.

- **Beta test versions:** Test versions given away for a limited trial period. The idea is that when the final version is available, you will buy it. By definition, beta test versions are full of bugs because the programming team isn't done getting the bugs out. Beta test versions of Netscape Navigator are available from the Web, bugs and all.

To find out which category your new program falls into, choose Help⇨About or look for other menu choices that offer information about registering. WinZip has, for example, a command called Help⇨Ordering Information.

If you're using a shareware program and you find it to be valuable, go ahead and pay up. It's never a great deal of money, and you become a registered user, entitled to receive information about updates and related programs. Besides, you feel great about what a wonderful, generous person you are, and you make it more likely that people will continue to write useful shareware. (*Note:* Neither of the authors of this book distributes any shareware programs, so we have no vested interest!)

Registering WinZip

To pay by check, send $29 to Nico Mak, P.O. Box 919, Bristol, CT 06011-0919. To pay by credit card, call the Public (software) Library (known as PsL) at 800-2424-PsL or 713-524-6394, or fax 713-524-6398. You can also mail credit-card orders to PsL at P.O. Box 35705, Houston, TX 77235-5705. Or go to this Web site to register:

http://www.winzip.com/order.htm

To congratulate Mr. Mak on a job well done, you can e-mail him at info@winzip.com.

For the latest information about paying for WinZip, choose Help⇨Ordering Information from the WinZip menu, and then click Help File. This command also enables you to print an order form to submit to your company for payment: After you see the help topic, choose File⇨Print Topic.

Part III

More Ways to Waste Time Online

In this part . . .

After you understand the basics of the Internet and are comfortable with e-mail and the World Wide Web, you may be wondering what else there is to do out there. Don't worry — plenty of cool stuff awaits you! In this part of the book, we describe "push" programs that turn your PC into a news ticker, Internet Relay Chat (IRC) software that turns your computer into one node in a crazy global chat conversation, Internet phone programs that turn your computer into a vaguely telephone-like device that can make long-distance calls for free, telnet software that turns your computer into an old-fashioned teletype, and MUDs and MOOs that turn your computer into a portal on hundreds of live, interactive fantasy games.

Other than that, we can't think of much you would want to do on the Internet.

Chapter 8

Advanced Surfing Techniques

● ●

In This Chapter

▶ Remembering where you have been and getting back there later

▶ Making your browser smarter by feeding it plug-ins

▶ Browsing the Web 24 hours a day, even when you're not at the computer

▶ Getting continuously updated news, weather, and stock prices

● ●

*G*etting started on the Web is easy — you start at a Web page and click links to get to other pages. When you spend some time on the Web, however, you need the tips and tricks we cover in this chapter.

Take Me Back!

Finding the information you want on the Web is difficult enough. What if you finally find exactly the page you need and later want to go back to it? You have several options:

✔ **Click the Back button on the toolbar (the leftmost button on most browsers) until you get back to the page you wanted.** This method works only if you have displayed the Web page during the current session with your browser; if you have exited your browser since you last saw the Web page you want, you're out of luck.

✔ **Choose Go from the menu.** Near the bottom of the menu that appears, you see a list of the Web pages you have visited recently. Choose one.

✔ **Choose Communicator⇨History or press Ctrl+H (in Netscape 4.0) or Window⇨History (in Netscape 3.0) or Go⇨Open History Folder (in Internet Explorer 3.0).** You see the History window, with a list of the Web pages you have looked at. Double-click one to see the Web page again.

✔ **Make a bookmark.** Read on for instructions.

Mark that book

When you see a Web page that you think you may want to come back to, add it to your bookmarks (favorites) list:

- **Netscape 4.0:** Click the Bookmarks icon, just below the Forward button on the toolbar, and choose Add Bookmark from the menu that appears.

- **Netscape 3.0:** Press Ctrl+D or choose Bookmarks⇨Add Bookmark from the menu.

- **Internet Explorer 3.0:** Choose Favorites⇨Add to Favorites from the menu.

Now your browser will remember the Web address (URL) of the page so that you can return to it later.

Adding a page to your bookmarks or favorites list is called *bookmarking* the page.

It takes me back. . . .

To return to a Web page you have previously bookmarked:

- **Netscape 4.0:** Click the Bookmarks button, just below the Forward button on the toolbar, and choose the Web page from the menu that appears. Choosing Communicator⇨Bookmarks displays the same list of bookmarks.

- **Netscape 3.0**: Choose Bookmarks from the menu and choose the Web page from the menu that appears.

- **Internet Explorer 3.0:** Click the Favorites button on the toolbar and choose the Web page from the menu that appears.

Bookmarks gone wild

After you have used the Web for a few days, your bookmarks or favorites list gets so long that its menu stretches down the screen, across your desk, and down on the floor. Some Web pages you bookmark turn out to be boring on a second visit, and others deserve to be saved. Also, you want to group together related Web pages on your bookmark list.

Both Netscape and Internet Explorer let you edit your bookmarks (favorites) list. Here's how:

✔ **Netscape 4.0:** Choose Communicator➪Bookmarks➪Edit Bookmarks from the menu, or press Ctrl+B, or click the Bookmarks icon (just below the Forward button on the toolbar) and choose Edit Bookmarks from the menu that appears. In the Bookmarks window, you can move a bookmark by dragging it; rename a bookmark by clicking its name, clicking again, and editing the name; and delete a bookmark by clicking it and pressing Del. To create a folder, choose File➪New Folder from the menu.

✔ **Netscape 3.0:** Choose Bookmarks➪Go To Bookmarks from the menu, or press Ctrl+B. You see the Bookmarks window, which works similarly to the Netscape 4.0 method.

✔ **Internet Explorer 3.0:** Choose Favorites➪Organize Favorites from the menu. You see the Organize Favorites windows, which lets you move, rename, and delete Web pages from your list of favorites. You can also create folders to contain groups of Web pages.

Making Your Browser Smarter

As a result of The Great Browser War, both Netscape Navigator and Internet Explorer have more features than a Swiss army knife. Web pages have new kinds of material all the time, however; some Web pages include sounds, movie clips, three-dimensional virtual worlds — you name it. To teach your browser to deal with these fancy Web page features and with even newer, zoomier stuff we may not even have heard of yet, you can graft new pieces of software, called *plug-ins,* onto your browser.

Netscape Navigator and Internet Explorer, for example, don't normally know how to show you three-dimensional virtual worlds (which are explained in Chapter 13). If you want to explore 3-D virtual reality, you can add a plug-in to Netscape or Internet Explorer that can handle 3-D worlds. When you go to a Web page with a virtual world — poof! — Netscape and Internet Explorer show it to you with nary a glitch.

Plug in, turn on, and browse out

To use plug-ins, you have to go get them and install them. This section explains how.

Plug-ins in Netscape

When you run into a Web page that contains stuff Netscape can't under-stand, you see the Unknown File Type window, as shown in Figure 8-1. Click the More Info button to see the Netscape Plug-In Finder. The page lists all the plug-ins that can handle the type of information you encounter on a Web page. Click the Download button next to a likely-looking plug-in, and follow the instructions on the Web page that appears. You usually have to download the plug-in program, exit from Netscape, and run the plug-in file you downloaded (that is, double-click its filename in My Computer, Windows Explorer, File Manager, or whatever). When you run Netscape again, the plug-in loads automatically.

Figure 8-1:
Oops —
you have to
download
and install a
plug-in.

To find out which plug-ins are already installed in your copy of Netscape, choose Help⇨About Plug-ins from the menu. You see something that looks like a Web page but that's really a report from the innards of your browser. Each installed browser appears on the list, with all kinds of gory technical information.

Plug-ins in Internet Explorer 3.0

Even though plug-ins were designed by Netscape to work with Netscape Navigator, Internet Explorer can use them too. In theory, when you display a page that asks for a plug-in you haven't installed, you see a Web page where you can download either the plug-in or an equivalent ActiveX control (the Microsoft answer to plug-ins).

In real life, however, Internet Explorer may display the message "Internet Explorer is opening file of unknown file type." It suggests that you open the file with a program you already have or save the file on your disk. If you don't already have a program that can work with the type of information you have encountered (a 3-D virtual world, video clip, or whatever), you probably would rather install a plug-in to deal with the file.

Unfortunately, it's not obvious how to install a plug-in in Internet Explorer. If it suggests downloading and installing a plug-in, follow its instructions to do so. Otherwise, go to the TUCOWS plug-in listing (see the following section, "Plug-in places"), download a plug-in, and try installing it. Who knows — it may work.

Plug-in places

Here's a list of our favorite sources of plug-ins:

- **Netscape's own plug-ins page:** Start at `http://home.netscape.com`, and look for a link for Netscape plug-ins. Netscape categorizes the plug-ins by type, such as audio-visual, 3-D and animation, image viewers, and presentations.

- **The TUCOWS plug-ins listing:** Start at `http://www.tucows.com`, choose a site near you, choose your operating system, and click Browser Plug-ins. TUCOWS rates the plug-ins, which Netscape doesn't do.

- **Stroud's plug-ins listing:** Start at `http://cws.iworld.com` or `http://www.stroud.com`, click 16-bit Apps for Windows 3.1 or 32-bit Apps for Windows 95 software, and click Plug-In Modules. Stroud lists Windows 3.1 and Windows 95 plug-ins, including ratings.

- **Dave Central:** Start at `http://davecentral.com`, and search for "plug-in." Dave Central lists only Windows plug-ins (nothing for the Mac).

Our favorite plug-ins

Here are some plug-ins we have found particularly useful or fun:

- **RealAudio:** The RealAudio plug-in (available from `http://www.realaudio.com`) lets you listen to sound files as you download them. Earlier programs required you to download the file and then start listening. Why wait when you can use *streaming audio* (a method of playing the first part of the sound file while downloading the next part)? RealAudio plays only sound files stored in RealAudio format, with the filename extension RA. We talk more about RealAudio in Chapter 10.

- **LiveAudio:** LiveAudio is a plug-in from Netscape (get it at `http://home.netscape.com`) that plays sound files in formats other than the RealAudio streaming format. If you encounter sound files with the filename extensions WAV, AU, MIDI, or AIFF, LiveAudio lets Netscape play the files.

- **QuickTime:** The QuickTime plug-in (you can get it from `http://quicktime.apple.com`) lets your browser play video files stored in QuickTime format, a popular format on the Web. If you use Windows, you also have to install the QuickTime for Windows Player, a stand-alone program the plug-in needs (available from the same Web site).

✔ **Shockwave:** If you want to see animations, video, interactive Web pages, and other cool stuff, you need the Shockwave plug-in (from `http://www.macromedia.com/shockwave`). Pages that include multimedia and interactive material requiring Shockwave are called *shocked* pages, and you find lots of them on the Web. Warning: The most shocking thing about them is often how huge they are and how long they take to download.

✔ **VDOLive and RealVideo:** Like RealAudio, VDOLive and RealVideo begin playing files while they're still downloading; VDOLive and RealVideo play video files, however, rather than audio files. Get the VDOLive plug-in from `http://www.vdolive.com` and the RealVideo plug-in from `http://www.realaudio.com`.

✔ **Live3D:** The Netscape Live3D plug-in lets you wander around in three-dimensional *virtual worlds*. See Chapter 13 for more about virtual reality.

✔ **Ichat:** If you like to participate in Internet text chats (which we don't, particularly), the Ichat plug-in is worth looking into (at `http://www.ichat.com`).

Because new plug-ins appear every day, check out the Netscape plug-ins page or the TUCOWS plug-ins listing to see what's new.

Browsing while You're Asleep

Yes, even when you're sleeping, your computer can browse the Web on your behalf. Thanks to new technology, your computer can cruise the Internet, looking for Web pages that may interest you and downloading them to your computer's hard disk. When you wake up and stagger over to your computer, you can check out the Web pages without going online and enjoy the quick load times you can get only from files stored on your own hard disk.

Offline browsers ask you to define which Web pages you want to see and when you want to see them. You enter the URL (Web address) of each Web site you want to download to your computer. You also tell the offline browser how many levels of links to follow from the page you specify: If you tell the program to download one level of links, you get the original page plus all the pages that are linked to from that page. If you ask for two levels of links, you get the original page, all the pages that are linked to from that page, and all the pages that are linked to from *those* pages — you can end up with thousands of pages on your hard disk if you're not careful.

You can tell some offline browsers to grab Web pages in the middle of the night or every hour or every ten minutes. After your offline browser has downloaded the Web pages, they're stored as files on your hard disk. Lots of files. More files than you would imagine — one text file for each Web page plus one graphics file for each picture on each Web page. You can look at the Web pages using your usual browser (Netscape or Internet Explorer or whatever). The pages load like lightning because they only have to make it from your hard disk to your screen instead of trekking across the vast spaces of the Net.

Here are a few programs that do offline browsing:

- **FreeLoader** (`http://www.freeloader.com`): You tell FreeLoader what kinds of Web sites interest you and then choose the specific sites you want to download. FreeLoader can download them daily, weekly, or only when you run the program. FreeLoader attaches itself to your browser, adding a row of buttons to the bottom of the browser window. The main drawback to this program is that it displays ads in the lower right corner of your browser window — and other places, at its own whim — to pay for this otherwise free software.

- **NetAttaché** (`http://www.tympani.com`): NetAttaché lets you create *briefs* — sets of Web pages or Web sites you want to download. You click a button on the NetAttaché toolbar to update the brief, downloading all the pages you specified. Figure 8-2 shows a brief that has been downloaded and is ready to view.

- **WebWhacker:** WebWhacker (which you can get from `http://www.ffg.com/whacker`) uses a disturbingly violent metaphor for downloading Web sites: Downloading a site is called a *whack* in this program. WebWhacker is the Cadillac of offline browsers, however, making it easy for you to create your own list of Web sites rather than select from a preset list. WebWhacker also makes it easy to transfer an entire Web site full of pages from one computer to another. For example, you can download a bunch of Web pages to your desktop computer and then move them to your laptop to peruse while you're riding the train on your commute home.

Don't go overboard with this offline browsing idea. If you tell an offline browser to grab the Microsoft Web site to a depth of five levels of links, you can eat up many, many megabytes of storage on your hard disk and waste lots of bandwidth (information transfer) on the Internet. Don't transfer information needlessly; grab only what you truly plan to read.

Also, a fair number of Web sites don't deliver Web pages to offline browsers, on the theory that they would rather use their bandwidth to deliver pages to live people who are looking at the pages now rather than to sleeping people who may look at them tomorrow, maybe.

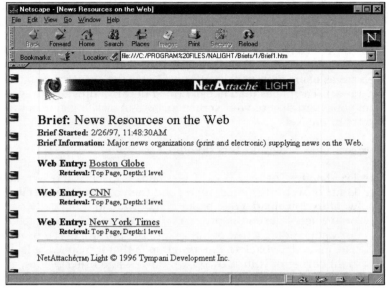

Figure 8-2:
NetAttaché
has down-
loaded the
latest news
for you.

The Web Is Coming to Get You

The problem with the Web is that you have to go out there and look at it.
E-mail comes and gets you; e-mail messages land in your inbox, where you
have to deal with them. Web sites are out there on the Web, though, and you
have to remember to browse over and look at them.

From an advertiser's point of view, this situation is dreadful. They have paid
good money for ads on Web pages, as have people who are selling products
from Web pages, and they want to make sure that you see their hard-earned
pages and spend your money accordingly, by golly, and they want you to see
them *now,* not when you get around to it. As a result, *channels* were born.

Several different programs offer you channels of information from the
Internet, including PointCast, Castanet, and BackWeb.

What's the PointCast?

When your computer is idle, how would you like to replace your screen
saver (flying toasters, inspirational message, or whatever you use now) with
frequently updated news? With PointCast, which you can download from
`http://www.pointcast.com,` **your screen saver can display the current**

news, weather, stock prices, and sports scores. When you install PointCast, you tell it which kind of news you're interested in, including which cities you want weather maps for and which stock prices you want to track.

After PointCast is installed, it downloads news headlines continuously when you're connected to the Internet. When you're not online, PointCast can't do its thing, of course, and the news gets stale. You can tell PointCast to connect to the Internet, update the news, and sign off once a day, hour, or other interval. PointCast can display the news in its own PointCast window, as shown in Figure 8-3, or as a screen saver that appears when your computer is idle.

PointCast is free because it charges advertisers to display ads along with the news. Not a bad deal for a news service on your desk!

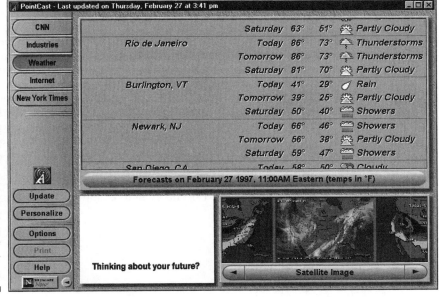

Figure 8-3: PointCast delivers news, sports, weather, and stock quotes to your computer screen.

Castanet wide

Castanet, from Marimba, gives you a "tuner" you can use to receive "channels" of information. Like a radio with preset buttons, you can tune in to the channels that interest you, from Marimba technical documentation to the Sesame Street KidSite channel. After you have selected a channel from a list of "transmitters," your Castanet Tuner program (which you can leave loaded all the time) downloads programs associated with that channel, stores them on your hard disk, and runs them.

The cool thing about Castanet is that the information in its channels arrives in the form of Java programs, which can display pages of information, run animations, or even play games with you. The Sesame Street KidSite channel, for example, may download a paint program that little kids will enjoy, and the Talk.com channel (at `http://www.talk.com`; it's run by HotWired, the online version of *Wired* magazine) lets you participate in online conversations almost as banal as those on IRC.

Castanet promises to get more interesting as software vendors offer software with automatic upgrades on Castanet channels. For example, Corel (the publisher of WordPerfect) has a channel from which you can download Corel Office for Java, a special version of its office suite.

BackWeb to the future

BackWeb, like Castanet, lets you choose channels to receive over the Internet. Information arrives in the form of *InfoPaks,* which are Web pages, programs, animations, or any other information your computer can download. InfoPaks from public TV station WGBH may be children's drawings of Arthur the aardvark (the star of his own public-television kids' show); InfoPaks from ZDNet are more likely to be Web pages with news about the computer industry. You can even sign up for channels that automatically download and install upgrades to the software you use. If you use the excellent McAfee virus-checking programs, for example, you can sign up for the McAfee BackWeb channel to get updates that guard your system against the latest viruses.

You can download the BackWeb program for free from `http://www.backweb.com`. To see a list of the available channels, take a look at this Web page:

```
http://www.backweb.com/chan/channels.html
```

Pushing back

If you have a permanent connection to the Internet, perhaps through your office local-area network, you may get an angry phone call from your system manager. A few dozen PointCast, Castanet, or BackWeb users can create a huge new demand for a constant flow of information and clog the corporate data lines.

This situation has made PointCast and its competitors quite unpopular with system managers who see the company's network capacity tied up reloading sports scores every half-hour. Before you install PointCast on a company computer, check with your system manager to see whether someone has installed a local PointCast server (a software package that uses a single outside connection and rebroadcasts info within the company, sold to companies at extra cost to solve the sports scores network overload problem — what a racket) or forbidden PointCast altogether.

Chapter 9

Internet Relay Chat: The Ultimate Solution to Free Time

● ●

In This Chapter

▶ How to connect to Internet Relay Chat

▶ How to discover who's out there to talk to

▶ How to waste unlimited amounts of time exchanging pleasantries (or, more commonly, unpleasantries)

● ●

*I*nternet Relay Chat, or *IRC,* is, in theory, a way for individuals around the world to have stimulating, fascinating, online discussions. In reality, IRC is more often a way for bored undergraduates to waste time. More than any other Internet service, IRC is what you make it. If you can find interesting people to have interesting discussions with, IRC is wonderful. If not, kiss your free time good-bye or stay away from IRC.

Like every other Internet service, IRC has client programs and server programs. The *client* is, as usual, the program you run on your local machine (or perhaps on your provider's system) that you type at directly. An IRC *server* resembles a large switchboard, receiving everything you type and sending your messages to other users and vice versa. What's more, all the different servers are in constant contact with each other. As a result, stuff you type at one server is relayed to the other servers so that the entire IRC world is one big, chatty family. In this chapter, we call the IRC client your IRC program because you don't run an IRC server program.

To add a degree of coherence, IRC conversations are organized into *channels,* with each channel dedicated to a single topic, at least in theory. Because any user can create a channel, you get some funky ones (not to mention downright *dirty*).

Where did IRC come from?

Finland, actually, where Jarkko Oikarinen originally wrote IRC in 1988. IRC has since spread all over the world and is today one of the standard Internet services.

The most notable hours of IRC were during the Gulf War, the recent California earthquake, and the 1993 coup in Russia against Boris Yeltsin, when IRC users at the scene sent reports to thousands of other users around the world.

The Theory of Chatting

You can use lots of different client programs for IRC that run on lots of different kinds of computers. Fortunately, however, the steps to use the different client programs are practically identical:

1. Establish contact with an IRC server.
2. Tell the server who you are.
3. Join a couple of channels.
4. Waste lots of time.

Networks, Servers, and Other Things You Don't Want to Know About

If you're at a university or use a commercial Internet provider, a server is probably at or near your site. Users at The World, for example, a Boston Internet provider, use an IRC server The World provides. Use a local server, if available, because using a local server is the polite thing to do and because it probably will respond faster than a server farther away.

Networks of servers

IRC servers are organized into networks of servers that talk to each other. Here's a list of the three biggest networks, in order of number of users, and their Web pages:

- ✔ **EFnet:** http://www.irchelp.org (the original network of servers)
- ✔ **Undernet:** http://www.undernet.org
- ✔ **DALnet:** http://www.dal.net

All EFnet IRC servers are connected to each other, all Undernet servers are connected, and all DALnet servers are connected. All the folks on EFnet can talk to each other regardless of which EFnet server they connect to. Servers on one IRC network don't connect to servers on other networks. Someone on EFnet can't talk to someone on Undernet, for example. When you choose a network, you choose the universe of people you'll be hanging out with on IRC. After you have spent some time on IRC, you probably will develop a preference for one network — the one where your friends hang out.

Lots of smaller IRC networks exist. Here are some, with the addresses of Web pages that have more information about them:

✔ **NewNet:** http://www.newnet.org

✔ **X-world:** http://www.x-world.org

✔ **Kidsworld:** http://www.kidsworld.org

✔ **AnotherNet:** http://www.another.org

✔ **StarLink:** http://www.starlink.org

✔ **GalaxyNet:** http://www.galaxynet.org

Choosing your server

Which server should you use? If your Internet provider runs an IRC server, use it. If you're sure that no local server is available, you can try one of the IRC servers listed in Table 9-1. Use the server closest to you. Because servers come and go frequently, be sure to consult the Usenet group alt.irc for more complete and up-to-date lists.

When you connect to an IRC server, you specify the *port,* which is a number. Unless it's specified otherwise, use port 6667 on any IRC servers. (You see in a minute where to tell your IRC program which port to use.)

Table 9-1	IRC Servers to Consider		
Address	*Ports*	*Network*	*Location*
irc.cerf.net	6666-6667	EFnet	U.S.
irc.frontiernet.net	6666-6667	EFnet	U.S.
irc-2.mit.edu	6665-6668	EFnet	U.S. (Massachusetts)
irc.ais.net	6650-6680	EFnet	U.S. (Chicago)
irc.mcs.net	6666-6668	EFnet	U.S. (Chicago)

(continued)

Table 9-1 *(continued)*

Address	Ports	Network	Location
irc.phoenix.net	6660-6669	EFnet	U.S. (Texas)
irc.texas.net	6666-6667	EFnet	U.S. (Texas)
irc.hp.net	6660-6669	EFnet	U.S. (Colorado)
irc.funet.fi	6666-6669	EFnet	Finland
irc.univ-lyon1.fr	6666-6667	EFnet	France
baltimore.md.us.undernet.org	6660-6669	Undernet	U.S. (Maryland)
washington.dc.us.undernet.org	6660-6669, 7777	Undernet	U.S. (D.C.)
chicago.il.us.undernet.org	6660-6669	Undernet	U.S. (Illinois)
stlouis.mo.us.undernet.org	6660-6669	Undernet	U.S. (Missouri)
dallas.tx.us.undernet.org	6661-6669	Undernet	U.S. (Texas)
austin.tx.us.undernet.org	6666-6667	Undernet	U.S. (Texas)
phoenix.az.us.undernet.org	6664-6668	Undernet	U.S. (Arizona)
montreal.qu.ca.undernet.org	6660-6669	Undernet	Canada (Montreal)
toronto.on.ca.undernet.org	6660-6669	Undernet	Canada (Toronto)
vancouver.bc.ca.undernet.org	6660-6680	Undernet	Canada (Vancouver)
dublin.ie.eu.undernet.org	6666-6667	Undernet	Ireland
oxford.uk.eu.undernet.org	6666-6667	Undernet	England
london.uk.eu.undernet.org	6666-6667	Undernet	England
au.undernet.org	6666-6667	Undernet	Australia
oslo.no.eu.undernet.org	6666-6667	Undernet	Norway

Address	Ports	Network	Location
amsterdam.nl.eu.undernet.org	6666-6667	Undernet	Netherlands
irc.dal.net	6661-6669, 7000	DALnet	U.S.
igc.dal.net	6661-6669, 7000	DALnet	U.S.
groucho.dal.net	6661-6669, 7000	DALnet	U.S.
sodre.dal.net	6661-6669, 7000	DALnet	U.S. (Florida)
hebron.dal.net	6661-6669, 7000	DALnet	U.S. (Indiana)
phoenix.dal.net	6666-6667	DALnet	U.S. (Texas)
glass.dal.net	6667	DALnet	U.S. (Ohio)
stlouis.dal.net	6666-6667	DALnet	U.S. (Missouri)
cyberverse.dal.net	6666-6667	DALnet	U.S. (California)
voyager.dal.net	6666-6669, 7000	DALnet	U.S. (California)
irc.ucs.net	6667	StarLink	U.S.
newyork.ny.us.starlink.org	6660-6669, 7000	StarLink	U.S. (New York)
rockhill.sc.us.starlink.org	6660-6670, 7000	StarLink	U.S. (South Carolina)
southbend.in.us.starlink.org	6667	StarLink	U.S. (Indiana)
denver.co.us.starlink.org	6667	StarLink	U.S. (Colorado)
aspen.co.us.starlink.org	6667	StarLink	U.S. (Colorado)
utrecht.nl.eu.starlink.org	6667	StarLink	Netherlands (with Dutch welcome message)
moof.xworld.org	6667	X-world	U.S.
trivia.xworld.org	6667	X-world	U.S.

What if you can't get in?

Frequently (most of the time, some days), when you try to connect to a server, you can't get in. Instead, you see an error message, such as "No Authorization" or "You have been K-lined." These messages mean that the IRC server is full or that too many people from your particular Internet provider are connected now or have been connecting frequently in the past. When this happens, just try another server.

Getting a Chat Program — mIRC

To participate in IRC, you need an IRC program (or, more properly, an IRC client program). For Windows users, we recommend mIRC; for Mac users, we suggest Ircle. Most of these fine programs are available from TUCOWS (http://www.tucows.com), the Web software repository we describe in Chapter 7. mIRC and Ircle aren't the only IRC programs available, but we like them because they are A.) easy to use B.) fairly reliable C.) cheap. (You can imagine which of these factors was our most compelling reason.)

If you use America Online or CompuServe, you can use mIRC or Ircle to use IRC. AOL and CompuServe don't provide IRC directly, but because you can use any Winsock or MacTCP programs with recent versions of the AOL and CompuServe software, mIRC and Ircle work fine. If you use a UNIX shell account, see the sidebar "Chatting for UNIX users: IRCII," later in this chapter.

In the rest of this chapter, we describe how to use IRC with the mIRC program; Ircle works similarly enough that you Mac users will get the idea.

Setting up mIRC

If you have just installed mIRC, you have to tell it a few things about you (although the figures in this chapter show mIRC running under Windows 95, mIRC works the same way using Windows 3.1):

1. **Start mIRC.**

   Before you can do anything else on IRC, you have a chance to admire a picture of the program's author, Khaled Mardam-Bey.

2. **When you have done so, click anywhere in the window (except on one of its buttons) to make the window go away.**

   You see the mIRC Setup dialog box, as shown in Figure 9-1. This dialog box lets you choose to which IRC server you want to connect as well as tell mIRC who you are.

3. **In the Real Name box, type your actual name.**

   You can use a pseudonym (see the section "Who's out there?" later in this chapter).

4. **In the E-Mail box, type your e-mail address.**

   Again, if you want to remain anonymous, leave this box blank.

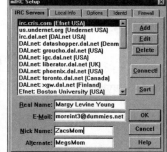

Figure 9-1:
The mIRC
server
setup
window.

5. **In the Nick Name and Alternate boxes, type nicknames by which you will be identified to all other IRC users.**

   All IRC nicknames must be different from each other, so try a peculiar variation on your name or a fanciful name. mIRC tries to use the name you enter in the Nick Name box; if that nickname is already taken, however, it tries the one you enter in the Alternate box.

   Don't use your username (the first part of your e-mail address) if you want to remain anonymous. IRCers can tell which Internet provider you're using and if your nickname is the same as your username, they can figure out your e-mail address.

   Now mIRC knows who you are (or who you want to pretend to be).

6. **Click OK.**

   The mIRC Setup dialog box disappears.

Connecting to an IRC server

You're ready to try connecting to a server.

1. **Click the Setup information button on the toolbar (the third button from the left, with a yellow folder on it). Or choose File⇨Setup or press Alt+E.**

   You see the mIRC Setup dialog box again.

2. **Click a server on the list of servers.**

   Choose a server on the network you want to try, and select one that's geographically near you.

Chatting for UNIX users: IRCII

In the old days, before the use of Windows and Mac Internet programs, everyone used UNIX IRC programs to participate in online chats. The most popular UNIX IRC program was (and still is) called *IRCII* (that's "IRC two"). You're most likely to run into IRCII if you type **irc** when you're using a UNIX shell provider's system. Because IRCII is so popular, most other IRC client programs use the same commands. As a result, we can slay a multitude of avians with a single projectolith by telling you about IRCII commands.

IRCII takes everything you type as lines of text. Two kinds of lines exist: commands to IRC and messages to other people. If a line begins with a slash, it's a command. If not, it's a message. (If only computers were this simple all the time.) The following command, for example, says to join the Hot Tub channel, a cheerful and usually crowded hangout:

```
/join #hottub
```

To see a list of channels, type **/list**, but you'll usually be appalled at how long the list is. Instead, specify that you want to see only channels with at least five people in them, by typing

```
/list -min 5
```

To join a channel, type **/join** followed by the channel name (don't forget the #), like this:

```
/join #dummies
```

Then type the messages you want to appear in the channel. When you tire of a channel, type **/leave**. When you're done with IRCII, type **/quit**.

Most of the other commands (that start with /) we describe in this chapter work in IRCII too.

3. **Click the Connect! button.**

   If everything works okay, welcoming messages from your server appear in the Status window within the mIRC window (usually with threats about all the naughty things that will get you kicked off). If you get an error message, go back to Step 1 and try another server.

After you're connected to a server, mIRC wants to know which channel you want to join.

Don't worry if you see Ping? Pong! in the Status window. This message just means that your IRC server checked that you were still there, and mIRC responded.

If the server you want to connect to doesn't appear on the mIRC Setup window's server list, you can click the Add button and fill in the information about the server: Type a description or name in the Description box, the address of the server in the IRC Server box, and the port (usually 6667) in the Port box.

What Channels Are On?

IRC discussions are organized (if you can call it that) into *channels*. Each channel has a name that begins with a sharp sign (#). We occasionally have a channel called #dummies, for example, for readers of the *Internet For Dummies* books. Some channels exist all the time, and others are around only at particular times. The big three networks of servers (EFnet, DALnet, and Undernet) have thousands of channels at any given moment.

Some channels have friendly conversations, some are specifically for new IRCers to ask questions, some are about kinky sex (would we kid you about a thing like that?), and some contain one bored, lonely person waiting for someone to take pity on him (yes, it's usually a him.) Choosing the right channel is the key to your IRC experience.

When you connect to a server with mIRC, the program displays a list of channel names, as shown in Figure 9-2. This is *not* the list of all available channels, which is really long. Instead, it's the list of the channels the program's author recommends for new IRC users.

Figure 9-2:
Which
channel do
you want
to join?

Why do all IRC channel names begin with # ?

We don't know. Maybe # means something special in Finnish. In principle, channels can also begin with an ampersand (&) and be limited to a single server, though nobody does that.

Joining a channel

To join a channel:

1. **Connect to an IRC server if you haven't already done so.**

2. **If you don't see the mIRC Channels Folder, click the Channels folder button on the toolbar (the fifth button from the left).**

3. **If the channel you want to join appears on the list, click it. Otherwise, type the channel name in the box at the top of the mIRC Channels Folder window.**

   If you have never done this, try the #irchelp, #newbies, or #mirc channel.

4. **Click the Join button.**

   A window appears for the channel. The window has three parts: a list of people in the channel (the rightmost column), the box in which you type what you want to say (the bottommost line), and the conversation occurring in that channel (the rest of the window).

Way too many channels

To find out which channels are available:

1. **Click the List channels button on the toolbar (the sixth one from the left, which has a globe and a list, or something).**

   The List Channels dialog box appears, as shown in Figure 9-3. To avoid having to download and wade through a huge list of thousands of channels, you can specify what kind of channels you want.

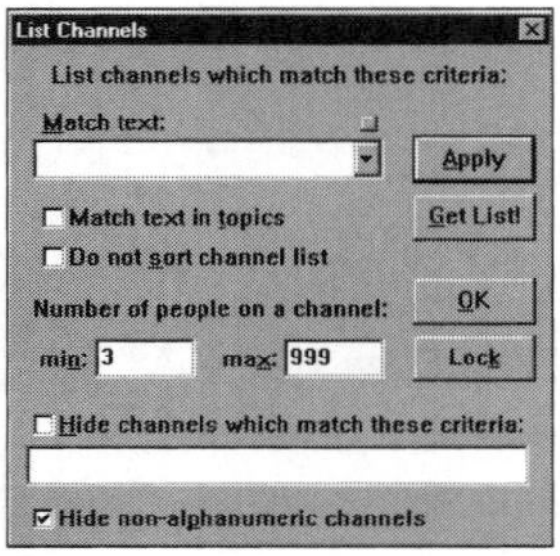

Figure 9-3:
What kind of channels do you want? Avoid channels with only one person.

2. **In the min box, type 3 (or more), to avoid channels with only one or two people.**

   You want a channel with a lively conversation going.

You can use the other boxes in this dialog box to specify part of the channel name (such as channel names that include *cats*) or to avoid channels with certain text in their names (such as channel names that include *sex* or *hot*).

3. Click the Get List! button.

A window appears, and the list of channels begins to appear. On a busy day, the list can take several minutes to arrive. mIRC sorts the channels alphabetically and shows the name, number of people in it, and description, as shown in Figure 9-4.

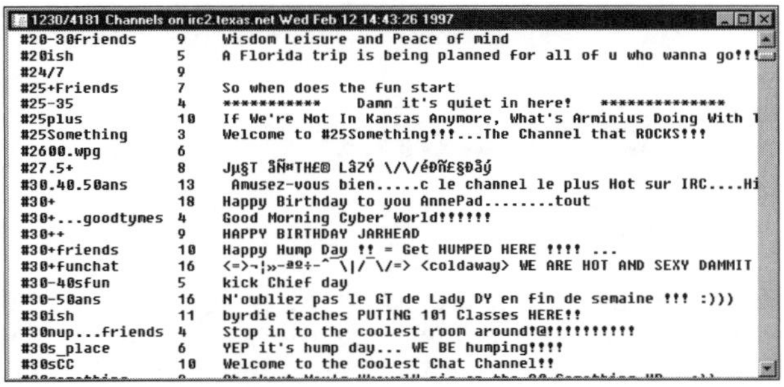

Figure 9-4:
Looks like a
quality
bunch of
conver-
sations,
doesn't it?

After you have displayed the list of channels, you can scroll up and down the list. To join a channel, double-click it.

Choosing a channel

Choosing the right channel can make the difference between a boring or offensive IRC experience and a good one. Which channels are good depends on which network of servers you use (EFnet, DALnet, Undernet, or another network). On all networks, try these channels:

- ✔ #newbies and #new2irc for getting started (DALnet has #DALnetHelp and #HelpDesk)
- ✔ #hottub and #chat for general hanging around
- ✔ #mirc, #new2mirc, or #mirchelp for getting help with mIRC
- ✔ #ircle for help with the Mac Ircle IRC program

You can also take a look for channels designed for folks in your age range, with names such as #teen, #21+, and #34_to_45. If you speak (type) a language other than English, try one of the many non-English channels out there — #espagnol, #francais, #brasil, #polska, and #42 (Finnish), for a start. IRC is a great way to practice that French you haven't spoken since high school.

Many channels have Web pages containing rules for the channel, information about people who frequent the channel, and suggested topics. For lists of Web pages about IRC channels, go to Yahoo (http://www.yahoo.com), click Computers and Internet, then Internet, then Chatting, and then IRC. You can click Channels (for miscellaneous channels). For EFnet channels, click EFnet and then Channels; for Undernet, click Undernet and then Channels; for DALnet channels, click DALnet and then Channels.

Channels that contain the word *warez* (such as soft*warez* — get it?) concentrate on illegally exchanging copyrighted software programs. We don't recommend them. (***Hint:*** If you can find those channels, the software vendors' security departments can too.)

Hey, Aren't We Ever Going to Do Some Chatting?

Oh, all right, we stalled as long as we could. After you have joined a channel, everything that people on the channel type appears in the window. Whenever someone joins or leaves a channel, a message is sent to all remaining participants; when you join a channel, everyone else immediately knows that you're a participant. Stuff that people type is preceded by their nickname, as shown in this example:

```
<JoeBlow> But what do you do with the woodchucks after you
          catch them?
```

mIRC displays a list of people in the channel on the right side of the channel's window so that you can tell whom you're up against.

Can I say something?

When you want to say something, make sure that your cursor is blinking in the box at the bottom of the channel window (click in the box if it's not). Then type your message and press Enter.

As is so often the case on the Internet, naive users can easily make fools of themselves. When you join a channel, lurk for a while. Don't immediately begin typing — wait to see the tenor of the conversation. Then type away. If you find that you like IRC, you may stay up all night and well into the next day after you have joined the conversation.

Staying out of trouble

Here are some rules of IRC netiquette:

- ✔ When you join a channel, listen for a few minutes until you pick up the thread of the conversation (or conversations). Don't immediately start saying "Hello!" to everyone.

- ✔ Don't use all capital letters; it's similar to shouting.

- ✔ Speak (type) the language that's appropriate for the channel and on the topic the channel is about (if any).

- ✔ Don't send inane messages, such as "Does anyone want to talk?" If you want people to talk to you, say something interesting. It doesn't have to be exactly erudite — "What about those Mets!" or "Cold enough for you?" should do. "I'd like to talk about movies" or "Anybody like cooking?" would be good too.

- ✔ If you have something to say to someone that isn't of general interest to the group, send it privately (see the section "Can we have a little privacy?" later in this chapter).

- ✔ Don't *flood* (send lots of messages real fast so no one else can get a word in edgewise).

Some people have a @ at the beginning of their nickname. These are *channel operators,* or *chanops,* or *ops.* Be nice to them: Channel operators can kick you off the channel if you don't behave. For more information, see the sidebar "Operator, is this the party to whom I am connected?" later in this chapter.

Attack of the robots

Most participants on IRC are people. Some participants aren't — some are robots. Hooking up IRC clients to programs, usually known as *bots,* is not too difficult. Bots can participate like a person can (more exactly, like a very *stupid* person can). Some bots are inoffensive and do such things as hold a channel open and send a cheery welcome message to anyone who joins. Some bots are really obnoxious and send large numbers of annoying messages to people whom the bot's creator doesn't like.

In many parts of IRC Land, bots are considered to be terminally antisocial and aren't the least bit welcome. Although we don't tell you how to create a bot, you should keep in mind that a particularly cement-headed user may have a microchip for a brain.

Commanding IRC

In addition to the buttons in mIRC, you can type commands. Commands start with a /, and you type them in the same box at the bottom of a channel window where you type messages for the channel. Rather than use the Channels folder or List channels buttons, for example, you can join a channel by using the /join command, like this:

```
/join #dummies
```

(This example assumes that you want to join the #dummies channel.)

You can change your nickname using the /nick command, like this:

```
/nick MegsMom
```

This command changes your nickname to MegsMom.

To get more information about the people in a channel, use the /who command, like this:

```
/who #dummies
```

The Status window (not the channel window, for some reason) shows the result of the /who command, with one line per person. The line for you includes the name and e-mail address you typed when you set up mIRC.

Who's out there?

To find out more about someone, type

```
/whois nickname
```

You type the person's nickname, not the word *nickname*. The result appears in the Status window and includes the person's e-mail address, the channel (or channels) the person is on, and which IRC server you're connected to.

After you know the person's e-mail address, you can *finger* that person (that is, ask the person's Internet provider for personal info) by clicking the Finger an address button on the toolbar (the tenth button from the left, with a hand on it), choosing Tools⇨Finger from the menu, or pressing Alt+G. You see in the Status window whatever information is available, which can include the person's name and other information.

Be sure to use the /whois and Tools⇨Finger commands to see what other IRCers can find out about *you*. Some Internet providers include your home phone number and other personal information in their finger information. Work or school accounts may include your department, dorm, or other personal information. If you meet some creep on IRC, you may not want him or her to be able to call you!

Take some action

You can send messages that describe what you're doing or what you want the folks in your channel to think that you were doing. You use the /me command, like this:

```
/me smiles slyly
```

The line appears like this (assuming that your nickname is ZacsMom):

```
* ZacsMom smiles slyly
```

Can we have a little privacy?

IRC lets you send messages directly to individuals and to channels. To send a message to an individual, assuming that you know her nickname, you type this command:

```
/msg nickname your personal message here.
```

A message to Johnny, for example, looks like this:

```
/msg johnny Can you believe how dumb that guy is?!!!
```

You can also converse privately with someone. When you type **/query** followed by the nickname of someone in your channel, the subsequent lines you type are sent to only that person. If someone uses a /query command with your nickname, mIRC opens a new window for your private conversation with the person. When you type **/query** with no nickname (or close the window), you're back to normal, sending lines to your current channel.

Your private conversation can be routed through a dozen IRC servers, and the operators of any of these servers can log all your messages. Don't say anything that has to be *really* private.

Lag and netsplits: the bane of an IRCers existence

Life on IRC isn't a bed of roses. (Indeed, sometimes it feels to us more like a den of vipers.) Two phenomena make life even worse: lag and netsplits. *Lag* refers to the terrible delay between the time messages are typed and when they appear on other people's screens. Sometimes one group of people in a channel are *lagged* while another group is not, and the first group's messages appear after delays of several minutes. Lags really foul up conversations. You can check on the amount of time a message takes to get from you to another person and back again by typing the command **/ping nickname** (replace *nickname* with the nickname of the person you want to ping).

A *netsplit* occurs when the connection between IRC servers is broken — the network of connected IRC servers gets split into two smaller networks. All the people connected to the IRC servers in one part can chat among themselves but can't communicate with the people connected to the IRC servers in the other part of the network. Eventually (after minutes or hours), the two networks reconnect and the netsplit is over.

To an IRC user, a netsplit looks like a whole bunch of people suddenly leaving your channel and then reappearing en masse sometime later.

A more private (privater?) way to converse is via DCC — Direct Client Connections. You don't have to be on the same channel as the person you want to talk to; you just have to know the person's nickname. You type this line (assuming that you want to talk to Freddie):

```
/dcc chat freddie
```

When someone tries to start a DCC chat with you, mIRC asks whether you want to chat with the other person. If you click Yes, mIRC opens a window for the discussion. Your DCC chat window is just like a minichannel with only two people in it.

You can also use DCC commands to send files to other people. For example, you could send a picture of yourself to a person you have just met. If someone offers to send you a file, however, we suggest declining unless you know the person. Unsolicited files tend to be unbelievably rude and disgusting.

Enough, Already!

You can leave a channel you tire of by typing **/leave** or closing the channel's window in the usual Windows manner (by clicking its Close button in Windows 95 or by double-clicking its upper left corner in Windows 3.1).

Then you can join another channel or exit. To exit, choose File⇨Exit from the menu.

Starting Your Own Channel

If you have nothing better to do, you can start your own IRC channel. Just make up a name and issue a /join command. IRC creates the channel automagically when you try to join it. In mIRC, click the Channels folder button on the toolbar (the fifth from the left), type the name of the new channel in the box, and click Join. A window appears for the new channel.

You can use the /topic command to display a topic line to other IRCers:

```
/topic #cephalopods Squid, cuttlefish, and their cousins
```

Then you wait, perhaps for a long, long time, until someone else joins your channel and begins talking. If you're the first person on a channel, you're considered to be the channel's operator, which gives you the greatly over-rated privilege of kicking off your channel any people you don't like (see the following sidebar, "Operator, is this the party to whom I am connected?").

When you lose interest, you leave your channel in the same way as you leave any other channel, by typing **/leave** or by closing its window.

Operator, is this the party to whom I am connected?

IRC channels and IRC servers both have *operators,* people with particular authority to give some kinds of commands. The first person on a channel is considered the channel's operator, and the operator can anoint other users as operators. In the list of nicknames in a channel, operators' nicknames are preceded by an at-sign (@).

The main command you get to use as a channel operator is /kick, which kicks someone off your channel, at least for the three seconds until he rejoins it. Kicking someone off is a thrill, but a rather small one, sort of like discovering that you have won 75 cents in the lottery. People usually get kicked off channels for being rude or obstructive or by sending so many garbage messages that they make the channel unusable.

Server operators manage entire servers and can kick unruly users entirely off a server — permanently. Don't let that happen to you; be a ruly user, please.

It's a Jungle Out There

The Internet is pretty anarchic, and IRC is one of the more extreme parts of the anarchy. In particular, all you really know about the people you're chatting with is their nicknames and who they purport to be. Unfortunately, some IRC users have a sick sense of humor and delight in offering other chatters "helpful speed-up files" that in fact delete your files or let these folks crack into your account. Also, many users have a completely different persona in IRC than they do in real life: These users alter details of their age, interests, lifestyle, gender — you name it. In some cases, the make-believe is fun; in others, it's just strange. Chat all you want — just keep in mind that not all your IRC friends may be who or what they claim to be.

If someone on IRC tells you to type a command, don't do it. No, no, no! Nefarious people may suggest that you type commands which can make it possible for other people to use your Internet account, scramble your disk, or otherwise diminish your quality of online life. (No, we're not going to tell you the commands!)

Also, IRC is no place for kids, unless you're right there looking over his or her shoulder. In our experience, IRC has the highest porn-to-nonporn ratio on the entire Internet.

Remember that IRC is a form of virtual reality and that some people find it addicting. Students have been known to miss entire semesters of classes because they spent every minute on IRC. Remember that IRC can be fun but that it's no substitute for real life.

For lots of good IRC background, take a look at the IRC Primer, at

```
http://www.irchelp.org/irchelp/ircprimer.html
```

Yahoo has good information too: Start at the Yahoo home page (`http://www.yahoo.com`) and click Computers and Internet, then Internet, then Chat, and then IRC.

Also check out this Internet Relay Chat Web site, maintained by Cliff "Edge" Wagner:

```
http://shoga.wwa.com/~edge/irc.html
```

Thanks to all the good folks in #irchelp, #newbies, and other channels for suggestions for this chapter.

Chapter 10

Speak to Me!

● ●

In This Chapter

▶ Telephony on the Net, such as it is

▶ Radio, recorded announcements, and other sounds you can hear

▶ Video, the final frontier

● ●

*F*or its first 25 years or so, the Internet was a bastion of text. If you couldn't read it, it didn't exist. During the late 1980s, people began sending around digitized versions of pictures on the Net (one guess what most of them were pictures of), and in the early 1990s the World Wide Web combined text with pictures, becoming the first Net *multimedia* application. (Multimedia in practice just means "something other than text.")

That opened the floodgates to animated pictures, three-dimensional pictures, sound, and video. In the next edition of this book, we will doubtless be describing scratch- — er, click-'n'-sniff attachments. In this edition, we stick to sound and pictures, though.

The Sound and the Fury

Sound on the Internet comes in two major varieties: one-way, such as recorded messages and radio stations, and two-way, such as telephones and chat party lines. The two-way stuff is much cooler than the one-way stuff, but because it doesn't work very well, the Sound is the telephone conversations you try to have, and the Fury is how you feel about it.

Internet Phone

The best-known telephone-type program on the Net is Internet Phone (from VocalTec). It works as well as any of them do, so we take a look at it here.

Does your computer have what it takes?

Sound and video on your computer take a little more hardware than do all the other applications we discuss in this book. In particular, for sound, you need a way to get the sound from the computer and, if you want two-way conversation, a way to get the sound into the computer. You also need a computer fast enough to keep up with the sound as it goes by.

Although all IBM-compatible computers have speakers, the traditional speaker control system is capable of doing little more than playing the occasional beep. (Quality sound would have cost another $2 per computer, so they didn't do it. Many peculiar things about PCs can be explained in this way.) These days, most computers come with a SoundBlaster card or the equivalent, which is plenty good for telephony. If your computer doesn't have a sound card, you can buy one for about $29 and a pair of speakers or lightweight headphones for another $25. To get sound into your computer, you need a microphone. If your computer doesn't have one built-in, any inexpensive microphone you can plug into your sound card will do.

If you're planning to use your computer for a great deal of phoning or chatting, you're better off with headphones than speakers because 'phones avoid the possibility of feedback from the speakers to the microphone, which can make the already crummy sound quality worse.

Macintosh users can feel superior because every Mac ever made has a fine sound card built right in. At most, you have to plug in a microphone.

Video is considerably more demanding. Although any 486/75 or better computer is fast enough to keep up with sound, you need at least a Pentium 100 to do video, and ideally something top of the line — Pentium Pro, MMX, or whatever this week's trendy abbreviation is. For video, you also need a fast screen card (cards vary widely in how fast they can pump picture changes out to the screen) and, if you want two-way video, a camera. For a little more than $100, you can get digital video cameras that look like oversized eyeballs.

Finally, you need a genuine Internet connection that makes your computer part of the Internet while you're online. Any PPP or SLIP provider offers this connection. If you're using a SLIP simulator, such as TIA or SLIRP, it won't work. Although AOL isn't a normal PPP provider, its system is close enough to PPP that it works, as do MSN, CompuServe, and Prodigy Internet.

Because Internet computers don't have phone numbers, all phone-type programs must have a way for the people on the two ends of a conversation to get in touch with each other. A small and shrinking fraction of the computers on the Net have what's known as a *fixed IP address*. Your computer's IP address is a four-part number that identifies it to other computers on the Net. With a fixed IP address, a computer always has the same number whenever it's connected to the Net. The alternative to a fixed address should be a *broken address* but is instead tactfully called a *variable*, or *dynamic*, *address*. Nearly every dial-up Internet provider uses dynamic addresses because IP addresses are hard to come by and using dynamic addresses means that they need only one address per phone line, not an address per customer.

What dynamic addressing means for *you,* the Internet user, is that your IP address, which is the closest thing to a phone number on the Net, changes every time you dial in. This system makes it more of a challenge for people who want to talk to you to find you. The solution (short of finding a fixed IP address, which is expensive) is to use a directory in which you register with a name and a nickname every time you dial in and where people can look for you.

One-on-one with Internet Phone

Using Internet Phone is relatively straightforward:

1. Install the program.
2. Start it up.
3. Call someone, or wait for someone to call you.

You can buy a boxed version of Internet Phone or download a time-limited demonstration version from the VocalTec Web site, at `http://www.vocaltec.com`. Click the Free Download button to download the current version for whatever type of computer you're using, as long as it's Windows 95, Windows 3.1, or a Mac. (Chapter 6 has more details about downloading and installing software.) You get a week's free trial with the demo version, which should be plenty of time to decide whether you can stand using it.

The installation process is straightforward. Run the installation program, and accept the suggested answer to nearly every question. It asks for your name, phone number, and nickname under which you want to be listed in its directory. (The last question it asks is whether you want to register the program — that is, pay for it right now. We suggest that you try it first.)

The first time you run Internet Phone after you install it, it runs an audio test to make sure that your microphone and speakers work. Click the Start Test button, speak into the microphone, and make sure that you can hear yourself on the speakers or headphones. (If not, nobody else can hear you either.) It gives you the choice of Quiet or Noisy environment; we suggest that you select Quiet if you're using headphones or Noisy if you're using speakers. Then click OK.

After a brief reminder that the company would love for you to register if you haven't yet, Internet Phone wakes up with two windows, as shown in Figure 10-1. One is Internet Phone itself, with a little cartoon guy who is supposed to be your connection-setting-up pal or something like that. The other is the global online directory, which is where you find people to talk to. The online directory window connects itself to one of several directory servers around the world and downloads a list of the "chat rooms" where people can register.

The list of rooms looks much like the list of Internet Relay Chat channels (refer to Chapter 9), although IRC is completely separate from Internet Phone. A bunch of chat rooms have names such as GENERAL 02, one of which you're assigned to by default. Because anyone can create a chat room, you probably won't be surprised to hear that a bunch of chat rooms have names such as SEX SEX SEX SEX SEX and NAKED GIRLS. (The latter, we expect, is populated entirely by young men who want to talk to, or at least about, unclad young women rather than by the young women themselves.) Chat rooms also exist for particular languages or countries — want to brush up on your high-school French?

Double-click an interesting-looking chat room, and then wait as the directory program downloads the list of people in the room, which can take quite a while if a large number of people are in the room. Double-click a likely-looking person, and Internet Phone then tries to contact that person, making authentic telephone dialing and ringing sounds. If the person is there and answers, you can begin talking. If someone calls you and you want to answer (the caller's name is on-screen so that you can tell whether it's someone you know), click Answer to start talking.

If you and a friend are trying to connect, use the Chat Room⇨New command to create a new room with an uninteresting name, something like "industrial sealants 3." Click Private if you want to keep the room name from showing up in the directory. If you and your friend both create a room with the exact same name, it's actually the same room; after you're both online, you see each other's entries, and one can call the other.

After you're done talking, click Hang up to hang up.

The bad news

After you have connected, you use Internet Phone sort of like a real telephone. You talk, and the other person eventually hears what you say. The "eventually" is the problem.

We tried a couple of experiments to see how usable Internet telephony is. First, we tried connecting from a computer on one side of the room to a computer on the other side of the room, connected by a network cable that ran across the floor. It worked great, just like a real phone — we could hear each other just as though we were in the same room. Because we *were* in the same room, of course, it wasn't all that impressive.

Our second experiment involved connecting from Internet For Dummies Central in upstate New York to the Internet For Dummies Poultry Research Station in Vermont. This setup was more similar to a typical user-to-user call. Although I For D Central has a high-speed direct link to the Net, our Vermont outpost uses a regular dial-up connection to a local Internet provider. Our experience wasn't promising. Although the sound quality wasn't bad, the delay ranged from 3 seconds to 20 or 30 seconds, giving a rather surreal quality to the conversation, sort of like talking to someone in orbit around the planet Neptune:

> Can you hear *Hello? Hello?* me? This is pretty hard to *Oh, now I hear you okay, but it took* follow. I wonder if everyone who *wait, I thought we already* uses this has as much trouble *no, dear, we're using the computer, you'll have to* let me try and fiddle with this [long pause] *wait your turn* [another long pause] *fiddle with what?*

Internet Phone has lots of other options, such as address books, white boards, answering machines, and voice mail. We didn't have the patience to try any of them. We believe that if you have a dedicated high-capacity network between you and your phone buddy, Internet Phone can sound sort of like a real phone. (If you have a dedicated high-capacity network between you, though, you usually have a real phone connection as well.)

Lots of other Internet voice programs

Many other voice programs are available as freeware, shareware, or commercial software, at software archives including our favorites: TUCOWS (at `http://www.tucows.com`) and Stroud's Consummate Winsock Apps Page (at `http://www.stroud.com`).

We couldn't get any of them to work. (Really.) They all crashed, hung, didn't connect, or otherwise did fascinating things not resembling talking on the phone. Maybe we're just unlucky, but we rate them all somewhere between Not Ready for Prime Time and Not Ready for Public Access Channel Z at Three in the Morning. Doubtless, there's some way to tease them all into working, at least somewhat; if *we* had this much trouble, though, we can't in good conscience recommend any of them.

The International Telecommunications Union is developing for voice on the Net a standard called *H.323.* Most of these programs plan to adhere to H.323, so if they ever work, people using any Internet voice program will be able to talk to people using any other Internet voice program. The title of standard H.323, by the way, is "Visual telephone systems and equipment for local-area networks that provide a nonguaranteed quality of service," which just about says it all.

Lots more Internet telephony advice

If you want to find out more about Internet voice programs from someone whose opinions are a little more upbeat about the topic than ours are, read *Internet Telephony For Dummies,* by Daniel D. Briere and Patrick J. Hurley (IDG Books Worldwide, Inc.).

Sound That Really Works

Now that we have gotten you all discouraged about Internet telephony, we want to cheer you up by telling you about *Internet radio,* the online sound that really works. The idea is sort of the same — sound sent over the Net; because it's one-way rather than two-way, however, it works much better. The most popular Internet radio system is RealAudio, from Progressive Networks, a Microsoft spin-off near Seattle. (Hi, Rob!)

Although installing RealAudio is a minor pain, using it is a snap because it acts like part of the Web. After you have RealAudio installed, you only have to click an audio link on a Web page, and a few seconds later, sound starts coming from your computer.

Packet wars

The questions about Internet voice programs aren't just about whether it works well enough to be useful. There are also big issues about the load it puts on the Net and the way it does or does not relate to regular telephony.

Whenever you use a regular Internet application, such as e-mail or the Web, data transfer over the Net uses a system known as TCP to make sure that all the data in a message gets through, even if the Net is slow and congested. (We discuss TCP in gruesome detail in Part VI.) Because TCP automatically adapts to the level of service available, when the Net is busy, it "backs off" and sends data more slowly than when the Net is less busy. This arrangement benefits everyone on the Net because TCP makes the best use of the bandwidth it has available. Telephony, on the other hand, doesn't need every single bit of data to get through because a missing packet or two just sounds like a pop in the phone conversation. Telephony uses a simpler scheme, UDP, rather than TCP. The problem with UDP is that it doesn't back off when the Net is busy — it just keeps pumping out data whether or not the capacity is available. A voice connection, therefore, uses many more Net resources than a data connection, and when the Net starts to slow down, voice connections make it even slower. As a result, some Internet providers are considering restricting or charging extra for voice users as a result of the extra costs they cause.

A few Internet telephony systems "leak" into the regular telephone network (that is, they let you dial out to a regular telephone). A few companies even plan phone-to-phone systems, where you dial from your regular phone into their system in one city and punch in your account number and the phone number you want to connect to, and it connects over the Net and dials out in a distant city. Guess what? If you're connecting phones in one city to another city, you're a long-distance phone company, regardless of whether what's in between them is a standard phone network, the Internet, or tin cans and string. A large pile of laws and court decisions dating back to 1919 regulate long-distance telephone companies and require, among other things, that they pay about three cents per minute to the local phone companies to which they connect at each end to defray the cost of connecting to the local phone network. (In theory, at least, this fee, which is called an access charge, keeps your monthly rates down.) Small long-distance companies have been loudly complaining that it's not fair competition for them to pay access charges and for Internet providers with phone users not to. As long as Internet telephony is computer-to-computer, it's not really like regular telephony (see the section "The bad news," earlier in this chapter); as soon as it's computer-to-phone or phone-to-phone, though, fair's fair, and access charges should be due, which is a huge headache for the Internet providers who would have to figure out who among their users is making phone calls over the Net and collect and remit the per-minute charges.

The three large long-distance companies have kept quiet about the access-charge issue. Why? Because they all have large Internet provider subsidiaries, so they figure that they will make money either way.

Setting up RealAudio

Progressive Networks gives away the basic RealAudio player and sells an enhanced version for about $30. To get either, visit http://www.real.com and click the Get RealPlayer button for the free version or the Get RealPlayer Plus button for the version you have to pay for. Because the free version is quite usable, we suggest that you try it out before deciding whether you want to trade up.

On the download page, you select your type of computer, the product you want (RealAudio Player 3.0 for sounds or RealPlayer 4.0 if you want to try video too), and your type of computer and then enter your name and e-mail address. Uncheck the box under your e-mail address if you don't want to get e-mail every time a new version of the player is available, and then click the large button to go to the download and instructions page. On that page, you get a list of sites from which you can download the software. Pick one close to you and download away.

At least two versions of RealAudio are available: the older one designed for 14.4 Kbps modems and the newer one intended for 28.8 Kbps and faster modems. The newer one sounds better with a good Net connection and a fast computer; with a congested Net connection or a slower computer (a 486 or less), however, the 28.8 Kbps version of a program can start to sound chopped up. For spoken programs, such as newscasts, the 14.4 Kbps version is entirely understandable, so try that if it's available.

After you have the player package downloaded, run it, and it installs itself. The installation process is a little complicated because it locates every Web browser on your computer and tells all the browsers how to play RealAudio files. You can just accept all the suggested answers to the questions, and the installation should work.

Are we ever going to hear anything?

Now that RealAudio is installed, using it is an anticlimax. Find a page with a RealAudio link, and click on it. The RealAudio player should start up and begin talking to you.

Because Progressive Networks has aggressively signed up sound providers, now you can listen, via RealAudio, to everything from garage bands to National Public Radio news shows to John's weekly radio call-in show. For NPR, visit http://www.npr.org. For the call-in show, visit http://www.iecc.com/radio.

What about video?

Now that we have one-way and (sort of) two-way sound over the Net, can video be far behind? Well, yes and no. You can download video clips from the Net, in formats such as MPEG, AVI, and QuickTime. Even with state-of-the-art data compression, video files are big; if you're patient, you can download little low-resolution video clips and watch them on your screen.

Real-time video is much more difficult. Everything that makes real-time audio difficult makes real-time video ten times as difficult. The amount of data is huge, and the amount of processing needed to turn camera images into Internet data is huger. Nonetheless, most audio packages have a video add-on, including Internet Phone and RealAudio, although we can't vouch for their usefulness.

If you have at least a Pentium 150 computer and a 128 Kbps network connection (an ISDN phone line, a cable-TV connection, or the like), it might be worthwhile to try some Net video. If not, and you want to watch TV-like moving pictures, we suggest that you cut out the middleman and just watch TV.

Other kinds of sound

RealAudio is called a *streaming* system because your computer plays the data as the data is fed to it. The older but still useful way to ship sound around on the Net is as sound files. You have to download a sound file completely before you can listen to it; after the file is on your disk, however, you can listen to it as often as you want. Sound files come in a wide range of incompatible formats, such as WAV (the Windows favorite), AU (the UNIX favorite), and others, such as AIFF and SND. Fortunately, they're all similar inside, and current versions of Netscape know how to play all of them. Because the sound clips are loaded as data files rather than as streaming data, no matter how slow your network connection is, you get the entire sound file downloaded; after the file begins playing, you get 100 percent fidelity.

For some good examples of sound clips, visit the *New York Times* Web site, at http://www.nytimes.com. Although you have to register to use it, it's free if you're in the United States. Many of the stories there have a green AUDIO tag. If you click one of those stories, you see links to sound clips that you can download and listen to.

Chapter 11

How to Break in to Computers on the Net

. . . .

In This Chapter

▶ Using telnet to log in to other computers

▶ Using Winsock telnet programs

▶ Some interesting computers to break in to

. . . .

Yes, indeed, it's true — while sitting at your own desk, you can quickly and silently log on to computers all over the world, without the owner of the computer even knowing! You can give commands, see information, and access files just like those teenagers in the movie *The Net.* How? By using *telnet.*

Before you get too excited, though, in reality you can "break in" only to computers that specifically give you permission to do so. Bummer — but them's the breaks. When you use telnet, you either have to have an account on the computer you want to use or you have to telnet to computers that allow public access. Some Internet hosts, primarily libraries, do allow public access. For example, libraries let you search their catalogs for books in their collections.

 When you use telnet to connect to a computer, the computer usually asks for a login or password. If you don't already have a password for that computer and it doesn't offer you a "guest" or "new" account to use, don't try to guess one. Breaking in to computers like that is at the least rude and in most places quite illegal.

Telnet, Telnet, Who's Got the Telnet?

When you use telnet, you log in to a remote *host* (telnet-ese for a computer) as though your *terminal* (workstation, PC, whatever) were attached directly to that host. Because all hosts on the Internet are officially equal, you can log in to a host on the other side of the world as easily as you can log in to a host down the hall; the only difference is that the connection to the distant host may be a little slower.

The key thing to remember when you're telnetting is that when you're logged in to another computer on the Internet, you have to use commands the other computer understands. If you use a PC running Windows and you telnet to a computer that runs UNIX, you have to give UNIX commands. Luckily, most host computers that let the public telnet in provide menus rather than require you to know a bunch of commands. Here's the other key thing to remember: When you finish using the other computer, log out!

To use telnet to log in to a computer over the Internet, you need a telnet program. If you use a UNIX shell provider, you can use the telnet command. If you use Winsock or MacTCP software, you have to get a telnet program. Telnet programs come with popular Internet programs (Windows 95 includes one called Telnet.exe), or you can get telnet programs from the Internet via FTP.

The best way to get a good Winsock telnet program is to use your Web browser to download a program from a public Internet software archive, such as Stroud's Consummate Winsock Applications or TUCOWS (The Ultimate Collection Of Winsock Software). They're at

```
http://www.stroud.com/
```

or

```
http://cws.iworld.com/
```

and at

```
http://www.tucows.com/
```

Choose the Terminal Apps section of the list, and pick a telnet program that looks good to you. We happen to like these two:

- **NetTerm:** This shareware telnet program is also available via FTP, from `ftp.neosoft.com` in the directory /pub/users/z/zkrr01. Download a file named nt32403.exe (Windows 95 and Windows NT) or nt16403.exe (Windows 3.1). The number may be larger for a later version.

- **EWAN:** You can also download this freeware telnet program from `ftp.best.com` in the directory /pub/bryanw/pc/winsock and in a file named ewan1052.zip (the number part may change).

Refer to Chapter 6 to find out how to download and install programs from the Net.

Among the commercial online services, only CompuServe offers telnet, although you can use Winsock telnet programs with AOL and NetCruiser.

Telnetting, for You UNIX Users

In the following true-life example, John telnets to his home computer and logs in as himself (no, you can't have his password — sorry). At the UNIX shell prompt (%, for example), he just begins typing:

```
% telnet iecc.com
```

The telnet program (Windows 95 or UNIX) replies:

```
Trying 205.238.207.65...
Connected to iecc.com.
Escape character is '^]'.

IECC ivan.iecc.com (ttyp6)
No public access.  Authorized users only.  All login
          attempts logged.
```

Then `ivan.iecc.com` (the computer John wants to use) asks him to log in (his responses are in bold):

```
login: john1
Password: xxxxx
Terminal type (default VT100):
...
```

Notice the following points:

- ✔ Some telnet versions report the numeric addresses of the hosts they contact (205.238.207.65, in this example). If your version reports numeric addresses, take note of that number in case of later trouble with the network connection.

- ✔ The thing that's absolutely essential to note is the *escape character*, which is your secret key to unhooking yourself from the remote host if the host becomes recalcitrant and stops doing anything useful. Winsock telnet programs often use a Disconnect menu item rather than an escape character.

- ✔ In our example, the escape character is ^], which means that you hold down the Ctrl key and press] (the right-bracket character on your keyboard). This escape character is the most common escape character used on UNIX systems.

After you're logged in, you can work pretty much as though you were directly logged in to the remote host. The primary difference is that characters take a little longer to appear on-screen — as long as a full second or more. In most cases, you can keep typing even when what you typed hasn't yet appeared; the remote host eventually catches up.

You're Not My Terminal Type

If you log in to a UNIX system and you want to use a full-screen program, such as the UNIX text editors emacs and vi or the mail programs elm and Pine, you have to set your *terminal type.* This problem shouldn't exist in the first place; because it does exist, though, you have to deal with it.

The problem is that about a dozen different conventions exist for sending screen-control messages, such as "Clear screen" and "Move to position (x,y)." The program you're using on the remote UNIX computer must use the same convention as your terminal (if you're using a terminal) or as your local terminal program (if you're on a PC or a workstation).

If the conventions are not the same, you get garbage (funky-looking characters) on-screen when you try to use a full-screen program. In most cases, the remote system asks you which terminal type to use. The trick is knowing the right answer:

- ✓ **ANSI:** The best answer if you're using a PC, because most PC terminal programs use ANSI terminal conventions. ANSI stands for American National Standards Institute. One of its several thousand standards defines a set of terminal control conventions that MS-DOS PCs — which otherwise wouldn't know an ANSI standard if they tripped over one — invariably use.

- ✓ **VT100:** A popular terminal from the 1970s (it became a de facto standard) that's a more likely answer if you're using an X Window-based system, such as Motif or Open Look.

- ✓ **3101:** An early IBM terminal, used in places in which a great deal of IBM equipment is used, that was also quite popular.

The ANSI and VT100 conventions are not much different from each other, so if you use one of these conventions and your screen is only somewhat screwed up, try the other convention.

Depending on how well implemented your local version of telnet is, telnet may automatically advise the remote system about which type of terminal you're using. With luck, you don't actually have to set your terminal type, or perhaps you just have to reply **y** when telnet says something like `Terminal type VT100 OK?`.

Help! I've Telnetted and I Can't Get Out!

The normal way to leave telnet is to log out from the remote host. When you log out, the remote host closes its end of the telnet connection, which tells your local telnet program that the remote host is finished. Easy enough — normally. Sometimes, though, the other end gets stuck and pays no attention to what you type. Or the remote host doesn't get permanently stuck but responds so slowly that you have no interest in waiting for a response anymore. (This slowness sometimes happens when network congestion occurs between you and the other host.)

Some versions of host software, which we won't name for looking-gift-horses-in-the-mouth-type reasons, get hopelessly slowed down by congestion, much more than the congestion itself causes. So you have to know how to escape from telnet, which is where the magic escape character comes in handy.

1. **First, you have to get telnet's attention by pressing the escape character.**

    (If nothing happens after a few seconds, try pressing Enter.) Telnet should come back with a prompt, telling you that it's there.

2. **Then type** quit **to tell telnet that you're finished.**

    You should see something like the following:

```
^]
telnet> quit
Connection closed.
```

Although you can give telnet a dozen other commands (press **?** to see them), none of the commands is anywhere near as useful as quit.

New, Improved Telnet with Whiter Whites

If you use a Macintosh, a PC under Microsoft Windows, or some other windowing system, you can start telnet differently from what you do on a UNIX system: You start the telnet program by double-clicking its icon.

Although Windows 95 comes with a telnet program, most folks don't see an icon for it anywhere. You can make an icon for it. In My Computer or Windows Explorer, open the Windows folder and find the file named Telnet.exe. Drag its filename out to your desktop. Windows 95 creates a shortcut icon for the program. Now you can double-click this icon to run the telnet program.

When you run a Windows or Mac telnet program, a window pops up with menu choices at the top. Connect (or something similar) is usually a choice. Click Connect (or Connect⇨Remote System in Windows 95) to see a Connect window. Figure 11-1 shows a typical Connect window, using the Windows 95 telnet program. Type the name of the host you want or choose the host name from a list, click OK, and away you go.

Figure 11-1:
Using the
Windows
95 telnet
program to
connect.

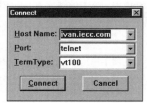

Figure 11-2 shows a connection to the same computer as shown earlier in this chapter, but this time from a Windows machine using the Windows 95 telnet program. When you run a Windows or Mac telnet program, you don't need an escape character because you do all the escape-type stuff from the program's menu. To disconnect from a recalcitrant host, for example, click a menu item called Disconnect (or something similar).

Figure 11-2:
When you
have
finished
using the
computer
you've
telnetted to,
choose
Connect⇨
Disconnect.

```
 Telnet - ivan.iecc.com                                    _ □ ✕
 Connect  Edit  Terminal  Help

 IECC ivan.iecc.com (ttyp4)
 No public access.  Authorized users only.  All login attempts logged.

 login: johnl
 Password:
 Last login: Wed Feb 12 22:51:50 from caetano
 Copyright 1992, 1993, 1994, 1995, 1996 Berkeley Software Design, Inc.
 Copyright (c) 1980, 1983, 1986, 1988, 1990, 1991, 1993, 1994
         The Regents of the University of California.  All rights reserved.

 BSDI BSD/OS 2.1 Kernel #14: Fri Jan 17 12:26:29 EST 1997

 Oct 4: New kernel, adds defenses against SYN floods and other trendy
                attacks
 You have mail.
 ivan:johnl:johnl$ ▮
```

Any Port in a Storm

When you telnet in to a remote host, you have to choose not just the host but also a port on the host. The *port* is a small number that identifies which service you want. The usual port for telnet is (for obscure historical reasons) the number 23, which means that you want to log in to the host. If you use the UNIX `telnet` program, you choose another port by putting the port name after the host name:

```
telnet ntw.org 13
```

If you use a Windows or Mac telnet program, you type the port number in the Connect window.

In case you were wondering, port 13 is the *daytime* port. Port 13 tells you the host's idea of the time of day and then disconnects. This exercise is not terribly useful, although occasionally you may want to see which time zone another host is in.

We're from IBM, and We Know What's Good for You

All the terminals discussed earlier in this chapter that are handled by telnet are basically souped-up teletypes, with data passed character by character between the terminal and the host. This type of terminal interaction can be called *teletype-ish*.

IBM developed an entirely different approach to terminal use for its 3270-series display terminals. The principle is that the computer is in charge. These terminals work more like filling in paper forms. The computer draws what it wants on-screen, marks which parts of the screen users can type in, and then unlocks the keyboard so that users can fill in whichever blanks they want. When a user presses Enter, the terminal locks the keyboard, transmits the changed parts of the screen to the computer, and awaits additional instructions from headquarters.

To be fair, this is a perfectly reasonable way to build terminals intended for dedicated data-entry and data-retrieval applications. The terminals on the desks at your bank and electric company, for example, are probably 3270s — or, more likely these days, cheap PCs *emulating* (pretending to be) 3270s. Because the 3270 terminal protocol squeezes a great deal more on a phone line than does teletype-ish, all 3270s in an office usually share the same single phone line, with reasonable performance.

The Internet is a big place, and plenty of IBM mainframes run applications on the Net. Some IBM mainframe applications are quite useful. Some library catalogs, for example, speak 3270-ish. If you telnet to a system that wants a 3270, the system usually converts from the teletype-ish that telnet speaks to 3270-ish so that you can use the system anyway. Some 3270 systems speak only 3270-ish, however; if you telnet to these systems, they connect and disconnect without saying anything in between.

To log in to a 3270-ish host from a UNIX system, use a variant of telnet that speaks 3270-ish called *tn3270*. If a system keeps disconnecting or you see full-screen pictures, as shown in Figure 11-3, try using the command tn3270 rather than telnet. Large amounts of UPPERCASE LETTERS and references to the IBM operating systems VM or MVS are also tip-offs that you're talking to a 3270. Even if a 3270 system allows regular telnet, you get a snappier response if you use tn3270.

Figure 11-3:
Using
tn3270 to log
in to the
Harvard
University
catalog.

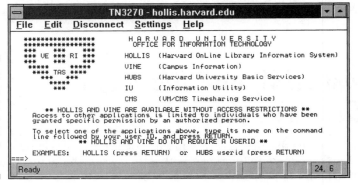

Fun Computers to Break in To

The Internet is a remarkably friendly place. Some systems let you telnet in with little or no prearrangement. Most systems listed in this section just let you telnet in without restriction. Other systems require that you register the first time you log in but still don't ask you to pay anything. These systems simply want to have an idea who their users are.

Libraries

Nearly every large library in the country (indeed, in the developed world) has a computerized catalog, and most catalogs are on the Internet. Most online catalogs also have other research info that is certainly more interesting than the catalogs themselves. This section lists the more prominent library systems and how to access them.

Library: Library of Congress
Address: locis.loc.gov
Access: via telnet or tn3270

The Library of Congress is the largest library in the world and certainly has the biggest catalog system, called LOCIS (your tax dollars at work, or maybe at play). Along with the regular card catalog, in which you can look up pretty much any book ever published in the United States, the Library of Congress has an extensive and useful congressional legislation system you can use to look up the bills that are in Congress. You can find out which bills have been introduced; what has happened to them (getting a bill through Congress is somewhat more complicated than getting someone canonized as a saint); who sponsored the bills; and what the bills say (in summary).

Note: LOCIS is supposed to be available only during library hours, generally 9 a.m. to 9 p.m. (Eastern time) on weekdays, with shorter hours on weekends. Other times, LOCIS sometimes disconnects immediately if it has been turned off for maintenance.

Library: Dartmouth College Library
Address: library.dartmouth.edu
Access: via telnet

Along with the card catalog, this service includes the full text of William Shakespeare's plays and sonnets and the works of other great authors. To search the plays, type **select file s plays**; for sonnets, type **select file s sonnets**.

Library: Yale Library
Address: orbis.yale.edu
Access: via tn3270

This large library is the only one in which you can find a copy of John's thesis, "A Data Base System for Small Interactive Computers," which may not matter to you, but we think that it's interesting. Type **orbis** to get started.

Many libraries are online. We generally find that the Library of Congress is the most useful for finding names of books, unless we're planning to physically visit one of the other libraries.

Other databases

As usual, you can find information about almost anything on the Internet, and telnet is no exception to this rule.

Database: GLIS
Address: glis.cr.usgs.gov
Access: via telnet

GLIS is the government's *Global Land Use Info System*. An enormous amount of map data is available in computer form, which GLIS enables you to locate and order. Impress your friends by whipping out a computerized map of your town, state, or planet.

Registration is required (that is, the first time you log in, you have to say who you are).

History databases
Database: University of Kansas
Address: ukanaix.cc.ukans.edu
Access: via telnet

You history buffs can find lots of good stuff in a variety of history databases around the Net.

Log in as `history` for databases on history, or as `ex-ussr` for databases on Russia and its neighbors. These databases list documents, bibliographies, and other info of interest to historians.

Book database
Database: CARL
Address: pac.carl.org
Access: via telnet

CARL contains book reviews, magazines, and articles, including fax article delivery. To use CARL, you have to sign up for an account and arrange to pay money.

For many of the services, you need a library card (or at least the number of a library card) from a participating library in Colorado or Wyoming, such as the Denver Public Library. Type **pac** to get started.

WorldWindow
Gateway: WorldWindow, the Washington University Electronic Information Gateway
Address: library.wustl.edu
Access: via telnet

WorldWindow is the best place to begin browsing if you like to telnet to far-off interesting places.

Log in as `services`. WorldWindow is a gateway to hundreds of other services around the Net. When you find an interesting service, make a note of its name (and port and login, if necessary) so that you can telnet in directly next time.

Chapter 12
Internet Classic

● ●

In This Chapter
▶ What is Gopherspace?
▶ Finding free files with Archie
▶ Fingering fun
▶ Ways with WAIS
▶ Pinging around the Net

● ●

*I*f you read the popular press (not including us, of course — we would never do anything popular), you might think that the only services on the Internet are the Web and maybe e-mail. The Net *was* around for about 20 years before the Web showed up, and some of the classic pre-Web services are still useful.

The three major classic services are telnet (refer to Chapter 11), FTP (refer to Chapter 6), and e-mail, all of which remain fairly popular. Less popular but still sometimes useful are the "transition" services that arose after the three classics and were mostly superseded by the Web. This chapter takes a look at Gopher and Archie, two of the transition services, as well as finger, ping, and traceroute, three minor classics.

In a nutshell, here's what these services are good for:

✔ Gopher is similar to the Web; rather than display pages of hypertext, however, it displays menus. Lots and lots of menus. See the following section, "Welcome to Gopherspace."

✔ Archie lets you find files on FTP servers, assuming that you know part or all of the filename. See the section "Ask Archie," later in this chapter.

✔ Finger lets you find out about a host computer or a user whose e-mail address you know. See the section "Fingering Far-Off Friends for Fun," later in this chapter.

✔ Ping lets you test your Internet connection, and traceroute traces the route that data takes to get from your computer to the Internet. See the section "Ping-a-Ding," later in this chapter.

Welcome to Gopherspace

FTP provided (and still provides) a handy way to retrieve information from all over the Net, as long as you're the type of person who thinks that it's handy to type lots of commands and equally handy to have to know where on the Net every file you might want is located.

Gopher solved both problems by reducing nearly everything to menus. You start up Gopher, you see a menu. You pick an item, you see another menu. After a certain amount of wandering from menu to menu, you get to menus with actual, useful stuff. Some menu items are files that Gopher can display, mail to you, or (usually) copy to your computer. Some menu items are telnet items that start a telnet session to a host that provides a particular service. Some menu items are search items that ask you to enter a *search string* and the name or partial name of what you're looking for and then use the search string to decide what to get next — more menus, files, or whatever.

You can look at Gopher as analogous to directories on your disk, in which some entries are files of various sorts and other entries are other directories. Whether you think of Gopher as a source for menus or for directories, it gets much of its power from the fact that any item on any menu can reside on any host in Gopherspace. Having a menu on which every item refers to a different host is common. Gopher automatically takes care of finding whatever data you want, no matter the data's location. You can use a dozen or more different Gopher servers in a single session without knowing that you're doing so.

This extremely simple model turns out to be very powerful, and until recently Gopher was usually the fastest, easiest, and most fun way to wander around the Net looking for and frequently finding the information you want. However, the World Wide Web has now eaten Gopher's lunch (in our modest opinion). The Web, like Gopher, is an easy-to-use method of accessing information from many different services. In fact, Web browsers can show you information from Gopher too! Because there's still lots of Gopher information on the Net, however, it's worth knowing how to find and use it.

The good, the bad, and the ugly

You use Gopher by running a *Gopher client program* or a Web browser that can handle Gopher (all the popular browsers do). If you use a UNIX shell provider, for example, you can use the UNIX `gopher` command. Gopher moved into the multimedia era with a vengeance, however, and the classic UNIX gopher program handles only text. For anything other than text, UNIX. Gopher goes into what one may call *cruel joke mode,* in which Gopher tells you that a swell picture you would love to see is available, but you can't look. A good Gopher client, on the other hand, wastes no time in finding the picture, copying it to your computer, and popping it up in a window on-screen. Graphic Web browsers, such as Netscape and Internet Explorer, handle pictures from Gopher with aplomb.

These days, most people who look at information from Gopher probably use a Web browser rather than a program designed just for Gopher. In this section, you see how to use the UNIX gopher program and a Web browser to cruise around in Gopherspace.

If you use Winsock software and are bound and determined to run a Gopher program rather than use a Web browser, we can't stop you. If you spend a great deal of time Gophering, you may prefer a Gopher program — who knows? If you like, download WS Gopher from `http://sageftp.inel.gov/`. You can also find this program at the Consummate Winsock Applications List (at `http://www.stroud.com` or `http://cws.iworld.com`) or at TUCOWS (at `http://www.tucows.com`). Refer to Chapter 7 to find out how to download and install software via FTP.

Among commercial online services, only AOL provides Gopher directly (go to the keyword GOPHER, of all things). If you use another online service, you're still in luck, though, because you can use the Web browser to see Gopher menus.

Gophering around in the Web

Enough of this Theory of Pure Gopherology — let's take Gopher for a test drive. These days the convenient way for people to use Gopher is by firing up their World Wide Web browser. (See Chapters 5 and 6 in *The Internet For Dummies,* 4th Edition (IDG Books Worldwide, Inc.), to find out how to use a browser, in case you've forgotten.) As you may recall, the Web gives each Web page a *URL*, which is a horrible-looking address that begins with `http://`. The secret to using Gopher via a Web browser is that Gopher menus have URLs too. Gopher URLs begin with `gopher://`. Simple enough?

Why is Gopher called Gopher?

They named it Gopher for two reasons: First, the gopher is an industrious little animal, always busy, scurrying about on behalf of its family. Second, Gopher is an obvious pun on "go fer" because Gopher "goes fer" your files.

The fact that a gopher is the mascot of the University of Minnesota, where Gopher was written, is, of course, *completely* irrelevant.

Gopher has been so successful that *Gopher+,* an improved version, has appeared. Fortunately, the main difference between the two is that Gopher+ can handle more and different kinds of information than plain Gopher can. Other than that difference, the two programs are so similar that they're interchangeable, and plain Gopher and Gopher+ items can intermix on the same menu.

Here's how to figure out a Gopher menu's URL if you know the name of the Gopher server the menu is on: Type **gopher://**, followed by the Gopher server name, followed by another slash. For example, for the University of Minnesota Gopher server (at gopher.micro.umn.edu), the URL is

```
gopher://gopher.micro.umn.edu/
```

When you type this URL in the Location or Address box of your Web browser, you see the main, or root, menu on the Gopher server. From that menu, begin choosing items until you get to the menu you want.

Someone may give you the URL of a specific menu on a specific Gopher server. The URL looks like

```
gopher://mudhoney.micro.umn.edu:4325/7
```

The stuff following the Gopher server host name tells your Web browser exactly where the menu is stored. Don't worry about what this stuff means — we don't!

To see a Gopher menu with your Web browser, type the URL into the box just below the toolbar and press Enter. (If your browser doesn't let you type in that box, get a better browser! In the meantime, choose File from the menu and look for a command such as Open Location.) Your Web browser gets the Gopher menu and formats the menu as though it were a Web page, as shown in Figure 12-1.

Figure 12-1:
When a
Web
browser
displays a
Gopher
menu, each
menu item
appears as
a link.

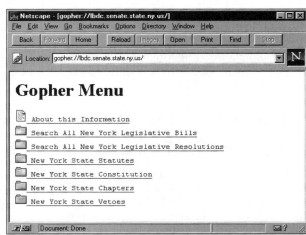

Gopher Menu

About this Information
Search All New York Legislative Bills
Search All New York Legislative Resolutions
New York State Statutes
New York State Constitution
New York State Chapters
New York State Vetoes

Each item on the Gopher menu appears as a link. To choose that item, click the link. Items on Gopher menus can be any of the following:

- **Another Gopher menu:** Some browsers display a cute little file folder to the left of these menu items. When you click one of these folder icons, another menu appears.

- **A text file:** These items usually have a little sheet-of-paper icon to their left. When you click one of these icons, your browser displays the text.

- **A search item:** Some browsers display little binoculars by these items. When you click a search item, a Web page appears that enables you to search Gopher menus for information. For example, Figure 12-2 shows the screen you get when you click a Gopher search item in Netscape. When you enter a word to search for and press Enter, Gopher returns a menu of items that contain the word you searched for.

- **A telnet item:** When you click telnet items (which have a little picture of a terminal to their left), you log in to an Internet host by using telnet (refer to Chapter 11). Most browsers run a separate telnet program. If clicking telnet items doesn't work, you may have to get a telnet program and configure your browser to work with it. If you use a commercial online service's built-in browser, you're out of luck. If you use Winsock software, refer to Chapter 11 to find out how to get a telnet program. To configure Netscape to use your telnet program, choose Options⇨Preferences from the menu, click Applications and Directories, and type the pathname of your telnet program in the Telnet box.

- **A graphics, sound, video, or other file:** These items are marked by a variety of adorable little icons. When you click one of these files, your browser downloads the file. If you click a graphics, sound, or video file that the browser knows how to display or play, your browser does so. Otherwise, the browser asks you where to store the file.

Figure 12-2:
To find Gopher items that contain a certain word, type the word you want to find.

These indexes are a mess

If you use Gopher much, you quickly notice a great deal of inconsistency from one menu to another. The inconsistency exists because Gopher is a totally decentralized system, like the World Wide Web. That is, anyone who wants to can put up a Gopher server. Putting up a Gopher server is relatively easy; the system manager only has to install a few programs and create some index files containing the text of the local menus. If one site wants to include in its Gopher menu a link to an item or menu somewhere else, the site can do so without requiring any cooperation from the manager of the item or menu linked to.

The *good* news is that thousands of Gopher servers are on the Net, put up by volunteers who want data retrieval to be easier. The *bad* news is that because almost none of these people has any experience in indexing and information retrieval (for that experience, you need a degree in library science), the same item may appear on five different menus under five different names, and no two Gopher menus are quite the same.

Figuring out where people have hidden stuff can take some experimenting and poking around, but that poking around is invariably worth the effort.

As you use your Web browser to surf the Net, you may find yourself looking at Gopher menus when you least expect it. Many Web pages contain links to items in Gopher menus. Now you know how to proceed when you see a Gopher menu on the Web.

Ask Archie

Archie is a system that does exactly one thing, but it does that thing well. What it does is to find an FTP server that has a particular file you want when you know the name, or at least part of the name, of the file. It's most useful for tracking down shareware or freeware.

Suppose that you know that you're looking for a file whose name starts with N32E40 (that would be a 32-bit version of Netscape 4.0, most likely). You send that name off to Archie, and he sends back a list of places where files with that name are available.

Archie on the Web

You can get to Archie in several ways. The most convenient is usually via the Web, but because Archie can be slow, it's sometimes easier to send him e-mail. A bunch of Archie gateway pages are on the Web, including:

```
http://www.nedesign.com/SITES/
http://www-ns.rutgers.edu/htbin/archie
http://www.thegroup.net/AA.html
http://hoohoo.ncsa.uiuc.edu/archie.html
```

You can also check the Yahoo list of Archie sites, at

```
http://www.yahoo.com/Computers_and_Internet/Internet/
            FTP_Sites/Searching/Archie/
```

No matter which of these servers you use, the steps are the same after you have the gateway page on your screen:

1. Type the name of the file you want in the "what to search for" window.

2. Set the search type to Exact if you know that you have typed the exact name of the file, including any extension such as EXE or gz. Set the search type to Case Insensitive Substring Match otherwise.

3. Leave the rest of the options alone.

4. Click the Search button.

5. Wait. Go make a new pot of coffee.

Did we mention that Archie is slow? Archie is really slow, sometimes taking five or ten minutes to do his thing. If you're using a Mac or Windows system, switch to another window and do something else in the meantime.

Archie by mail

Because Archie is slow anyway, you might rather get his advice by e-mail. The e-mail version has a zillion options, almost none of which is useful. Send a message containing

```
find filename
```

in the text of the message, not in the subject line, to any of these Archie server addresses:

```
archie@archie.unl.edu
archie@archie.ans.net
archie@internic.net
archie@archie.rutgers.edu
```

You get the results of the search by return mail. If you're wondering what the rest of the options are, send a message that just says help.

If you have a telnet program, you can also telnet directly to Archie. Telnet to any of the servers just listed (leave out the `archie@` part), log in as `Archie`, type **find *filename*** the same as you would put in the e-mail message, and join the waiting game. The server should eventually start listing the places where your file can be found. If the listing stops at the end of the screen and displays a colon, press space to continue. At the end of the list, when it displays `(END)`, you have to press Q to confirm that you know that it's done. When you're done with the telnet game, type **quit** to get out. (In case it's not obvious yet, Archie is a system designed by nerds for nerds.)

Although in theory all the Archie servers have the same list of files, in practice they vary somewhat, so if you don't find the file you want on one server, try another. The servers also vary a great deal in speed.

After Archie has found you a list of sites where your file lives, be sure to use a site that's reasonably close to you. If you're in the United States, sites whose names end with `edu`, `com`, `net`, `org`, and `us` are likely to be nearby. Sites whose names end with other, two-letter combinations are in faraway countries connected with slow links.

Other places

As the Web has grown, much of the software that used to be available only by FTP has popped up on the Web. Here are a few places to look:

- `www.jumbo.com`: An enormous archive of shareware and freeware
- `www.shareware.com`: Less enormous, but better organized
- `www.tucows.com`: Internet-related shareware and freeware
- `www.stroud.com`: Windows Internet-related shareware and freeware

Be sure to visit `http://net.dummies.net/software`, where we keep our latest updated list of hot software sites.

Fingering Far-Off Friends for Fun

UNIX systems always (well, ever since about 1971) had multiple users, and nosy nerds always wondered who else was using their computer and when. The UNIX `finger` command started as a way to find out who else was logged in to the computer you were using and rapidly grew to become everything from a mail directory to a homemade database inquiry system.

Fingering on the Web

Unless you happen to have a special-purpose finger program lying around, the easiest way to use finger is on the Web. The best-known finger page is here:

```
http://www.cs.indiana.edu:800/finger
```

In the box labeled Enter search keywords on that page, you type the address you want to finger, in the same format as an e-mail address, and press Enter. The next Web page you see tells you the result.

Fingering from UNIX

To **run** finger from a shell prompt, type **finger *username@hostname*** and press Enter. To finger someone whose e-mail address is, for example, elvis@bluesuede.org, you type this line:

```
finger elvis@bluesuede.org
```

You get back something like the following:

```
Login name: elvis           In real life: E. Aaron Presley
Directory: /usr/elvis        Shell: /bin/sh
On since Jun 30 16:03:13 on vt01    1 day 9 hours Idle Time
Project: Working on "Hound Dog"
Plan:
Write many songs, become famous.
```

The exact format of the response varies a great deal from one system to another because fiddling with the finger program is a bad habit of many UNIX system hackers.

Fingering with a SLIP/PPP account

What if you don't have a UNIX shell account, don't feel like using the finger page on the Web, and have nowhere to type the finger command? Have no fear, because the Windows and Mac version of Eudora can finger people for you. In Eudora 3.0, choose Tools➪Directory Services (or press Ctrl+Y) to see the Finger window. Type in the Command box the address you want to finger and click Finger. The results appear in the big text box, as shown in Figure 12-3. Press Ctrl+F4 to close the Finger window.

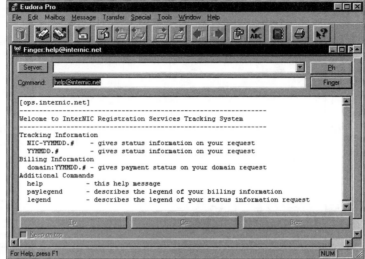

Figure 12-3:
Eudora can open a window that lets you do some fancy fingering.

If you use Windows, an intrepid programmer out in Netland named Lee Murach has created just for you a Winsock program called WS Finger. You can get WS Finger via FTP from `sparky.umd.edu` in the /pub/winsock directory, among other places.

Finger works only if the fingeree's Internet provider runs a program called (intriguingly enough) a *finger daemon*. It doesn't hurt to try fingering; the worst that will happen is a "Connection refused" message.

Project that plan! (Or is it plan that project?)

The response to the `finger` command on UNIX systems comes back with a *project* and a *plan*. If you have a shell account, you too can have a project and a plan so that you look like a well-informed, seasoned network user (appearances are everything).

Your project is a file called `.project` (yes, it begins with a dot), and your plan is a file called `.plan` (it begins with a dot too). You can put in them anything you want. The `finger` command shows only the first line of the project but all of the plan. Try not to go overboard. Ten lines or so is all people are willing to see, and even that's stretching it if it's not really, *really* clever.

The industrial-strength finger

Some places, universities in particular, have attached their `finger` programs to organizational directories. If you finger `levine@bu.edu` (Boston University), for example, you get the following response:

```
[bu.edu]
 There were 55 matches to your request.

  E-mail addresses and telephone numbers are only displayed
          when a query matches one individual.  To obtain
          additional information on a particular indi-
          vidual, inquire again with the index_id.
```

The finger program lists all the matches. When you see a listing you want to check further, use the index_id:

```
finger Nxxxxx@bu.edu
```

where `Nxxxxxx` is the index_ID you saw listed when you first fingered your friend.

Other universities with similar directories include MIT and Yale. It's worth a try — the worst that can happen is that it will say `not found`.

Ping-a-Ding

One of the most disconcerting and annoying parts of being on the Net is Mysterious Network Failure, in which a host that you know is there just disappears.

Plain old ping

Ping is the SONAR of the Internet, as seen in old submarine warfare movies. It sends a few packets to a host somewhere on the Net and lets you know what, if anything, it got back. (A few people claim that it stands for Primitive Internet Network Groper, or something like that, but really now.)

To use ping, you tell the ping program the name (or number) of an Internet host computer that is willing to bounce your ping message back to you. For example, you can ping `www.yahoo.com` or `home.netscape.com` or `www.internic.net`, among other large Internet hosts.

Windows 95 comes with a standard albeit poorly documented ping program called, remarkably, Ping.exe. You run it in an MS-DOS window, as shown in Figure 12-4 (choose Start➪Programs➪MS-DOS Prompt to open a DOS window, type **ping** followed by the Internet host name, and press Enter). Ping reports back a bunch of numbers, most of which are of no interest except to network aficionados. The one number that *is* interesting is the time, which tells how many milliseconds ($^1/_{1000}$ second) it took for the response to the ping to come back. Anything under 500 ms, which is half a second, is okay. If you get no response or it takes thousands of milliseconds, consider trying that host later unless you're really desperate and really patient.

Figure 12-4:
Come in,
IDG, do you
read me?

UNIX systems have a similar ping command. (The Windows 95 version is a copy of the UNIX version, in fact.) The Mac has a freeware MacPing, available from http://www.dartmouth.edu/netsoftware/macping.html. On Windows 3.1, you're out of luck because most 3.1 Winsock packages are lacking a crucial feature that ping needs.

Over the network and through the woods

If ping doesn't give you enough geeky details, the next step up is traceroute, the program that shows you the route your packets take as they fly through the Internet.

The original UNIX version is called traceroute, and the Windows 95 knockoff is tracert, which you run in an MS-DOS window. As with ping, you give traceroute (or tracert) the name of an Internet host computer to trace a route to. Figure 12-5 shows a trace from Internet For Dummies Central to the AT&T WorldNet Service Web site, a pretty typical trace. The packets first go to our local provider in Pennsylvania (hops 2–4); then out to the Sprint network access point in Pennsauken, New Jersey (hops 5–6); then to BBN Planet, the AT&T provider (hops 7–12); and then through the AT&T internal network (hops 13–15). The times show how long it takes to get to each of the intermediate systems, again measured in milliseconds.

Figure 12-5:
The long, lonesome road to AT&T WorldNet Service.

If you're trying to contact a host computer on the Net and have trouble, traceroute can tell you where the problem is. In particular, the connection points between networks (for example, sprintnap, which is short for the Sprint network access point — hops 6 and 7 in Figure 12-5) tend to be overloaded and to cause a great deal of delay. Finding out where the congestion is can make you feel better, of course, but there's usually not much you can do about it.

If you see that your packets are getting into your own Internet provider's network and never escaping, that's their problem, and you can call them up and suggest that they check into it. We have found that the hardest thing is to find someone who understands the problem. More than once, we have called up our provider and reported that one of its internal links was broken — even specifying which link it was and what the likely problem was — and the response was "Huh?" Sigh.

Chapter 13

Fun and Games on the Net

• •

In This Chapter

▶ Playing in the MUDs

▶ Getting lost in 3-D space

▶ Participating in chat-based games on IRC

▶ Pro wrestling by e-mail

▶ And much, much more!

• •

*T*o hear us talk, the Internet is just about working — sending chapters by e-mail, checking stock yields on the Web, and reading up on new software trends in `comp.whatever`. The Internet has some services that are pure fun too, and this chapter talks about them. No work-related stuff here, so don't let your boss see you reading this chapter.

For a wide variety of Internet-based fun programs, start at the TUCOWS software Web site (`http://www.tucows.com`), select your mirror site, select your operating system, and click Entertainment and Games. Refer to Chapter 6 to find out how to download and install programs from TUCOWS.

Rolling in MUDs and MOOs

MUDs? MOOs? Internet terminology is always strange; in the area of online gaming, however, the acronyms get totally out of control. Worse, no one can agree on exactly what the acronyms stand for. *MUDs* are Multi-User Dungeons, Multi-User Dimensions, or Multiple User Dialog, depending on whom you ask. *MUSHes* are Multi-User Shared Hallucinations, which speak for themselves. *MOOs* are the same thing, but with *object-oriented* programming capabilities (which we explain in a minute). *MUDs* are imaginary worlds in which you can participate using the Internet and some software. Lots of other people may be participating — MUDding — in the same world at the same time, and you may run into them. To figure out what's going on in a MUD, you give commands that let you look around, move from place to place, say things, kiss someone passionately, or engage in armed combat (as appropriate).

Exactly what you can do in a MUD depends on how it's set up: what the setting is, what objects you find there, what commands are available, and what are the unwritten rules of behavior between people in the MUD. A MUD may simulate a beach resort, a university campus, Arthurian England, or Planet X in the Galactic Empire.

Each MUD has folks who are in charge of running it and enforcing its rules. These people are called *wizards* or *gods,* and you had better be nice to them.

We stayed away from MUDs for years for fear of getting totally addicted and spending weeks or months at the keyboard without a break. As with IRC (refer to Chapter 9), you can waste, er, spend, a great deal of time in a MUD just trying to figure out what's going on.

MUDding basics

To connect to a MUD, you can use one of two methods:

- **Telnet in:** That is, run the telnet program (described in Chapter 11) to log in to the computer on which the MUD runs. Then type commands to participate in the MUD. Because telnet is limited to text, you can't see any graphics or use your mouse. (See the section "Telnetting in to MUDs," later in this chapter.)

- **Use a MUD program:** A MUD client program is a program designed specifically for participating in MUDs. A MUD program can keep track of the MUDs you frequent, and it makes the screen easier to read than a regular telnet program. (See the section "Better-quality MUD," later in this chapter.)

After you're connected (using either telnet or a MUD program), you start exploring. Some MUDs require you to register, connect to an existing character, or create your own character.

Types of MUDs

MUDs have been around for more than ten years, and hundreds of them are out there. As a result, you can choose from lots of different kinds, including these:

- **TinyMUDs** are socially oriented MUDs in which people hang around and chat.

- **LPMUDs, DikuMUDs,** and **AberMUDs** are online role-playing adventure games, sort of like Dungeons and Dragons. The wizards in an LPMUD can actually change and extend the world of the game by giving special commands.

> ✔ **MOOs** are usually also social in nature, but can be about anything. Players can create and change the objects in the world of the MOO, using an object-oriented programming language.
>
> ✔ **Talkers** are for talk only, with no games, no monsters to fight, no quests, and no bizarre rules to learn. All you do is talk and make new friends. Talkers are much like IRC, except that rather than join a channel, you move into a room.

To get started, you have to choose a MUD to try out. A good way to choose a MUD is to start at the Yahoo list of MUDs that have Web home pages and find one that looks congenial. Many MUDs (like, hundreds) have their own Web page, and you can find them by starting at Yahoo (`http://www.yahoo.com`) and clicking Recreation, then Games, then Internet Games, and then MUDs, MUSHes, MOOs, and so on.

A MUD's Web page should tell you how to connect, including these important facts:

> ✔ **Host name:** The name of the computer on which the MUD is running.
>
> ✔ **Port number:** The *port* on the host computer that connects you to the MUD game. Most Internet host computers do a number of things at the same time. Specifying the port number connects you to the MUD program.

For example, the Diversity University MOO runs on the host computer `moo.du.org` using port 8888.

Of course, some MUD home pages have all kinds of information except how to connect! Stealth's MUD List (`http://www.gulf.net/~kverge`) contains a history of MUDs and a list of current MUDs with their addresses. If you find a MUD that looks interesting based on its Web page, you can use Stealth's MUD List to find out how to connect to the MUD.

Another source of information about MUDs is the Usenet newsgroup `rec.games.mud.announce`, which includes lists of active MUDs.

Telnetting in to MUDs

Telnet (described in detail in Chapter 11) lets you log in to the computer on which the MUD is running as though your computer were a terminal on that computer. You can type commands and see the results. If you use Windows 3.1 or a Mac, you need a telnet program (Windows 95 comes with one).

To participate in a MUD using your telnet program:

1. **Start up your telnet program and connect to the computer on which the MUD is running.**

   Refer to Chapter 11 to find out how to run your telnet program. If you're looking at a Web page with a telnet link, just click the link to fire up your telnet program and connect to the MUD. (See the following sidebar, "Telling your browser how to telnet," if clicking a telnet link doesn't work.)

   You see welcome information and a prompt to log in. (If you don't, the MUD is not working or has moved.)

2. **Follow the instructions to log in.**

   This process works differently for each MUD, so we can't be much more specific.

3. **Explore the MUD!**

   See the section "MUD, MUD, glorious MUD," later in this chapter, for suggestions for getting to know MUDs. Figure 13-1 shows the Ancient Anguish MUD, an exploration-and-adventure game situated in a medieval-like land with dwarves, elves, knights, and monks. (Ancient Anguish, an LPMUD, is at `ancient.anguish.org`, port 2222.)

Figure 13-1:
When you use telnet to participate in a MUD, you type commands and you see the results in the telnet window.

4. **Sign off by typing** quit **and pressing Enter.**

   The telnet connection ends, and your telnet program tells you so.

5. **Exit from the telnet program.**

Telling your browser how to telnet

It's a good idea to tell your Web browser about your telnet program. The home pages of most MUDs include a telnet link — that is, a link with a telnet URL (Chapter 2 tells you what URLs are) for the MUD. A telnet URL looks something like

`telnet:moo.du.org:8888`

If your browser knows about your telnet program, clicking the telnet link runs the telnet program and connects automatically to the MUD's host computer.

To tell Netscape 3.0 which telnet program you use, choose Options⇨General Preferences

(in Netscape 3.0) or Edit⇨Preferences (in Netscape 4.0) to display the Preferences window. Click the Apps tab along the top of the window, and then click the Browse button to the right of the Telnet Application box. Find your telnet program and click the Open button. (The Windows 95 built-in telnet program is usually named in C:\Windows\telnet.exe.) Then click OK to dismiss the Preferences window.

Internet Explorer already knows about the Windows 95 telnet program.

Telnet programs work fine for using MUDs, and lots of MUDders use them. Sometimes, however, you can't see what you're typing or the conversation in the room gets mixed up with the results of commands you type.

Some MUDs' home pages have built-in telnet programs you can use to connect to the MUD if your Web browser can run Java programs (Netscape and Internet Explorer both can). If a MUD's home page has a link to join the MUD, try clicking it.

Better-quality MUD

A better way to connect to a MUD is by using a MUD client program: a program specifically designed for MUDding. A MUD program is really a telnet program that has had various MUD-related commands added.

You can find MUD programs at the TUCOWS software Web site (`http://www.tucows.com`). Go to the TUCOWS page, select your mirror site, select your operating system, and click Entertainment and Games. (Refer to Chapter 7 to find out how to download and install programs from TUCOWS.) You can find MUD programs for Windows 95, Windows 3.1, and the Mac.

For example, Figure 13-2 shows zMUD, a Windows 95 MUD program, connected to the Ancient Anguish MUD. zMUD lets you

✔ Store the names and passwords of the MUDs you usually use

✔ Display the MUD text in a larger window so that you can see more than just the last 20 or so lines

✔ Scroll the window up to review stuff that has scrolled off the top of the screen

✔ Change the text and background colors and font, to make the text more readable (although some MUDs seem to overrule the settings you make)

✔ Program your function keys or other key combinations to type commonly used commands and names

✔ Record the route to commonly visited locations in the MUD (if you usually go to the hot tub in a particular MUD, for example, you can record the commands required to get there so that you don't have to type them all every time you want to go there)

✔ Help you create maps of a MUD as you explore it

Figure 13-2:
zMUD
makes
MUDding a
little more
convenient.

MUD, MUD, glorious MUD

Whether you use telnet or a MUD program to connect to your MUD, your first move is to figure out what's going on and what you can do. Here are some suggestions:

- ✔ Type **help** to get some general help with using the MUD. This command usually tells you how to get more detailed information about moving around, communicating with other MUDders, and your other options.
- ✔ Type **news** to read the recent announcements about the MUD.
- ✔ Type **look** to look around the room or area where you start out.

Most MUDs have commands like these:

- ✔ To move to another room or area, type **move** or **go** followed by a compass direction.
- ✔ To pick something up, type **get** or **take** followed by the thing you want to pick up. To put it back down, type **drop** or **throw** and the name of the thing.
- ✔ To find out what's around you, type **look**. Or type **look** and the thing you want to look at or the direction in which you want to look.
- ✔ To talk to another person, type **say** followed by your message. Most MUDs let you type a double-quote character as an abbreviation for "say."
- ✔ To perform an action, such as smiling at someone or falling down in a dead faint, type a colon (:) followed by the action. For example, if you type

```
: leaps into the air and turns into a bat.
```

then everyone sees the following message (assuming that you're a character named CountDrac):

```
CountDrac leaps into the air and turns into a bat.
```

- ✔ To find out which objects you have picked up and are carrying around, type **inventory**.

Not all MUDs use these exact commands; the results of the help command tell you which commands work in the MUD you're in.

Most MUDs let you page wizards or other players who are in charge. If you run into serious trouble, page a wizard and ask for help.

Staying cool in the MUD

As usual on the Internet, MUDs have unwritten rules of netiquette. Either follow them or get ignored, killed, or otherwise spurned:

- Don't demand things. No one in the MUD owes you anything. If you're not polite, no one has to be nice to you.

- Don't whine; ask nicely. If you can't get help, just stand around and watch the action for a while.

- Don't follow people around without their permission.

- Don't page wizards who are off-duty or page the same wizard over and over or page wizards who have asked you to stop. Wizards can throw you out.

- In MUDs that involve combat, don't steal things from corpses that someone else has just killed. Killers get first dibs on the stuff their victims are carrying.

Getting more MUD info

It can take months to learn your way around a MUD. For help getting started, several Usenet newsgroups discuss MUDs:

- `rec.games.mud.admin`: Administrative matters

- `rec.games.mud.announce`: Moderated newsgroup for announcements about MUDs

- `rec.games.mud.diku`: DikuMUDs

- `rec.games.mud.lp`: LPMUDs

- `rec.games.mud.misc`: Miscellaneous postings

- `rec.games.mud.tiny`: Postings pertaining to the TinyMUD and related MUDs

You can also find information at Yahoo; start at the Yahoo home page (`http://www.yahoo.com`) and click Recreation, then Games, then Internet Games, and then MUDs, MUSHes, MOOs, and so on.

Games on the Web

Thousands of Web pages have games on them, from trivia games to chess to the classic Hunt the Wumpus (see Figure 13-3). These games include single-user games, in which you play against the program on the Web server, and multiuser games, in which you interact with other people who are using the same Web page.

Yahoo is a great place to look for Web-based games; start at the Yahoo home page (`http://www.yahoo.com`) and click Recreation, then Games, then Internet Games, and then Interactive Web Games.

Figure 13-3: Beware of the wumpus! Click the Instructions link to find out how to hunt him.

Games on IRC

Lots of games are available on Internet Relay Chat (IRC) channels too (refer to Chapter 9 for an introduction to IRC). Because IRC consists of lots of people typing text, IRC-based games are limited to text too. You can play trivia games or word-finding games or enter a simulation of *The X-Files* (the television show, for you folks who don't have a TV).

For a list of IRC games, start at the Yahoo Web page (`http://www.yahoo.com`), and then click Computers and Internet, then Internet, then Chat, then IRC, and then Games.

Games by E-Mail

You can also play games by e-mail. Although the play isn't as breathtakingly speedy as games on the Web or on IRC, e-mail is an excellent way to play games that call for some thought, like chess. You can participate in e-mail-based fantasy baseball, VGA Planets (a galactic multiplayer strategy game), Diplomacy (negotiations and back-stabbing in pre–World War I Europe), and wrestling (we are not making this up).

For a list of games by e-mail, start at the Yahoo Web page (`http://www.yahoo.com`), and then click Recreation, then Games, then Internet Games, and then Play By E-Mail.

Wandering in Virtual Reality

Web pages can contain something called *virtual reality,* and you can view virtual reality pages with a specially equipped Web browser. At first, virtual reality images look just like regular pictures on a Web page. When you click in the image, however, you can "enter" the world of the picture and move around inside it in three dimensions. As you move around (using your mouse), the picture changes. That's why virtual reality is also called *3-D,* because it simulates a 3-D world.

Virtual reality images (also called *virtual worlds*) are written in a programming language called VRML (virtual reality modeling language), and files in this format usually have the extension WRL. Although Netscape and Internet Explorer don't know how to display virtual worlds, you can add plug-ins to either browser to teach them how. Refer to Chapter 8 to find out how to use plug-ins to extend the capabilities of your browser. Most versions of Netscape Navigator come with the Netscape 3-D plug-in, Live3D, already installed.

For a virtual world to enable multiple people to participate in the same world and see each other's images (called *avatars*) on-screen, you need special software. For example, AlphaWorld is a virtual world that encourages Internet users to visit and create their own little piece of the world — you can create a home or business in AlphaWorld using its world-building tools. To visit AlphaWorld, you have to download and install the Active Worlds browser (see `http://www.worlds.net/alphaworld` for more information). The first time you try to visit AlphaWorld, you're mailed an "immigration number" you can use to connect. Figure 13-4 shows avatars (the images that show where people are) in AlphaWorld.

Because Microsoft has one of every other type of program in the universe, it should be no surprise that it has a virtual interactive program called V-Chat, which you can download from `http://vchat1.microsoft.com`.

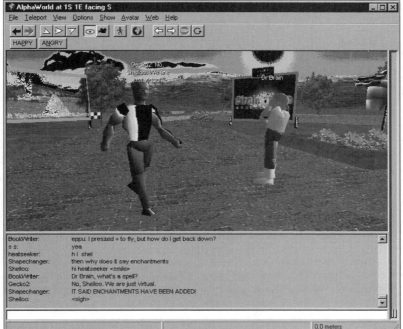

Figure 13-4:
Just
hanging
around in
AlphaWorld.

Finding virtual worlds

To find a virtual world with a game in it, look at these Web sites:

- ✔ **The Yahoo list of 3-D games:** Start at Yahoo (http://www.yahoo.com) and click Recreation, then Games, then Internet Games, and then Virtual Worlds.

- ✔ **Hot Links to the Virtual Worlds Industry** (http://www.ccon.org/hotlinks/hotlinks.html): This pages lists lots of different kinds of worlds, including those that work with Web browsers and those that require special software. It also includes MUDs and MOOs, which are like non-3-D virtual worlds.

- ✔ **Proteinman's Top Ten VRML Worlds** (http://www.clark.net/theme/proteinman): Dennis McKenzie and Adrian Scott compile this useful list and update it from time to time.

What to do, virtually

When you're "in" a virtual world, you can do the following (these instructions work with the Live3D plug-in and some other programs):

- ✔ **Move around:** Hold down the left mouse button while you move the mouse where you want to go. As you move, the view of the virtual world changes. To turn your "head," hold down the right mouse button while you move the mouse.

- ✔ **Take a closer look:** Hold down the Ctrl key while you click something. Your view "zooms in" to give you a closer look.

- ✔ **Move to a predefined viewpoint:** The creator of the virtual world may have defined *viewpoints,* or spots that are useful to go to. When you enter a virtual world, you see the *entry view,* which is always one of the predefined viewpoints. To see a list of viewpoints, right-click anywhere in the virtual world and click Viewpoints from the menu that appears. To go to one of the viewpoints, click it in the list.

For more information about virtual worlds, read *VRML & 3D On The Web For Dummies,* by Dave Kay and Doug Muder (IDG Books Worldwide, Inc.).

More Fun

New kinds of Internet fun appear every day, usually in the form of new Web pages or new Internet-based programs. To see a list of Internet game software, go to TUCOWS (`http://www.tucows.com`), select your mirror site, select your operating system, and click Entertainment and Games. To see lists of Web sites that run games of all types, go to Yahoo (`http://www.yahoo.com`) and click Recreation, Games, and Internet Games.

Chapter 14

Cool Stuff Is Out There!

• •

In This Chapter

▶ Finding information about the Net on the Net

▶ Frequently asked questions (FAQs) and their answers

▶ The Usenet urban folklore quiz

▶ Weather, news, stock prices, and sports

▶ Kids' and educational stuff

▶ Fun, adventure, and total silliness

• •

*T*he Internet is such a huge place that no single book can possibly list all the resources and services available. Even if it did, the book would be out-of-date the day it was published. Fortunately, the Net itself is the ideal place to find out more about its resources. (Think of using the Net as looking up the word *dictionary* in the dictionary, except that you're more likely to find something you didn't already know. By the way, have you heard that by lexicographer's tradition, the word *gullible* doesn't appear in any dictionary?)

In this chapter, we look at our favorite sources of information about the Internet, other useful information, and just plain silly stuff. For each service, we list the *URL,* the *Uniform Resource Locator,* of the server. Chapter 2 tells you how to use URLs to access stuff by using Gopher, WAIS, and — first and foremost — the World Wide Web. URLs that begin with *http* are World Wide Web pages. URLs that begin with *news* are Usenet newsgroups. URLs that begin with *ftp* are files available from FTP servers. And, URLs that begin with *gopher* are Gopher items.

Yuck! I Hate Typing URLs!

This chapter is full of URLs, and they're a pain to type. *We* didn't have to type them, of course, because we used cut-and-paste commands to copy the URLs from our Web browser to the word processor we used to write this chapter. But you're stuck typing them into *your* browser. Or are you?

The Internet comes to the rescue! Simply type this one URL:

```
http://net.dummies.net/update/
```

You see The Internet For Dummies Central, the home page about this book and other books by the same great group of authors. (Not to mention humble!) Follow the links to see the update page about *MORE Internet For Dummies,* and you see all the URLs we mention in this chapter. Rather than type the URLs, you simply click. We also update on this Web page any URLs that have changed.

The Net on the Net

We start with information about the Internet itself, including indexes to information about the World Wide Web.

The Usenet urban folklore quiz (Part I)

Face it — more interesting things exist than chapters full of lists. One of our fellow ...*For Dummies* authors calls these types of chapters Ten Coffeepot Chapters. To perk things up, direct from the world-famous Usenet group `alt.folklore.urban`, it's the Usenet Urban Folklore Quiz.

Each section has ten true or false questions. The answers are at the end of this chapter. Don't cheat by looking at the answers first!

Part I: Science

True or false:

1. You can make as much ice faster by starting with warmer water.

2. Boiled water freezes faster than ordinary water at the same initial temperature.

3. Daylight sky appears dark enough to see stars from the bottom of a deep well.

4. Fluorescent lamps light up when held near a high-voltage line.

5. Leather saddles used to be treated with llama dung to avoid scaring horses.

6. If the entire population of China jumped up at the same time: A.) The Earth's orbit would be disturbed or B.) The entire United States would be swamped by a tidal wave.

7. You can see glass flow in the windows of old buildings.

8. A newspaper once substituted "in the African-American" for "in the black."

9. Scientists once concluded that bumble-bees can't fly.

10. The F-51D fighter plane can flip because of engine torque.

Indexes to the Net

```
http://www.yahoo.com
http://www.yahooligans.com
http://www.lycos.com
http://altavista.digital.com
http://www.excite.com
http://www.infoseek.com
http://index.opentext.net
```

If you're looking for information and decide to see what the Web has to offer, any of these indexes can take you to interesting places. Most indexes contain a blank you can fill in to search for a word or phrase on almost any page on the World Wide Web. Yahoo and Excite also contain a detailed topic list so that you can browse through the information on the Web. Lycos and AltaVista let you search huge databases of Web pages, larger (we think) than the Yahoo database. (The AltaVista database contains more than 31 million Web pages, as of February 1997.) AltaVista indexes articles in Usenet newsgroups too. Excite also reviews Web pages. InfoSeek provides a free Internet search service, or you can sign up for an account that enables you to search the text of wire service news stories, business magazines, and newspapers. Yahoo has special index pages ("Yahooligans") for kids as well as for some large metropolitan areas.

The Internet Tourbus

```
http://www.tourbus.com
```

The Internet Tourbus is a service that sends an e-mail message twice a week with news about the Net and recommendations about interesting sites. The Tourbus, written by Patrick Crispen and Bob Rankin and sponsored by America Online, also brings Internet scams to the attention of its readers. A subscription ("bus ticket") to the Tourbus is free; Patrick and Bob support this service by including ads.

Finding people

```
http://www.four11.com
http://www.switchboard.com
```

If you want to find someone's e-mail address or phone number, one of these Web sites will probably do the trick. You enter the information you know about the person, click a button, and see what's in the database. Switchboard provides phone numbers, not e-mail addresses, and lets you find businesses by city and category.

Who's got dandruff.com?

```
http://www.internic.net
```

The InterNIC (Internet Information Center) is in charge of registering the big four types of domain names (com, edu, net, and org). You can use its whois server to find out who has registered a domain name, such as something.com or whatever.org. (It turns out that Something Consulting, in Hoboken, New Jersey, has something.com and someone in Washington State has whatever.org. It figures.)

Us

```
http://net.dummies.net
```

Here at Internet For Dummies Central, we have quite a bit of information about the Net, including

- ✔ Two-letter country codes that appear at the end of Internet host names (such as ca for Canada and br for Brazil)
- ✔ Internet resources for kids
- ✔ Resources for Macintosh users
- ✔ Instructions for UNIX shell account users
- ✔ Our favorite Internet software and where to find it to download it
- ✔ Mailing lists and newsgroups we like
- ✔ Information about writing Web pages

Online Magazines

In a place as big and busy as the Internet, keeping up with what's new can be difficult because it changes every day. Fortunately, you're not on your own — lots of magazines, both on paper and online, can help keep you up to date. Because paper magazines are hopelessly retro, in this section we look at the online sources.

The Atlantic

http://www.theAtlantic.com

The Atlantic Monthly has been around for more than 100 years and concentrates on culture and politics. It's a top-class rag, and we would say that even if we weren't friends with Corby Kummer, a senior editor and food columnist. Figure 14-1 shows a recent page from the magazine.

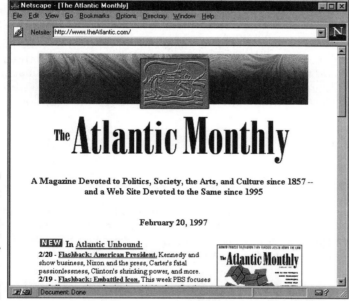

Figure 14-1:
Here's a page from *The Atlantic Monthly* online magazine.

The Electronic Newsstand

http://www.enews.com/

The Internet Company (which, despite its grand name, consists mostly of two guys named Rob and Bill) developed the Electronic Newsstand, which offers a variety of magazines and online information services. All magazines offer tables of contents and selected articles and let you order single issues or discounted subscriptions online. A few offer the entire magazine electronically. The magazines run the gamut, from *American Demographics* to *Canoe & Kayak* to *The New Yorker* to *Yellow Silk*.

You can also see a huge list of online magazines at this site:

```
http://www.yahoo.com/Business_and_Economy/Magazines.
```

The Economist and Barron's

```
http://www.economist.com
http://www.businessweek.com
http://www.forbes.com
http://www.barrons.com
```

The Economist is the weekly newsmagazine for hard-core news hounds. Some of the magazine's content is online at its Web site, and the publisher plans to add more soon. *Business Week* and *Forbes* put their magazines online too, and *BW* offers lots of extra information for people who register at its Web site. *Barron's* requires that you register too, but for now, it's free.

Word

```
http://www.word.com
```

Word has nothing to do with Microsoft Word, the word-processing program. Instead, it's a quirky, independent pop-culture magazine that has received excellent reviews for writing and reporting. *Word* has ads, which can be a bit annoying, but it's nice to get an interesting magazine for free.

Suck and HotWired

```
http://www.suck.com
```

If you're interested in reading a daily magazine with a bad attitude, this Web site is for you. Suck contains just one article, which changes every day. Suck has been bought by HotWired, another popular Web magazine, which brings the graphical eyestrain of the dead-tree *Wired* magazine alive online, at

```
http://www.hotwired.com
```

The Usenet urban folklore quiz (Part II)

Still with us? Amazing!

Part II: Computing and medicine

True or false:

11. Apple used a Cray supercomputer to design hardware systems; Cray used an Apple.

12. Bill Gates has a $750,000 Porsche 959 he can't use because it can't be made to comply with emission laws.

13. A Russian mechanical translator program translated "out of sight, out of mind" into "blind and insane," and "Spirit is willing, but the flesh is weak" as "the drink is good, but the meat is rotten."

14. In 1947 a moth was found in a relay of the Harvard Mark II computer and was taped into the logbook as the "first actual case of bug being found."

15. Computing pioneer Grace Hopper coined the term "bug" as a result of this event.

16. A London doctor was fired for inveigling Turkish peasants to donate a kidney.

17. Flowers are bad in hospital rooms because they suck oxygen from the air.

18. Some people sneeze when they're exposed to bright light.

19. Drinking large quantities of deionized or distilled water over a long period of time can screw you up because of ion imbalances.

20. You can catch a cold by being chilled.

And Now, the News

The online services (America Online, CompuServe, Prodigy, and Microsoft Network, among others) provide up-to-the-minute news from big, fancy new services, such as AP (Associated Press) and Reuters. Don't be disappointed if you have an Internet account — the Web has lots of up-to-date news too!

Yahoo news

http://www.yahoo.com/headlines/news

Yahoo, the Web index described earlier in this chapter, also lists the day's top news stories, courtesy of Reuters NewMedia. You can even read news stories from the preceding seven days. Windows 95 users can also download a news ticker program that runs all the time you're on the Internet, showing the top news headlines and stock prices.

Yahoo also lets you create your own news page, customized to include the kind of stories you're interested in. To make your Yahoo news page, start at this URL:

```
http://my.yahoo.com
```

The New York Times

```
http://www.nytimes.com
http://nytimesfax.com
```

The New York Times has gone online in a big way, with all of each day's major stories on the Web as well as some background material not printed in the wood pulp edition. AP updates are available every ten minutes. You have to register to use it, but it's free, supported by unobtrusive advertising. (The *Times* says that it may eventually charge users connecting from outside the United States.)

Also, the *Times* has distributed an eight-page summary of the news by fax for several years, and now the same version is available online. To read the summary, you need an Adobe Acrobat reader, a program you can download from `http://www.adobe.com/`. A link to the Adobe page is right on the *TimesFax* page. (Acrobat is available for Windows, Macs, and a few kinds of UNIX workstations.)

This site can be really busy in the morning but clears up in the afternoon, after all those busy executives have gotten their news fix.

Mercury News

```
http://www.merc.com
```

Mercury News delivers news, sports, weather, soap opera updates, and other information to your Internet mailbox every working day. Use its Web page to subscribe and to specify which information you want. We rely on its NEWSpot Morning Edition report to find out what's happening in the world (or at least what has happened since the morning radio report from NPR).

Clnews

```
http://www.news.com
```

CNET, Inc., has created an excellent news site with an emphasis on business and computer news. It also runs Shareware.com (`http://www.shareware.com`), a good source of shareware programs.

ClariNet

```
http://www.yahoo.com/News/Newswires/ClariNet
```

or

```
news:newsgroupname
```

ClariNet distributes news, features, and commentary in the form of articles in Usenet newsgroups. The newsgroup names all begin with `clari`, and we have listed some interesting newsgroups in Table 14-1. To read the newsgroup, use your newsreader or Web browser (if it can read newsgroups). The URL for a newsgroup consists of `news:` followed by the newsgroup name. The URL for `clari.world.top`, for example, is `news:clari.world.top`.

Note: Not all Internet providers carry the ClariNet newsgroups because ClariNet charges providers for the news.

Table 14-1	Some ClariNet Newsgroups
Newsgroup Name	*Description*
`clari.biz.briefs`	Business news briefs
`clari.biz.urgent`	Late-breaking business news
`clari.nb.online`	Newsbytes about the Internet and online services
`clari.news.briefs`	Hourly news briefs about the United States
`clari.news.weather`	Weather news and reports
`clari.sports.briefs`	Sports scores
`clari.sports.features`	Sports feature stories
`clari.sports.top`	Top sports news
`clari.world.americas.canada`	General Canadian news
`clari.world.briefs`	News briefs from around the world
`clari.world.top`	Top world news stories

To see lists of all the ClariNet newsgroups, go to the Yahoo URL listed at the beginning of this section.

Live from the Internet

The global village even has radio stations. You can download sound files and play them on your computer. Be warned, however, that sound files are *large,* like many megabytes. Don't try downloading sound files unless you have a fast Net connection. You can make yourself extremely unpopular if you download 15MB files in the middle of the day from a server on another continent. Check the list of sites to find a server close to you, and do your heavy-duty downloading at off-peak times, such as in the middle of the night or on weekends.

RealAudio takes a different approach, feeding your computer the data to play sound as necessary. Although the sound quality isn't quite as good as a downloaded file, sound clips start up in seconds rather than in hours. To listen to RealAudio sound files, you need a RealAudio player, which you can download from `http://www.realaudio.com/` (see Chapter 10 for more details).

National Public Radio

`http://www.npr.org`

After NPR began giving out e-mail addresses on all its news programs, could a Web site be far behind? You can hear the day's newscast, the NPR favorite story of the day, and an archive of recent news programs in RealAudio format.

ABC News Reports

`http://www.realaudio.com/contentp/abc.html`

ABC provides hourly news, at 15 minutes after every hour, in RealAudio format. You can also hear sports, commentary, and special reports.

Air Force Radio

`http://www.brooks.af.mil/realaudio`

This five-minute news broadcast is updated daily.

Yahoo Net Events

`http://events.yahoo.com`

Yahoo lists all the Internet events that are happening today, including IRC chats, CU-SeeMe video events, RealAudio concerts, and other live events and events that change daily (see Figure 14-2).

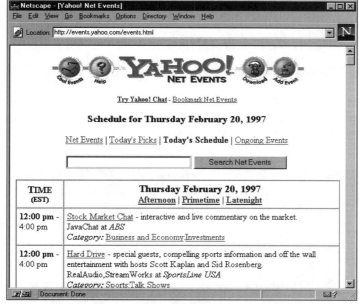

Figure 14-2: Wow! The Internet is popping today!

(Text and artwork copyright 1996 by YAHOO!, INC. All rights reserved. YAHOO! and the YAHOO! logo are trademarks of YAHOO!, INC.)

How's the Weather?

Everyone talks about the weather, but nobody does anything about it, right? Although you still may not be able to do anything about it, at least you can be well informed.

See the "ClariNet" section, earlier in this chapter, for one source of up-to-the-minute weather reports.

The Weather Bureau

```
http://www.nws.noaa.gov/cgi-bin/page?pg=netcast
http://iwin.nws.noaa.gov/iwin/main.html
```

You have already paid for the U.S. government weather forecast — might as well take advantage of it. (You won't be the only one — the second site listed here says that more than 4,500 links on the Web point to it, and it gets more than 200,000 visits per day.)

The Weather Channel

```
http://www.weather.com
```

The Weather Channel provides a Web site with up-to-date weather forecasts, as shown in Figure 14-3, along with background information about the weather and forecasts for skiing and other sports.

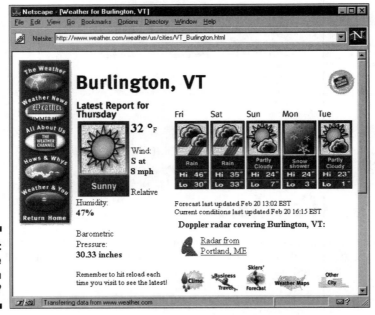

Figure 14-3:
How's the
weather in
Vermont?

Yahoo Weather Pages

`http://weather.yahoo.com`

Hey, Yahoo provides every other kind of information on the Web — why not weather reports? You can get weather reports, including satellite maps, for almost any country in the world.

Touchdown! Goal! Home Run! Wicket!

Whatever your sport, you can find lots of information about it on the Net.

See the "ClariNet" section, earlier in this chapter, for one source of up-to-the-minute sports news.

The Tennis Server

`http://www.tennisserver.com`

The Tennis Server page contains all kinds of information about tennis, from the rules of the game to current tennis news to pictures of the players. It also has links to dozens of other tennis ties on the Web.

Sports Network

`http://www.sportsnetwork.com`

Sports Network concentrates on scores and news rather than on background information about sports. If you want to see scores for today's games in baseball, football, basketball, tennis, hockey, golf, boxing, horse racing, and the Olympics (when they're on), this is the page for you. This page also has news, statistics, and odds for each sport.

ESPNet Sportszone

`http://espnet.sportszone.com`

ESPN, the cable sports new network, has put together a Web service as well. This service is so popular that getting through to the ESPN Web server on the day of a big game can be tough. If you subscribe (for about $5 a month), you can also get more in-depth sports information.

Sports Illustrated

```
http://pathfinder.com/si
```

Yes, it even has the swimsuit issue, with videos.

The Literary Life

Until the online revolution reaches its final victory, many old-fashioned books will still be made in the traditional way, by pressing ink on thin layers of dissolved, deceased trees. (You have one of them in your hands now.) In the meantime, a bunch of bookstores are on the Net, many with online catalogs and all of which welcome online orders. (Wouldn't this be a good time to buy another dozen copies of this book to give to your friends? How about just one or two?)

This section presents a selection of online bookstores.

Amazon.com Books

```
http://www.amazon.com
```

Amazon Books exists only online (it doesn't have a retail store) and claims to carry more than one million titles. Its goal is to carry every book in print (good luck!). You can search for a book by keyword, title, or author, and you can even ask Amazon to notify you when a book is available in paperback or when an author publishes a new title.

The Amazon catalog is getting a little messy now that it has been online for a few years, and some of the entries are inaccurate or downright hard to decipher, but it does have many more books available than anyone else. You can always e-mail these folks with questions, though.

Wordsworth

```
http://www.wordsworth.com
```

Wordsworth is a large, general-interest bookstore in Cambridge, Massachusetts, that sells most books at a discount. It carries all ...*For Dummies* books, many autographed by us. (Its book buyer said of one of your authors: "I have to buy all his books. He's friends with my dog.") The Wordsworth search system isn't as complete as the one at Amazon.com, but because it does carry a large number of books in stock, you can probably get them sooner.

The Tattered Cover Bookstore

http://www.tatteredcover.com

The Tattered Cover, in Denver, Colorado, is a bookstore with a following. The physical bookstore is huge and has an amazing inventory. Via its Web site, you can order any of the books in the store, and someone there will order any other book for you if it's not in stock.

Future Fantasy Bookstore

http://futfan.com

This specialty sci-fi store in Palo Alto, California, holds readings and events in addition to selling books. An extremely cool logo appears on its WWW page. This tiny little store gets a large percentage of its orders from the United States and overseas by way of the Internet.

Computer books, anyone?

http://www.softpro.com
http://www.quantumbooks.com
http://www.roswell.com
http://www.clbooks.com
http://www.cbooks.com

Softpro has stores near Boston and in Denver. Quantum has stores in Cambridge, Massachusetts, and Philadelphia. Roswell is a large, Canadian computer bookstore located in Halifax, Nova Scotia. Computer Literacy Books is the premier computer bookstore chain in the country, with three stores in Silicon Valley and one near Washington, D.C. All are computer specialty bookstores with extensive catalogs of computer books, including all the ...*For Dummies* books, of course, and all accept orders over the Internet.

The Usenet urban folklore quiz (Part III)

Hey, don't you have anything better to do than take quizzes? Well, if you insist:

Part III: The groves of academe

True or false:

21. A professor listed a famous unsolved math problem; a student thought that it was homework and solved it.

22. At some colleges, if a roommate commits suicide, it gets you an automatic A for all your courses.

23. A student got his tuition money by asking in a newspaper ad for a penny from each person.

24. A professor allowed students to "bring in what they can carry for the exam;" one student carried in a grad student.

25. A student submitted a 20-year-old paper for class. The professor gave it an A, say-ing that he had always liked it but that he got only a B when he wrote it.

26. The eminent Stanford professor Donald "Art of Computer Programming" Knuth's first publication was in *MAD* magazine.

27. A philosophy professor's one-word exam was "Why?" He gave an A to a student who replied, "Why not?"

28. A low-grading professor graded the same exam in successive semesters; he gave it a higher grade each time. The fourth time around, he wrote, "Like it more each time."

29. Science class students took swabs from the inside of their cheeks and examined them under a microscope. One group saw odd organisms and called the professor, who looked and declared that it was sperm.

30. Albert Einstein did poorly in school.

Let Your Mouse Do the Walking

More and more normal businesses are getting connections to the Net, usually with glitzy Web pages, where you can find out about their wares and, usually, order them.

The Internet Mall

`http://www.internet-mall.com`

The Internet Mall is an extensive list of cybershops on the Net, selling everything from culinary herbs to fossils to computer books.

I don't like Spam!

A few businesses, unfortunately, have taken to blanketing the Net with obnoxious advertisements. Early in 1994, a pair of Arizona lawyers caused an enormous furor by blanketing Usenet newsgroups with thousands of copies of an electronic advertisement offering to file applications in an upcoming U.S. immigration lottery, known as a "green card lottery." They claimed, not very plausibly, that nothing was wrong with what they had done and that people who objected were just fuddy-duddies who hated all advertisements. For their troubles, the pair managed to get their pictures in *The New York Times* and to get interviewed on CNN.

The lawyers also got many, many megabytes of online complaints, enough that their Internet provider (which had no advance notice of their plans) had to disconnect from the Net for a while. To put it mildly, the lawyers didn't make themselves popular. Internauts all over the world ground their teeth in fury for weeks.

Their technique was quickly dubbed *spamming,* from an old "Monty Python" skit of actors in Viking costume who, with almost no provocation, would break into a song about Spam. (Yes, it's the same stuff that comes in little blue cans and sort of resembles meat.) With luck, as commercial providers become more sophisticated, spamming will be nipped in the bud and attempted spammers booted off the Net; at the moment, however, it's a plague.

For more info, you can visit `http://spam.abuse.net`, the responsible Net commerce Web site (partially maintained by one of us authors).

The Internet Shopping Network

`http://www.internet.net`

This Web page, brought to you from the Home Shopping Network, points you to thousands of hardware and software items for personal computers and workstations in addition to reprints from *InfoWorld.* It has snazzy graphics too, though they take a while to appear unless you have a fast modem. Most products are sold at a discount. Although you have to be a member to order, membership is free. Anyone can browse and look at prices, descriptions, and even reviews of the products.

The Branch Mall

`http://www/branchmall.com`

This Web site is another mall, offering a florist, gift food baskets, and other goodies.

We're from the Government, and We're Here to Help You

The U.S. government maintains hundreds of Web sites in an effort to make information available to Joe Average Citizen. Here are a few sites you may find useful.

United States Postal Service

```
http://www.usps.gov
```

Okay, we know that the post office is not officially part of the U.S. government, but it's not all that independent, either. The USPS Web site lets you look up the zip codes for U.S. postal addresses and find out the postage for packages by weight.

Edgar, Prince of Profit

```
http://www.sec.gov/edgarhp.htm
```

Interested in money? We thought so. The U.S. Security and Exchange Commission, the government agency that regulates stock markets, has a system called EDGAR that contains data filed by all the thousands of publicly held companies it regulates. Every time a company sneezes, it has to file stuff with the SEC, so you can find out a great deal from EDGAR about your favorite company. Check out companies in which you hold stock, companies in which you might want to hold stock, the company where you work, and the company where you plan to work next. (For those last two, it wasn't us who suggested that you do that.) You can also find out a surprising amount of detailed financial information, including Bill Gates's salary.

It's patently obvious

```
http://patents.cnidr.org
```

There has been much excitement (and anger) in the computer business about patents issued for software. You can find out about recent software patents and any other patents issued since 1994.

Here's another URL:

```
http://patent.womplex.ibm.com/
```

This patent server is run by IBM and has full copies of nearly every patent issued since 1971 as text and as scanned photographic images, which let you see the figures. Don't miss the Gallery of Obscure Patents, featuring the combined bird trap and cat feeder and the human slingshot. (No, we didn't make these up.)

The Census Bureau

```
http://www.census.gov
```

or

```
ftp://ftp.census.gov/pub
```

The Census Bureau, repository of far more information than it is healthy to have in one place, has a comfortable home in cyberspace (as it should, because the Census Bureau has among the best records of government agencies for protecting personal privacy). Figure 14-4 shows one of the country maps you can display.

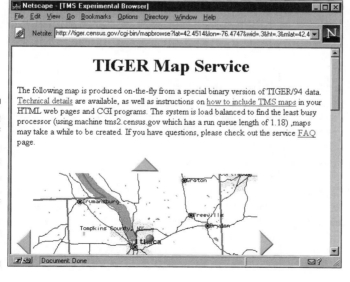

Figure 14-4: A map of scenic Tompkins County, New York, courtesy of the U.S. Census Bureau.

You can find statistical and financial data of many varieties. You don't find detailed statistical data (too bulky, evidently), but statistical briefs (beautifully formatted in PostScript form so that you have to retrieve them and then print them by using a PostScript viewer) full of interesting info are available. We found out from one brief, for example, that although Americans of Asian and Pacific Island backgrounds are only slightly more likely to graduate from high school than are whites, they're almost twice as likely to complete college and go on to a graduate degree. At certain kinds of cocktail parties, that sort of factoid can be darned handy.

Stock Prices, Almost Live

Everyone wants to know whether you can get live, up-to-date stock price quotations on the Internet. The answer is yes, but not for free. You can get prices that are delayed by 15 to 20 minutes, though. Here's how.

Quote.com

```
http://www.quote.com
http://quote.yahoo.com
```

Quote.com provides lots of financial information online, including end-of-day prices for stocks, commodity futures, mutual funds, money market funds, and indexes. Some balance sheet data is available too. Although you have to subscribe to use Quote.com, subscribing is free. The Yahoo version has similar information but a different (we think better) layout.

Search for your stock

```
http://www.secapl.com/cgi-bin/qs
http://www.pathfinder.com/money/quote/qc
http://www.dbc.com/quote.html
http://www.lombard.com/PACenter
```

A number of Web pages allow you to enter the stock ticker symbol for a stock and get its stock price, usually delayed by about 15 minutes. Some companies require you to register, but they don't charge for the quotes.

The Usenet urban folklore quiz (Part IV)

Holy petunias, you're still here.

Part IV: The entirety of human knowledge

True or false:

31. The song "Happy Birthday" is copyrighted.

32. Studies indicate that the majority of U.S. currency has traces of cocaine.

33. A woman had epileptic seizures after hearing "Entertainment Tonight" anchor Mary Hart's voice.

34. Some parents got a video for their children and found that it was recorded over an old porn tape.

35. Unless fast food shakes are marked "dairy," they aren't milk: instead, they're mostly carrageenan (seaweed extract) gel.

36. Lead leaches from lead crystal decanters into drinks, which is not good for you.

37. People have been poisoned by eating food cooked on burning oleander branches.

38. A woman removed the label from a "tuna" can and found a cat-food label underneath.

39. There's a basketball hoop at the top of the Matterhorn replica at Disneyland.

40. There were (are?) Japanese soldiers hiding out on islands in the Pacific who believed that WWII was still on.

41. Gerbils are illegal in California.

Kids' Stuff

More and more Web sites are geared to kids, partly because many grants have gone toward creating educational Web sites and partly because companies love to advertise to kids. Here are some sites our kids like.

Yahooligans

```
http://www.yahooligans.com/
```

Yahoo, the popular Web index and directory, has a version just for kids.

PBS Online

```
http://www.pbs.org
http://nyelabs.kcts.org
```

PBS, the public television broadcasting network, has lots of stuff online for kids, including pages for *Mr. Rogers' Neighborhood, Wishbone,* and *Reading Rainbow.* Bill Nye the Science Guy, who has an educational show by the same name, has a Web site full of "way cool free stuff of science!"

Great Tapes for Kids

    http://www.greattapes.com

We're biased because Margy runs this Web site, but Great Tapes for Kids lets you find hard-to-find, charming, non-overcommercialized video- and audio-tapes for kids. Some books, too. End of commercial announcement!

Arts and Crafts

Culture is alive and well on the Net. Here are some sites to browse.

The Smithsonian Institution

    http://www.si.edu

The Smithsonian Institution, which, because it's supported by U.S. tax money, you probably have already paid for, includes a bunch of interesting museums (our favorite is the National Air and Space Museum). Lots of stuff from the museums is available on its Web site.

The Metropolitan Museum of Art, New York

    http://www.metmuseum.org

You want culture? This place has culture out the wazoo, although that is not, perhaps, exactly the description the folks there would use.

The Louvre

    http://mistral.culture.fr/louvre

The Louvre Museum Web site is in French, with links to English, Spanish, and Portuguese versions. The Web pages contain news and information about the museum and its programs, but few images of the art itself — maybe because Bill Gates has bought the copyright to most of them!

The WebMuseum

```
http://sunsite.unc.edu/wm (North Carolina)
http://watt.emf.net/wm (California)
http://www.netspot.unisa.edu.au/wm (Australia)
http://www.southern.net/wm/ (England)
```

The WebMuseum is a project of Nicolas Pioch, a French Web consultant, and includes images of art from every imaginable period. If you aren't in the eastern United States, choose the *mirror site* (an Internet host that stores exactly the same set of Web pages as the original site) nearest you.

Travel

Internauts are a peripatetic crowd, always on the move. More information is about travel than about anything else (except for information about the Net itself). Because the Net is truly global, it has tons of information about specific countries available from the countries themselves.

U.S. State Department travel advisories

```
http://travel.state.gov/travel_warnings.html
```

Wondering how dangerous it is to go to Djibouti? The U.S. State Department publishes for every country in the world (except, for some reason, the United States) a travel advisory that discusses travel facilities, entry requirements, political instability, medical facilities, and availability of U.S. embassies and consulates. (As developing African countries go, Djibouti is not particularly unsafe.)

This Web page has links to all the current travel advisories so that you can Know Before You Go. Many experienced travelers find these advisories to be somewhat alarmist (Egad! You can't get Big Macs in Timbuktu!), so you may also want to take them with a grain or two of salt.

CIA Fact Book

```
http://www.odci.gov/cia/publications/pubs.html
```

This page has a link to the latest CIA *World Fact Book,* which has political and economic information for countries all over the world and links to home pages for a few countries.

The Railroad Page

```
http://www-cse.ucsd.edu/users/bowdidge/railroad/
            rail-home.html
```

The Railroad Page displays mailing lists, FTP archives, commercial services, online maps — everything for the well-informed rail fan. Although the owner isn't maintaining the page anymore, it still has a fabulous connection of links to other train-related Web pages.

The Metro Server

```
telnet://metro.jussieu.fr:10000/
```

Are you troubled by getting lost on the subway? As long as you live in Vienna, Hong Kong, Montreal, Palermo, Toronto, Mexico City, Lille (France), Amsterdam, Lyons (France), Madrid, Marseilles, London, Paris, Boston, Toulouse (France), New York, Frankfurt (Germany), San Francisco, Munich, Washington, D.C., or Athens, today is your lucky day. The Metro server figures out your route for you. Telnet in, and you're immediately in the Metro system. You tell it the name of the city and the departing and arriving stations, and it gives you the best route and the travel time.

When the server asks whether you want to use the X Window system, say no. You can abbreviate stations to the shortest amount of the name that isn't ambiguous.

The On-line Airline Information Page

```
http://iecc.com/airline
```

A remarkable amount of information is available about flight schedules, fares, special offers, destinations, and other related topics on the Web. This site tells you where to find it all. A second page lists travel agents on the Net.

The Funnies

Enough travel. Let's relax and read the funnies.

Dr. Fun

```
http://sunsite.unc.edu/Dave/drfun.html
```

The Internet has its own daily cartoon, Dr. Fun, in the tradition of *The Far Side*. It ranges from the strange to the extremely strange; one caption was "Silly String and Crazy Glue — a Deadly Combination." (The picture was not unlike what you would expect.)

The Doctor appears every weekday as an attractive, full-color graphic. Don't miss him.

The Dilbert Zone

```
http://www.unitedmedia.com/comics/dilbert
```

United Media, the company that distributes *Dilbert,* puts it on the Web too. *Dilbert* is every nerd's favorite strip (because everything he says about us is true). In addition to the *Dilbert* strip of the day, you can see the preceding two weeks of *Dilbert* cartoons, an interview with Scott Adams (its creator), and even a photo tour of the very room in which Scott draws the strips.

Yahoo, there are lots of comics!

```
http://www.yahoo.com/News_and_Media/Daily/Comics
```

Yahoo, the index to the World Wide Web and described earlier in this chapter, lists a bunch of comics — five, anyway, at the time this book was written. As more comics appear on the Net, Yahoo will list them.

Um, It's Personal

Lest we forget that even nerds have personal lives, read on.

Match.com

```
http://www.match.com
```

With more than 45,000 registered members, this site is a good place to meet other singles and look for Ms. or Mr. Right.

Fun and Games

And now for something completely different!

GameCenter

```
http://www.gamecenter.com
```

GameCenter has news, reviews, and tips about playing all kinds of computer games.

The Spot — an online soap opera

```
http://www.thespot.com
```

Click the links to read the journal entries of the groovy Gen X-ers who share a house in Santa Monica, California. Then go to the SpotBoard and send e-mail to The Spot to tell the soap opera characters what they should do next.

Attention, klutzes!

```
http://www.juggling.org
```

Ever want to learn how to juggle? The Juggling Information Service features news, advice, pictures, vendors of juggling equipment (flaming Indian clubs have to come from somewhere), software, and lots of gossip.

Puzzle of the Week

```
http://www.vni.net/~panthera/pow.html
```

Several sites post a new puzzle every week (some even post one every day!). The first site on the list is a monthly puzzle for Mensa members, so you had better be smart to get near it.

Anagrams (A ram sang?)

```
http://www.genius2000.com/anagram.html
http://www.ssynth.co.uk/~gay/anagram.html
http://mmm.mbhs.edu/~bconnell/anagrams.html
http://www.wordsmith.org/awad-cgibin/anagram
```

Want to find out some cool anagrams for your name? These anagram generators are just the trick. The first one listed also turns them out in Dutch.

We submitted the phrase Sarah Willow (the name of a charming one-year-old of our acquaintance) and got back this list:

air owl shawl	allow his raw
also whir law	hail slow war
hair swallow	how will rasa
howl was liar	i shallow war
oar will wash	oral law wish
	wail or shawl

Food, Food, Wonderful Food

Finally, we get to something we all can agree is interesting and important.

Like to cook?

```
http://www.gulf.net/~vbraun/food.html
```

Vicki Braun maintains a vast list of food- and drink-related Web sites, which is well worth browsing if you're looking for a recipe or general cooking information.

Online soda machines

```
http://www.cc.columbia.edu/~pepsi
http://www.cc.columbia.edu/~cocacola
```

Soda machines have been on the Net for almost as long as there's been a Net. Nothing annoys a hard-hacking nerd more than walking down the hall to get a life-sustaining carbonated sugar beverage, only to find out that the machine is empty or, worse, was just filled and the soda is warm. To avoid this unspeakable horror, machines were quickly networked for the benefit of local users. The Net being the Net, of course, querying a machine from 10,000 miles away is as easy as querying one from 10 feet away.

To check on the status of a soda machine, you used to have to master the esoteric `finger` command, found mainly on UNIX systems. Thank heavens, soda machines are now found on the World Wide Web. All soda machine Web pages tell you the basics — whether the soda is sold out. Some machines also add other crucial details, such as the soda's temperature — in Celsius, naturally — and whether change is available.

The Trojan Room

```
http://www.cl.cam.ac.uk/coffee/coffee.html
```

In England, hackers evidently drink coffee rather than Coke, and going down the hall is pointless if the pot is empty. In the finest hacker tradition, they pointed a video camera at the coffeepot with some extremely complicated software to digitize the picture once a second and send the image to their Web server. Now people all over the world can tell — if they happen to fly to Cambridge — whether the coffee is ready, as shown in Figure 14-5. This particular coffeepot is so famous that, according to *The Economist,* people have asked at the local tourist booth where the coffee pot is.

Sometimes the picture is pitch black. Nothing's wrong; it's probably the middle of the night and the lights are turned out.

Figure 14-5:
Somebody
had better
make more
coffee.

Answers to the Usenet urban folklore quiz

For much, much more information about these and other topics of vital interest, visit the Usenet groups `alt.folklore.urban` and `alt.folklore.suburban`.

1. False.

2. True.

3. False.

4. True.

5. True.

6. Both false.

7. False.

8. True, but it was a reporter's prank.

9. False.

10. True.

11. True.

12. True.

13. False.

14. True.

15. False.

16. True.

17. False.

18. True; doctors call it the "photic sneeze effect."

19. True.

20. False (take that, Mom).

21. True; the student was mathematician George Dantzig.

22. False.

23. True.

24. False.

25. False.

26. True (*MAD* #33, "The Potrzebie system of weights and measures").

27. False.

28. False.

29. False.

30. True.

31. True.

32. True.

33. True.

34. True.

35. True.

36. True.

37. True.

38. True.

39. True.

40. True.

41. True [CA Reg. Title 14, Sec. 671 (c)(2)(J) 1].

Part IV
Home Page, Ho!

The 5th Wave　　　　　By Rich Tennant

In the end, it was Edward Scissorhand's cousin, Jonathan Hammerhead, who brought the group to a consensus on a client/server architecture.

©RICHTENNANT

In this part . . .

Everyone who's anyone has a home page on the Web, right? We certainly do! You can join the hordes of people with personal home pages or (more interestingly) create a Web site for your company, school, church, club, extended family, or hobby. Whatever your reasons for creating Web pages, this part of the book tells you how and suggests ways to let other internauts know that your Web page is out there.

Chapter 15

Home-Page Bound

*E*veryone who's anyone on the Net (and just about everyone else) has a World Wide Web home page. Sometimes the pages are interesting, sometimes they're exciting, sometimes they're pretty stupid. Because we're sure that you fall into one of the first two categories, in this part of the book, we tell you how to create your own Web pages.

The Big Picture

Here's what you have to do to put a home page, or any Web page, on the Net:

1. **Write the page on your own computer, inserting all the special codes that control the page's appearance in Web browsers.**

   Because Web pages are basically plain text files, you can create them with any text editor you want, even Windows Notepad or WordPad. You can just type them, using codes we explain in this part of the book.

   If you want your page to have pictures, you create the pictures using a scanner or a paint program (or both), storing each picture in a separate graphics file. Special codes in the Web page text file specify where on the page each picture appears.

2. **Check to make sure that the page looks like what you envision.**

   Your page rarely looks the way you want it to on the first try. Fine-tune the page until you're happy with the result. You can use your regular Web browser to look at it and then fix mistakes in the text editor.

3. **Copy the page to your Internet provider's computer, where the page will be available to everyone on the Net.**

4. **Repeat these steps forever, as you keep adding and updating your Web pages.**

The bad news about writing Web pages

To create a Web page, you have to wear three different hats:

- ✔ A writer, to create the text

- ✔ A graphics designer, to create the images and the overall appearance of the page

- ✔ A programmer, to create the special coding required to make the page look the way you want it to in a browser

Not many people can do even two of these things well, and only an exceedingly rare person can do all three well. That's why you find lots and lots of Web pages that are badly written, badly designed, and badly coded.

Big, rich companies solve this problem by hiring Web-building teams that include professional writers, designers, and programmers. If you're the only one making your pages, what are you going to do? Our answer is *don't try too hard.* For example, when we made the pages for Internet For Dummies Central at http://net.dummies.net, we figured that we knew a little about writing and programming (that's our job, after all) but practically nothing about graphic design. We kept the design of our pages simple, figuring that the less we tried to do, the less we could mess up.

We suggest that you start simple too because a simple page that's attractive and readable will attract many more fans than a complicated and ugly one.

Who Cares about HTML?

You do. *HTML,* short for *Hypertext Markup Language,* is the language that makes the Web go. HTML codes tell your browser what's text, what's a heading, where the links go, where to put the pictures, and everything else about your page. Some HTML editors purport to let you create pages without knowing anything at all about HTML. We discuss a few of these editors in Chapter 16, but we have found that without a smattering of HTML, you will have much more trouble figuring out why your page doesn't look the way you want it to. Be sure to read the next few sections and get yourself smattered.

HTML codes use a consistent syntax, with each code enclosed in angle brackets, such as <P>, to start a new paragraph. For example, the HTML in the file in Figure 15-1 makes Netscape display the page shown in Figure 15-2.

HTML in its full glory is, to put it mildly, rather complicated. Fortunately, you can create entirely respectable-looking pages using only a handful of simple HTML codes.

```
<HTML>
<HEAD>
<TITLE>Your Name Here's Home Page</TITLE>
</HEAD>
<BODY>
<H1>Welcome to Your Name Here's Home Page</H1>
<P>
I've been reading the most fabulous book ever written,
<I>MORE Internet For Dummies, 3rd Edition</I>.
I'll add more stuff to this page, but first I have to go
buy 15 more copies of the book to give to all my family
and closest friends.
</BODY>
</HTML>
```

Figure 15-1:
A simple
HTML file.

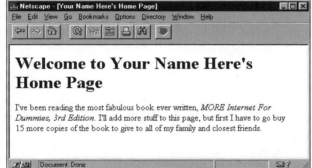

Figure 15-2:
The same
file,
displayed in
Netscape.

Gentlemen, Start Your Software

You can create files with HTML-coded documents in lots of different ways. In keeping with this chapter's philosophy of not trying overly hard, we suggest that you start with something like Windows Notepad or Windows 95 WordPad, the simplest text editors around.

You probably will have a bunch of Web pages, so before you start up your text editor, create a folder called \Web in which to store them.

Where did HTML and the Web come from?

An atomic physics laboratory in Switzerland, in fact. (For the best effect, say this sentence with a mad-scientist accent.)

CERN is an international laboratory near Geneva, Switzerland, where atomic physicists do atomic physics-type experiments. These experiments generate mountains of data, to the extent that simply organizing and presenting the data is a big problem. In 1990, Dr. Tim Berners-Lee, an English researcher who was then at CERN, built an online hypertext system inspired by Ted Nelson's Xanadu (see the next sidebar, "And where did hypertext come from?") that evolved into the World Wide Web we know today.

HTML is a version of *SGML,* the *Standard General Markup Language* adopted as an international standard for encoding documents in computers. SGML is a high-level language, and any actual useful SGML requires what's known as a Document Template Description, or DTD, a template that describes what can be included in some category of documents. HTML is basically a DTD that is a template for Web pages.

The original Web system handled primarily text, not pictures or other data. In the early 1990s, at the National Center for Supercomputer Applications, two student programmers, Marc Andreesen and Rob McCool, were working on their own Web software for the UNIX-based X Window system. (Legend says that the two were supposed to be doing something else at the time.) Because an X Window program without graphics isn't much fun, Andreesen and McCool added features to the Web's HTML language so that they could mix pictures into their Web pages. Their programs, Mosaic (for the user) and the NCSA HTTPD (for the server), quickly became the Web programs people wanted to use, partly because they were so cool and partly because they were free. Andreesen left NCSA to join a Web software start-up now known as Netscape. You may have heard of it.

And where did hypertext come from?

Most people think that hypertext is a recent invention, but it's not. Our friend Ted Nelson first conceived of hypertext in 1965, in an era when most people who thought about computers at all thought of them as machines that turned stacks of punched cards into telephone bills.

Ted has labored on for years, trying to persuade people that hypertext is an important idea and not getting very far. During some 15-minute time period in the 1980s, hypertext metamorphosed from a cockamamie idea that nobody who *really* understood computers would take seriously into the inevitable framework for literature of the future. Ted's vision of hypertext has been wrapped up in his Project Xanadu, an online publishing concept that, after years of work and many dead ends, may yet come to fruition on the Internet, using the Web as its underpinning.

Web Page, Take One

We start with a really simple page, the one we showed you in Figure 15-2. Type the text from Figure 15-1 into your text editor, save it in your \Web folder, and call the file Mypage.htm. If you're feeling creative, go ahead and put in your own name.

That should have been easy enough. How do you look at your new page as a Web page? Simply open the file in your Web browser. In Netscape 3.0, for example, you choose File⇨Open File and select the file. In Netscape 4.0, you choose File⇨Open Page, click the Choose File button, select the file, and click Open. In Internet Explorer, choose File⇨Open, click the Browse button, and select your file. Poof! The Web page appears. (It appears quickly, too, because the page is loaded from the disk, not over the network.)

Unless you have superhuman typing skills, the chances are pretty good that the page on-screen doesn't look quite right because you have typed one of the codes wrong. (We know this problem because we have never gotten a page right on the first try either.) Look at your page in the browser, and look for the first place where the page looks wrong. That place is usually pretty close to the mistake. Switch back to your text editor, find and fix the mistake, save the page again, switch back to your browser, and load the revised page by pressing the Reload button. After a few rounds of editing, browsing, and revising, you should be able to get your page looking okay.

Although this nit-picking is a pain, it's inevitable with any system like HTML. The *tags* in HTML, the stuff in angle brackets, are interpreted by computers, and those computers are, unfortunately, extremely dumb and unforgiving when it comes to coding errors. (In case you were wondering, this sort of error picking is what programmers spend about half of their time doing.) If you have a great deal of trouble getting the tags right, *HTML editors,* which automate much of the tagging process, are available. We talk about HTML editors in Chapter 16. (We don't really find HTML editors worth the trouble, which is why we start you out with writing your own tags.)

What Are All These Tags, Really?

Take a closer look at all the tag glop in that Web page. Many different tags exist, but most have a pretty simple structure.

Each HTML tag is enclosed in angle brackets, like this: `<GLOP>`. Many tags bracket information that's supposed to be treated in a particular way, in which case the end of the material is marked with a tag that starts with a slash, like this: `</GLOP>`. The EM tag, for example, means emphasized text, which you write as `<EM>stuff to emphasize</EM>`.

How many kinds of HTML are there?

Too many, unfortunately. HTML has evolved at a furious rate over the years. The most recently standardized version is HTML 2.0, and every browser you're likely to come across can handle all tags defined in HTML 2.0. A lack of additional standards hasn't slowed down browser writers, though, and every browser has features beyond what 2.0 offers. Netscape has been the most enthusiastic adder of features, but nobody can resist adding a few of their own.

The World Wide Web Consortium (W3C) is working on a 3.2 update to the spec, having tried and failed to standardize a 3.0 version; some new features will definitely be included (tables, for example), and some won't (blinking text — ugh.) But many details have yet to be decided.

Until 3.2 comes out, you have to either be sure that you use only 2.0 features, which everyone's browser handles, or try your pages in lots of Web browsers to be sure that they all look reasonable. You can create reasonable-looking pages with 2.0, so start with that version's features.

In most cases, spacing and indentation don't affect the appearance of your Web page, so arranging the material so that you can see the structure of the tags is a good idea. You can put in handy comments, which don't affect the page's appearance, to remind yourself of what you were doing when you come back after a month to look at your page:

```
<!-- this is a comment. The exclamation point and the two
           dashes at the front and end are required-->
```

Your minimal set of tags

Because you write Web pages in HTML, a Web page has to begin with a tag that says, "Here comes some HTML," and end with a tag that says, "That's the end of the HTML," like this:

```
<HTML>
... contents of the page
</HTML>
```

(Computers, because they're extremely dim, don't find the fact that your HTML document consists of HTML obvious.)

Furthermore, you need two sections within the HTML: the header and the body:

```
<HTML>
 <HEAD>
...header stuff here...
 </HEAD>
 <BODY>
...contents of the page here...
 </BODY>
</HTML>
```

You have to put only the page's title, which most browsers display in their title bar at the top of the screen, in the header. Here's a complete header section:

```
<HEAD>
<TITLE>The Combination to the Vault at Fort Knox</TITLE>
</HEAD>
```

Note the `<TITLE>` and `</TITLE>` that bracket the text of the title.

Body language

The actual contents of the page go between `<BODY>` and `</BODY>` tags. You can put any material you want in the body — HTML doesn't require that you structure your page's body in any particular way.

Do I really have to put in all these tags?

Well, since you ask, many Web browsers let you get away with some pretty sloppy tagging. Even if you leave out many of the required tags, the browsers display something anyway.

No browser *promises* to do the right thing if you have missing tags. Although your page may look okay today, when the next version of Netscape or Internet Explorer or whatever comes out, your page may not work anymore. Put in all those tags — you will be glad you did.

Look at the body of our sample page:

```
<BODY>
<H1>Welcome to Your Name Here's Home Page</H1>
<P>
I've been reading the most fabulous book ever written,
<I>MORE Internet For Dummies, 3rd Edition.</I>
I'll add more stuff to this page, but first I have to go
buy 15 more copies of the book to give to all my family and
            closest friends.
</BODY>
```

The first thing is an H1, a first-level heading, which is displayed at the top of the page. (The page's title repeated as a heading is common because not all browsers display the title.) The `<P>` code introduces a paragraph of plain text. In that paragraph, we italicize the book's name by putting the name inside `<I>` and `</I>` tags.

That's what's required to make a Web page. You can put your newly created Web page on a server for all the world to see. In Chapter 16, we come back to making the page prettier.

Going Public

Okay, you have a Web page. You think that your page is ready for prime time. How do you release your page to the world? In principle, showing off your page is easy; in practice, however, a wee bit of confusion is possible.

For other people to see your Web pages, you have to load your handiwork on a machine with a public Web server. Although nearly every Internet provider has this type of server, no two providers handle the uploading process in quite the same way.

Although you have to check with your provider to get the details, here's the general strategy for loading your Web page:

1. **Run your FTP program.**

   We use WS_FTP (described in Chapter 6), but any FTP program or even Netscape will do.

2. **Log in to your provider's Web server, using your own login and password.**

   The server's name is usually something like `www.gorgonzola.net`, though providers differ. At TIAC, one of the providers we use, you log in to `ftp.www.tiac.net` when you're uploading Web pages. In Netscape, open `ftp://username@gorgonzola.net/` (suitably adjusting both your user name and the server name), and type your login password when it asks. Internet Explorer doesn't handle file uploads.

3. **Change to the directory (folder) where your Web home page belongs.**

The name is usually something like /pub/elvis, /pub/www/elvis, or /pub/elvis/www. Your provider will tell you what to use. In a Web browser, just click your way to the appropriate directory.

4. **Upload your Web page.**

Use ASCII mode, not binary mode, because your Web page is a text file. In Netscape, drag the file from the Internet Explorer or File Manager into the Netscape window, or choose File⇨Upload File.

If your page on the server is called mypage.htm, its URL is something like

```
http://www.gorgonzola.net/~elvis/mypage.htm
```

Again, URLs vary by provider. Some providers don't follow the convention of putting a tilde (~) in front of the name. Others name their users' pages something like /user/elvis rather than ~elvis. You have to check with your provider to find out its convention.

You should generally call your home page, the one you want people to see first, index.html. If someone goes to your Web area without specifying a page name, such as `http://www.gorgonzola.net/~elvis`, a nearly universal convention is to display the page named index.html. If you don't have a page by that name, most Web servers construct a page with a directory listing of the pages in your Web directory. This listing is functional enough because it lets people go to any of your pages with one click, but it's not cool.

Sprucing Up Your Page

After you have gotten over the hurdle of creating and installing a Web page, you can add fancier contents. We finish this chapter with suggestions of ways to add more interesting text to your Web pages.

Because pictures and hyperlinks are topics of their own, we're saving them until Chapter 16.

To update your page, edit the copy on your own computer, debug it using your Web browser, and then upload it to your Internet provider, replacing the preceding version of the page.

Let's Get Organized

Web pages can be organized like an outline, with as many as six levels of headings. You mark headings with tags such as `<H1>` and `<H2>`, up to `<H6>`. You mark the end of each heading with `</H1>` and the like. Figures 15-3 and 15-4 show some corresponding headings.

```
<HTML>
<HEAD>
<TITLE>Headings</TITLE>
</HEAD>
<BODY>
<H1>This is a first level heading</H1>
<H2>And a second level heading</H2>
<H3>A third level heading, yet</H3>
<H4>Is anyone really organized enough to need a fourth
level heading?</H4>
Oh yeah, you can have some text, too.
</BODY>
</HTML>
```

Figure 15-3:
A lot of
headings.

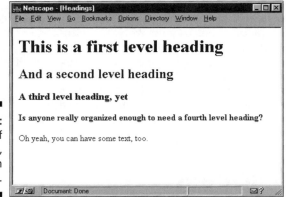

Figure 15-4:
A lot of
headings,
displayed in
Netscape.

Be sure to put an end-of-heading tag at the end of each heading. The tag goes at the end of the heading, not after any material that may be under that heading.

Although you can use as many as six levels of headings, we rarely use more than two or three. An <H1> heading usually goes at the top of the page, and <H2> indicates any intermediate headings you want.

Run, Text, Run

You usually have paragraphs of plain old text within your document. (We know people who have done entire pages as headers, but the result looks brutal.) You use paragraph tags <P> to separate paragraphs of running text. You can also use <BR> to force line breaks without the extra space the browser puts between paragraphs. Figures 15-5 and 15-6 show paragraphs and line breaks.

```
<HTML>
<HEAD>
<TITLE>Paragraphs</TITLE>
</HEAD>
<BODY>
<P>Here is a paragraph of running text.
Run, text, run.
You'll notice that the Web browser moves the text from
line to line so that the lines it displays
are all more or less the same length.
<P>
This is a good thing, since when you write your Web page,
you can't tell how wide a user's screen will be when she
displays your page, so this lets the page look reasonable
regardless of the screen width.
<P>
Paragraphs are separated with white space. Line break
tags don't add any space, which can be useful when your
material should be displayed together, as in the lyrics
of this song:
<P>
We knew a man whose name was Lang
<BR>
And he had a neon sign
<BR>
But Mr. Lang was very old
<BR>
So we called it Old Lang's Sign!
</BODY>
</HTML>
```

Figure 15-5:
Some
paragraphs
and an ode.

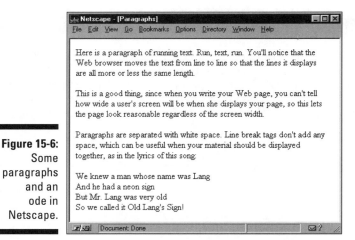

Figure 15-6:
Some
paragraphs
and an
ode in
Netscape.

The Strong, the Bold, and Other Typography

HTML has quite a few codes for various kinds of text; each code begins with an HTML tag and ends with the same tag preceded by a slash:

- <EM>: Emphasized text
- <STRONG>: Strong emphasis
- <CITE>: Citations of book titles and the like
- <CODE>: Examples of computer code
- <SAMP>: Sample text of some sort
- <ADDRESS>: Addresses, usually the page author's address
- <PRE>: Preformatted text, which, unlike all other text in a Web page, is displayed with spacing and line breaks unchanged

Most browsers don't really have separate styles for all these tags but in fact display them in variations of bold, italic, and fixed-spacing text. You can also specify typography directly:

- <B>: Bold text
- <I>: Italic text
- <TT>: Typewriter (*fixed pitch*) text

HTML also throws in one graphic element, <HR>, for a horizontal rule (a line across the page).

Figures 15-7 and 15-8 show a badly designed Web page that displays all these typographic elements. We suggest keeping the fancy formatting to a minimum because a great deal of formatting looks awful.

The absolute number-one error novice typographers make — and that's what we all are when we begin designing Web pages — is to overformat material. Experienced users disparagingly refer to documents with too many fonts and other typographic elements as "ransom notes."

```
<HTML>
<HEAD>
<TITLE>A Ransom Note</TITLE>
</HEAD>
<BODY>
This text is <EM>emphasized</EM>, while this text has
<STRONG>strong emphasis</STRONG>.
<P>
My favorite book is <CITE>MORE Internet For Dummies, 3rd
Edition</CITE>.
<P>
It's hard to come up with a plausible example that has
both <CODE>examples of computer code</CODE> as well as
<SAMP> sample text</SAMP>, so we won't try. And examples
of <B>bold</B>, <I>italic</I>, and <TT>typewriter</TT>
text are just as hard.
<P>

<PRE>
If you FTP text files in binary rather than ASCII mode
you'll find that the
                        line breaks usually
                                            come out like
this.
So don't do that.
</PRE>
<!-- It's common to put a horizontal rule above the
address-->
<HR>
<ADDRESS>
The Internet for Dummies Authors' Cabal<BR>
http://net.dummies.net/
</ADDRESS>
</BODY>
</HTML>
```

Figure 15-7:
The HTML for a really ugly Web page.

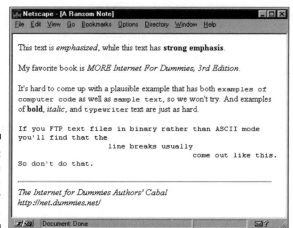

Figure 15-8:
Netscape
displays the
really ugly
Web page.

Chapter 16

Pretty As a Picture — and Well Connected Too

In This Chapter

▶ Adding graphics to your Web pages

▶ And links

▶ And backgrounds

*O*kay, in Chapter 15 we explain how to make Web pages. In this chapter, you can discover how to make *good* Web pages . . . or, at least, more aesthetically appealing pages.

Picture This

Most Web pages contain graphics of some sort. As usual where computers are concerned, adding graphics to your pages is easy in principle but a little more complicated in practice.

Even on Web pages that look like they're mostly text, you frequently see a number of graphics "dressing up" the page. In Figure 16-1, for example, you certainly notice the graphic of the *...For Dummies* guy, but 24 other graphics also appear in the figure. In front of the words ABOUT, NEWS, and ORDER are little ball icons, which appear in color on-screen, as well as the NEW! icons. This sort of layout is typical of Web pages these days.

The theory of putting graphics on your pages is easy enough: You put the graphic in a separate file and then add a reference to that file in your Web page so that your browser fetches the graphic and displays it on the page. The practice is complicated by the facts that pictures are stored in at least two common file formats and that some browsers understand pictures better than other browsers do.

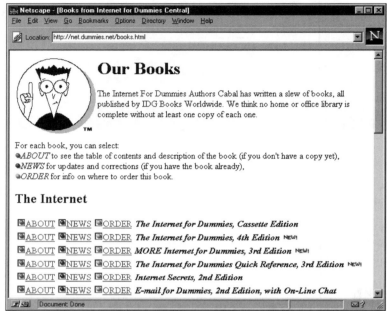

Figure 16-1:
A typical
Web page
with more
graphics
than you
may notice.

Format wars

"How many different ways can you have to store a picture in a computer?" you may ask. Dozens, maybe hundreds — that's how many. On your Windows machine, you may run into BMP, PCX, DIB, GIF, JPG, TGA, and other files, all of which contain various kinds of pictures. If, for some reason, you want more details about this convoluted state of affairs, you probably aren't surprised that we suggest *Graphic File Formats,* 2nd Edition, by David Kay and John Levine (Windcrest, 1994), and *Programming for Graphics Files in C and C++* (Wiley, 1994), which John wrote by himself.

Fortunately, only two picture formats are in common use on the Web. These formats are known as GIF and JPEG. Many lengthy . . . er, *free* and *frank* discussions have occurred on the Net concerning the relative merits of these two formats. Because John is an Official Graphics Format Expert, by virtue of having persuaded two otherwise reputable publishers to publish his books on the topic, Table 16-1 lists his opinions on the subject.

Table 16-1	JPEG and GIF Duke It Out
JPEG	*GIF*
Best format for scanned photographs	Best format for computer-drawn cartoons and icons

JPEG	GIF
Handles "true color" better	Can have transparent backgrounds (which we discuss at the end of this chapter)
Files are usually smaller	Files are usually larger
Doesn't handle large areas of solid color or sharp edges well	Handles solid color areas well
Some older browsers don't handle JPEG	All graphical browsers handle GIF
Slower to decode	Faster to decode

If you have a picture in any other format, such as BMP or PCX, you must convert it to either GIF or JPEG before you can use it on a Web page. Many graphics-wrangling programs are available; check out the Consummate WinSock Applications page, at `http://www.stroud.com`, for some suggestions.

So I've got some images already

After you have your image file, plugging it in to your Web page is simplicity itself. You put a tag identifying the file to display at the place on your page where you want the image to appear. The following example is this type of tag:

```
<IMG SRC="filename">
```

The following tag, for example, tells the browser to locate a file named monalisa.jpg on the Internet For Dummies Central computer and display that file on your page:

```
<IMG SRC="http://net.dummies.net/greatart/italian/
        monalisa.jpg">
```

Make sure that the filename ends with the gif extension if the file's a GIF and jpeg or jpg if it's a JPEG file so that people's browsers can determine how to decode the file.

The SRC value in the IMG tag is, in theory, a full Web Uniform Resource Locator (URL); 99 percent of the time, however, the image is in a file in the same directory as the Web page itself or in a directory nearby, so you can abbreviate the URL to just the filename, along with the relative directory path if necessary, similar to the following example:

```
<IMG SRC="icons/elbow.gif">
```

This tag tells the browser to display a file named elbow.gif in the icons subdirectory of the directory in which the Web page is stored. (Use forward rather than backward slashes because UNIX servers understand only forward slashes as filename and directory separators.)

You should always put your image files in either the same directory with your Web pages or a nearby directory that you call icons or images or something similar. That positioning enables you to check your pages and images locally on your own machine. Then you can upload all the pages and images to your Web server, and as long as the relative positions of the files don't change, your pages are sure to work.

Making your image fit into your pages

In the simplest cases, images are just spliced into your Web page as though they were large text characters. If your image is a tiny icon, such as the little balls and NEW! that were shown in Figure 16-1, you can get away with this effect, but the process tends to produce rather unsatisfactory results with larger pictures. Figure 16-2 shows what happens when the following HTML splices in a graphic as text:

```
<HTML>
<HEAD><TITLE>An ugly picture</TITLE></HEAD>
<BODY>
<H1>This is my picture</H1>
Here comes my picture.
<IMG SRC="ugly.gif">
That was my picture. Bye.
</BODY>
</HTML>
```

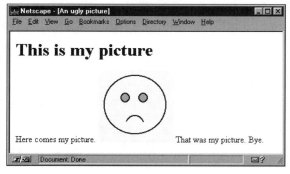

Figure 16-2: This example isn't an attractive Web page.

Fortunately, you can improve the layout of your page in several ways so that the images and text look reasonable. The simplest approach is to put the picture in a separate paragraph, as the following bit of HTML does:

```
<IMG SRC="pretty.gif">
<P>
This is a bunch of text ...
```

Now the text appears beneath the picture, which usually looks okay, rather than in the middle of a line of text, which doesn't.

Modern browsers, such as Internet Explorer and Netscape, have added options that enable you to "float" the image to the left or right side of the window, which in most cases results in a better look than positioning the picture by itself. You add the option `ALIGN=LEFT` or `ALIGN=RIGHT` inside the image tag, as in the following example:

```
<IMG ALIGN=LEFT SRC="filename">
```

The following HTML example results in the display shown in Figure 16-3:

```
<HTML>
<HEAD><TITLE>A less ugly picture</TITLE></HEAD>
<BODY>
<H1>This is my picture</H1>
<IMG ALIGN=LEFT SRC="pretty.gif">
<P>
This is a bunch of text that will be displayed along side
my picture and will flow around underneath it when it gets
long enough.
<P>
We've found that floating a picture to the left like this
is usually the easiest way to put a large image into a page
and have it look decent.
<P>
Remember that different browsers will use different sizes
of text and different sizes of window, so you can't count
on exactly where the text will flow under the picture.
</BODY>
</HTML>
```

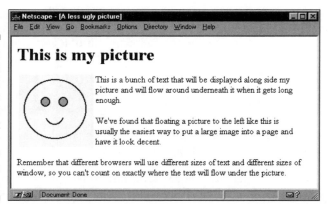

Figure 16-3:
Using the
ALIGN
feature
makes a big
improvement
in how your
graphic
appears on
your page.

Although the `ALIGN=LEFT` and `ALIGN=RIGHT` options are widely supported, some Web browsers still in use don't understand them. That's why we put the `<P>` tag right after the image; if someone's browser doesn't understand how to left-align the picture, the browser places the picture in its own paragraph above the text so that the page doesn't look entirely stupid.

How about us text lovers?

Ah, yes. A fair number of users still use Lynx, the UNIX Web browser that handles only text. To save time, many people who use Netscape or other graphical browsers set them up so that the browsers don't load the images on each page. Can you do something for them?

Yes, indeed. In each IMG tag, you can — and usually should — put an "alternative text" tag that tells the browser what to display if it can't display the picture. For example, we changed the IMG tag line in the preceding example as follows:

```
<IMG ALIGN=LEFT SRC="pretty.gif" ALT="The Mona Lisa">
```

Now, if a user views this page without graphics, the page looks like the one shown in Figure 16-4.

Where can I get some images?

That's a good question. You can always draw them by using a paint program or scan in photographs; unless you're a rather good artist or photographer, however, your graphics may not look as nice as you want. (See, for example, the images in Figures 16-2, 16-3, and 16-4. Luckily for us, we don't claim to be artists.)

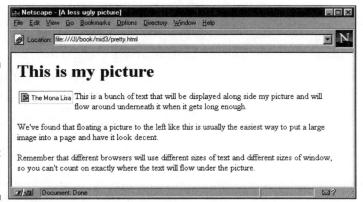

Figure 16-4:
Here's the same page as shown in Figure 16-3 — but without the graphic.

Fortunately, you can locate lots of sources of graphical material, as described in this list:

- ✔ Plenty of freeware, shareware, and commercial clip art is available on the Net. Yahoo has a long list of clip art sites at `http://www.yahoo.com/Computers_and_Internet/Multimedia/Pictures/Clip_Art/`. Also try searching for *clip art* in any other Web directory or index.

- ✔ If you see on a Web page an image you want to use, you can write to the page's owner and ask for permission. More likely than not, the owner will let you use the image.

- ✔ Lots of regular old software programs totally unrelated to the Internet, such as paint and draw programs, presentation programs, and even word processors, come with clip art collections.

- ✔ You can buy CD-ROMs full of clip art, which tends to be of higher quality than the free stuff. These items usually aren't all that expensive, particularly considering how many images fit on one CD-ROM.

Clip art, like any art, is protected by copyright. Whether the art has already been used on a Web page or whether a copyright notice appears on or near the image doesn't matter. It's still copyrighted.

If you use someone else's copyrighted art, you must get permission to do so. Whether your use is educational, personal, or noncommercial is irrelevant. If you fail to secure permission, you run the risk of anything from a crabby phone call from the owner's lawyer to winding up on the losing end of a lawsuit.

Most people are quite reasonable whenever you ask for permission to use something. If an image you want to use doesn't already come with blanket permission to use it, just check with the owner before you decide to add it to your own Web page.

Slo-o-o-o-w-lo-o-oading pages

Many Web pages we see are burdened with images that, although beautiful, take a long time to load — so long that many users may give up before the pages are completely loaded.

You can take a few steps to make your Web pages load more quickly. The main step, of course, is to limit the size of the images you use. A 20K image takes twice as long to load as a 10K image, which takes twice as long to load as a 5K image. You can estimate that images load at 1K per second (on a dial-up connection), so a 5K image loads in about 5 seconds, which is fast, and a 120K image takes two minutes to load, so that image had better be worth the wait.

If your images are in GIF files, images with fewer colors load faster than images with more colors. In many cases, if you use a graphics editor to reduce a scanned GIF from 256 colors to 32 or even 16 colors, the appearance hardly changes, but the file shrinks dramatically. If you set up your graphics program to store the GIF file in *interlaced* format, browsers can display a blurry approximation of the image as it's downloading, which at least gives the user a hint of what's coming.

If your images are JPEG files, you can adjust the "quality" level in the JPEG, with a lower quality making the file smaller. In our experience, because of the limited resolution of most computer screens, you can set the quality quite low with little effect on what appears on users' screens.

You can also take advantage of the *cache* that browsers use. The cache keeps copies of previously viewed pages and images. If any image on a page being downloaded is already in the browser's cache, that image doesn't have to be loaded again. When you use the same icon several places on a page or on several pages visited in succession, the icon's file is downloaded by the browser only once, and the same image is used for all examples on the pages. Although the page in Figure 16-1, for example, contains 25 images, only five different files are downloaded (the ...*For Dummies* guy, the three colored balls, and the NEW! icon), so the page loads relatively quickly. In creating your Web pages, you should try to use the same icons from one page to the next, both to give your page a consistent style and to speed up the process of downloading its images.

The Missing Link

We saved the best for last (or at least almost last): hyperlinks. Hyperlinks are the things that make the Web the Web. A *hyperlink* (which we call merely a *link* from here on because we're lazy typists) enables a user to hop from one page to the next at the click of a mouse.

Plain links

You install links on your page by using HTML tags called *anchors*. An anchor performs two functions: It identifies the page to which your page is linked and displays some text or image on the page that the user can click (or the keyboard equivalent) to tell the browser to follow the link. An anchor looks like this example:

```
<A HREF="URL">text</A>
```

The URL in the anchor identifies where to jump after the user clicks the link. The text is the text of the link — the text that appears blue and underlined on the Web page. You can see these components in this example:

```
<A HREF="http://net.dummies.net">
          Internet For Dummies Central</A>
```

The link starts with an <A> tag, which contains an HREF with the URL of the page to link to. Following that is the text to display on the current page and an end tag, </A>. The text Internet For Dummies Central then appears on your Web page as a link. Here's the full HTML source that displays the text and link shown in Figure 16-5:

```
<HTML>
<HEAD><TITLE>A sample link</TITLE></HEAD>
<BODY>
<H1>Your Gateway to the Best Site on the Net</H1>
I've searched all over the net, and there's no question
that my favorite site of all is
<A HREF="http://net.dummies.net">
          Internet For Dummies Central</A>
<P>
See you there!
</BODY>
</HTML>
```

If you link to a page of your own that's on the same server as the page containing the link, you can and should use the same kinds of abbreviated references for images, as described in the section "So I've got some images already," earlier in this chapter — as in the following example:

```
<A HREF="poptart.htm">My favorite main course for dinner</A>
```

Figure 16-5:
A Web
page
containing
a link to yet
another
Web page.

By using these types of abbreviated references, you can create and test your pages in a single directory on your own computer; then you can upload them as a group to your provider's server — and the references all still work.

Fancy links

You aren't limited to using just text in your anchors. You can also use an image or a combination of text and image in an anchor. You can even use an image as a link, as set up in this example:

```
<A HREF="http://net.dummies.net">
          <IMG SRC="wow.gif" align=left></A>
```

You can use all the fancy text formatting in an anchor that you can use in any other place on your pages.

In theory you can use images and text in a single link, although it looks strange if you do so. Use an image or use text, but don't use both in the same link. You can make two separate links to the same place, one with an image and one with text.

For example, we added a link using an image and overformatted the existing text link (using Strong and Italic tags) as follows to create the Web page shown in Figure 16-6:

```
<HTML>
<HEAD><TITLE>A sample link</TITLE></HEAD>
<BODY>
<H1>Your Gateway to the Best Site on the Net</H1>
<A HREF="http://net.dummies.net">
          <IMG SRC="wow.gif" align=left ALT="Wow! "></A>
```

```
I've searched all over the net, and there's no question
that my favorite site of all is
<A HREF="http://net.dummies.net">
<STRONG><I>Internet For Dummies Central</I></STRONG>
</A>
<P>
See you there!
</BODY>
</HTML>
```

Figure 16-6:
Links,
beautified
with an
image and
formatted
text as
links.

Colorizing Your Pages and Other Advanced Hackery

In case you're still with us, this section describes two more simple elements you can add to make your Web pages more attractive: transparent GIF images and colored Web page backgrounds.

Transparently better

One simple element is *transparency.* In Figure 16-7, notice that the starburst on the left has an ugly, white rectangle around it and the one on the right has no border outside the star. That's because, in the GIF file for the right star, we made the white border transparent, which tells the browser to use the regular background color for that area. Whenever you have a GIF of an image that isn't really rectangular, making the area outside the image transparent always makes the image look better. Because transparency adds only ten bytes to the size of a GIF, it doesn't affect the time to load or display the file.

Figure 16-7:
The star on
the right is
transparently
better.

You need to use a graphics program that can mark one color in a GIF as transparent. In Windows, using the shareware program LView Pro or Paint Shop Pro is the most popular way to do that. On UNIX systems, a little shareware program called giftools can mark one color as the transparent one. DOS users can use GIFTRANS. Some Web pages also can "transparentize" a GIF for you. The following pages are among those that can do so:

```
http://www.mit.edu:8001/tweb/map.html (U.S.)
http://www.inf.fu-berlin.de/~leitner/trans/english.html
        (Europe)
```

Colorful pages

Many Web pages have background patterns. Because we think that background patterns are almost without exception ugly and difficult to read, however, we're reluctant to tell you how to use them (although we do in the next section).

Plain *background* and *foreground colors* on your pages look much better. They let you feature, for example, black text on a white background or vice versa — as long as a user's browser supports that effect, of course. (It's another addition that originated with Netscape, but it's widely supported.)

You set the colors by adding BGCOLOR and TEXT fields to the <BODY> tag at the beginning of the body of your Web page:

```
<BODY BGCOLOR=#FFFFFF TEXT=#000000>
```

All set? Well, you do have to deal with the minor detail of that #FFFFFF glop, which is an extremely nerdoid way of identifying colors. A color is considered to consist of a mixture of red, green, and blue, with the amount of each color ranging from 0 (none) to 255 (the brightest). You convert each of the three amounts to a two-digit hexadecimal number (anywhere from 00 to FF) and then glom the three numbers together.

If the preceding explanation is less than obvious to you, Table 16-2 provides a list of some likely colors and their corresponding codes.

Table 16-2	Web Page Color Coding
Code	*Color*
#FFFFFF	White
#000000	Black
#FF0000	Red
#00FF00	Green
#0000FF	Blue
#FFFF00	Bright yellow
#999999	Medium gray

We find that you must always fiddle with colors to make them look good. Remember that many PC users can display only a limited number of colors on their screens at one time. If you use other than basic colors, Windows approximates your colors with *dithered* colors (using a geometrical pattern of basic colors) that are utterly illegible. Remember too that some people are more or less color-blind, so make sure that you provide plenty of contrast between your text color and your background. Although white on black and black on white may seem boring, these combinations have certainly stood the test of time.

A deep background

Okay, here's the scoop on background patterns. Background patterns are really images, just like the ones we discussed earlier in this chapter, except that they happen to be displayed behind the rest of the page. Unless you have an enormous background as big as the entire page (not recommended), your background is *tiled* to fill the window. That is, starting at the upper left corner of the window, your browser fills the window with repeated copies of the background image.

 The only type of background images we have found that work well are ones that are very wide and not very tall. For example, Figure 16-8 shows the Zig-Zag page, with the elegant zigzag stripe next to this paragraph down the left side.

Figure 16-8:
Check out
that elegant
zigzag.

How did we do it?

That page has a background image that's 30 pixels (screen dots) high and 1,000 pixels wide. The image has one black zig and one zag at the left side, and the rest of the image is white. We made it the background image on our sample page, using the HTML shown in Figure 16-9. Because the image is so wide, when the browser tiles it, it makes a vertical stack of zigzag images, producing the reasonably attractive image you see in Figure 16-9.

```
<!- - This isn't exactly the HTML for this page
      see "On the Table", Chapter 17, to find out why not.
- ->
<HTML>
<HEAD><TITLE>The Zig-Zag Page</TITLE></HEAD>
<BODY background="zigzag.gif" text=#000000>

<H1>Welcome to The Zig-Zag Page</H1>

Hi.  That sure is a zig-zag over there, isn't it?

</BODY>
</HTML>
```

Figure 16-9:
Ready to
zigzag.

What would have happened if the background image was just the size of the zigzag without all the white space that pads it out to 1,000 pixels wide? In that case, the browser would fill the background with copies of the zigzag, producing the traffic-accident effect in Figure 16-10. Practice safe backgrounds — don't let this happen to you!

Figure 16-10:
This page
looks like it
was run
over by a
truck.

Chapter 17

Everything Else We Know about Web Pages

Since we wrote the last edition of this book, we have designed a few more Web pages of our own and found out a few more ways to make fancier Web pages. Here they are.

On the Table

One relatively recent (a year-and-a-half ago, or 13 Web years) addition to the HTML language is tables. They let you lay out material in rows and columns in what you might call a tabular form. It turns out that tables are also the easiest way to push stuff around on your Web page to arrange the stuff the way you want. For example, look at Figure 17-1. It doesn't particularly look like a table — it looks like three pictures with descriptive text. In HTML, however, the way you get them to line up is to put the pictures and text in a table. Figure 17-2 shows the same table, with some borders around the boxes so that you can tell where they are.

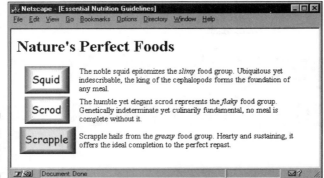

Figure 17-1:
Where's the
table?

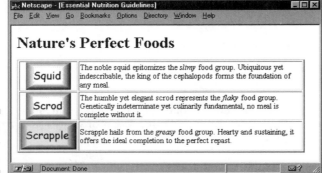

Figure 17-2:
Aha —
there it is.

Tabling details

Tables are simple in concept, but (no, you never would have guessed) can be kind of tricky to get all the details right because the HTML you write doesn't look much like the table you end up with. An HTML table consists of a bunch of rows, and each row contains a bunch of cells. The entire table is enclosed in TABLE tags:

```
<TABLE>
contents of table
</TABLE>
```

Each row of the table is enclosed in TR tags:

```
<TR>
contents of row
</TR>
```

Each cell in each row is contained in TD (table data) tags:

```
<TD>
contents of the cell (the actual stuff)
</TD>
```

We have put them all together in Figure 17-3, the HTML for the nutrition plan shown in Figure 17-1. First comes the <TABLE> tag and then the first row (squid), the second row (scrod), and the third row (scrapple). In each row, the first cell contains the button image; the second cell, the descriptive text.

Figure 17-3:
The inside scoop on perfect foods (slightly simplified).

```
<TABLE>

<TR>
<TD><IMG SRC="squid.gif"></TD>
<TD>
The noble squid epitomizes the <I>slimy</I> food group.
Ubiquitous
yet indescribable, the king of the cephalopods forms the
foundation of any meal.
</TD>
</TR>

<TR>
<TD><IMG SRC="scrod.gif"></TD>
<TD>
The humble yet elegant scrod represents the <I>flaky</I>
food group.
Genetically indeterminate yet culinarily fundamental, no
meal is
complete without it.
</TD>
</TR>

<TR>
<TD><IMG SRC="scrapple.gif"></TD>
<TD>
Scrapple hails from the <I>greasy</I> food group.
Hearty and sustaining, it offers the ideal completion to
the perfect
repast.
</TD>
</TR>
</TABLE>
```

You can put within each table cell any HTML elements you want. Although we have kept this table relatively simple, you can put HTML links, fancy paragraph formatting, and even tables within tables.

Real tabling details

We have to admit that we lied a little — Figure 17-3 isn't the real HTML code that produces our nutrition table. Although Web browsers do a respectable job of laying out tables, sometimes you have to give them some hints about how you want your table to appear. We wanted the buttons to line up in a centered column (by default, they're left-aligned), so we put some alignment hints in the cell descriptions, like this:

```
<TD ALIGN=CENTER><IMG SRC="squid.gif"></TD>
```

You can set ALIGN to LEFT, CENTER, RIGHT, to control the left-to-right alignment. There's also VALIGN, which you can set to TOP, BOTTOM, or CENTER, to set where the contents appear vertically within the cell. We also dressed up the descriptions of the images, but we save that for the next section.

Tables and backgrounds

At the end of Chapter 16, you can see the HTML for a page with a zigzag background stripe down the left side. Because Web browsers are pretty dumb (despite being so big and slow), without some assistance they would start the text right on top of the background stripe. The best way to offer that assistance is with a table that has two columns, a blank column on the left (to leave room for the stripe), and the actual contents of the page in the right column. Here's how we left room for the zigzag:

```
<TABLE>
<TR><TD WIDTH=30> </TD>
<TD>
<H1>Welcome to The Zig-Zag Page</H1>

Hi.  That sure is a zig-zag over there, isn't it?
</TD>
</TR>
</TABLE>
```

The first column is started by `<TD WIDTH=30>`, which tells the browser to make the cell and hence the column 30 pixels (screen dots) wide because we happen to know that's how wide the zigzag is. There's nothing in that column — it's just a placeholder to leave room for the background. The second cell contains the entire text of the page, both the header and the following text. This looks like a strange sort of table, but it's probably the most common kind on the Web now. Any page that has a column on the left with either a border pattern or a list of icons or index links is set up in this way.

Border patrol

Sometimes your tables are real tables rather than page-formatting hackery (fancy that), in which case you may want to put some borders around the cells to make the table look more, well, tabular, as we showed you in Figure 17-2. That's easy because it needs only this addition to the TABLE tag at the beginning of the table:

```
<TABLE BORDER=2>
```

This line requests a two-pixel wide border, which is usually about the right width. You can create a variety of pompous-looking effects using combinations of borders. Figure 17-4 shows the HTML for a table in a table in a table, with each table having a single row with a single cell but each table having a border, to get the Louis XIII border effect shown in Figure 17-5. This example is a gross abuse of tables, but it's common too, and some people think that it looks nice. There's no accounting for taste.

Figure 17-4:
Great
excitement
in an
elegant
three-level
frame.

```
<HTML>
<HEAD>
<TITLE>Great excitement</TITLE>
</HEAD>
<BODY>

<TABLE BORDER=6><TR><TD>
<TABLE BORDER=4><TR><TD>
<TABLE BORDER=2><TR><TD>

<IMG SRC="hey.gif">

</TD></TR></TABLE>
</TD></TR></TABLE>
</TD></TR></TABLE>

</BODY>
</HTML>
```

Figure 17-5:
Great
excitement,
displayed in
Internet
Explorer.

Tabular wrap-up

By this time you probably have found out more about HTML tables than you thought you wanted to know. Table 17-1 summarizes the table tricks. Be sure to put your tricks on the right kind of HTML tag: ALIGN, VALIGN, and WIDTH go with a TD tag, and BORDER goes with the outer TABLE tag. (Yes, this system is kind of arbitrary. Computers are like that.)

Table 17-1	A Table of Table Tricks
Code	*What It Does*
`<TD ALIGN=CENTER>`	Centers the contents of this cell horizontally; also can be LEFT or RIGHT
`<TD VALIGN=CENTER>`	Centers the contents of this cell vertically; also can be LEFT or RIGHT
`<TD WIDTH=30>`	Makes this cell (and this column) 30 screen dots wide; can also use a percentage, such as WIDTH=25%, to use one-fourth of the screen width
`<TABLE BORDER=2>`	Puts a two-dot border around every cell

Despite the disparaging things we say about Web page editing programs later in this chapter, if you're doing tables, a good page editor can make the job much easier because the editor rather than you writes tags and adds the glop for sizes, alignment, borders, and so on.

Making Your Graphics Load Snappily

Here's a quick tip that makes your pages look much more professional: Whenever you include a GIF or JPEG image in your page, put the size of the image in the reference to the image. For example, in Figure 17-1 (which by this time probably doesn't seem all that clever anymore), the Squid graphic is 50 pixels high and 80 pixels wide, so the reference to that image really looks like this:

```
<IMG SRC="squid.gif" HEIGHT=50 WIDTH=80 ALT="[Squid]">
```

The reason that this reference helps is that when someone looks at your page, the browser first fetches the page and then fetches the individual images. If you tell the browser how big the images are, it leaves the right amount of space as it lays out the page and pops in the images as they're available. If you don't tell the browser how big the images are, it leaves a tiny box that then erupts to the actual image size when the image is available, in a manner somewhat reminiscent of an unpleasant skin condition. (We would be more specific, but our editor's not crazy about the word *zit*.)

Another advantage of putting in the image sizes is that even if a visitor has turned off images to make pages load faster, your pages are still laid out on-screen the same as though the images were there.

Helping Your Fans Send You Mail

If you're proud of your pages, you probably will want a way for people to tell you how much they liked them. The easiest way to let people do that is to put a `mailto` link on your page, which lets them send you e-mail. This type of link has the form `mailto:user@domain`, as shown in this example:

```
<A HREF="mailto: moreint3@dummies.net">How'd you like
        the book?</A>
```

When someone clicks that link, the browser opens a new mail message (in the browser's mail window, if it has an integrated mail program, like Netscape does, or in a separate mail application if not), and the user can send you a message that arrives with the rest of your e-mail.

We occasionally get strange messages from people who seem to think that a `mailto` link gives them a license to send you any old junk they want to send. We treat that like any other kind of unsolicited mail: Ignore it if the sender looks merely confused, or send a complaint back to the person's Internet provider if it looks like bulk advertising.

Getting Noticed

After you have built some beautiful Web pages, you may want to get people to come and visit. Here are a few ways to do it:

✔ Visit your favorite Web directories and indexes, such as Yahoo (point to `http://www.yahoo.com`) and AltaVista (you can find it at `http://altavista .digital.com`), and submit your URL (the name of your page) to add to their database. They all have a line on their home pages called something like "add a new page."

- ✔ Visit `http://www.submit-it.com`, a site that helps you submit your URL to a whole bunch of directories and indexes. You can get submitted to 30 popular searching sites for free or pay money if you want them to submit your URL to a much larger list.

- ✔ Find and visit other similar or related sites, and offer to exchange links between your site and theirs.

You probably will end up doing all of these things. Even for the most wonderful of sites, it takes a while to build up traffic, so patience, as always, remains a virtue.

HTML Tags — Yuck!

If you just hate the thought of writing HTML yourself, a bunch of HTML editors more or less automate the process for you.

The newer versions of Microsoft Word and WordPerfect can now create Web pages all by themselves. Using your own word processor probably is the easiest way to go to create simple Web pages, although they're both a pain to use for more complex formats.

If you use Microsoft Word 6.0, you can download and install a free add-on that enables you to edit documents and save them as HTML. Check out the following site, which explains how to download and install Microsoft Internet Assistant:

`http://www.microsoft.com/word/internet/ia`

Microsoft frequently moves pages around on its site, so if that URL doesn't work, start at the Microsoft home page, at `http://www.microsoft.com`, click the Products button, click the Select a Product box, choose Internet Assistant for Word, and click the little Go button.

A number of stand-alone HTML editors also are available. Two that are well regarded are HoTMetaL (`http://www.sq.com/products/hotmetal`), which comes in both a limited freeware version and a more complete commercial version, and HotDog (`http://www.sausage.com`), a commercial product with standard and professional versions you can download for a 30-day test. Netscape Navigator Gold is also available on the Net for evaluation (`http://home.netscape.com`), and it combines the regular Netscape Navigator 3.0 browser with a decent HTML editor. Netscape Communicator includes Composer, a Web page editor.

We personally haven't found writing HTML tags to be all that difficult a process, so we have never found any of these editors worth the effort to use; if you're less tag-tolerant than we are, however, your opinion may well be different. If you're doing many tables, using the editors can be easier than matching up all the tags that begin and end tables, rows, and cells.

Much more elaborate and expensive Web authoring systems also are available. These systems can help you keep track of the relationships among a group of pages, create the necessary server programs to process forms, and otherwise automate the maintenance of a Web site. These systems tend to be big, expensive programs, however, that are severe overkill if all you want to do is put up a few personal pages of your own. Microsoft FrontPage is the best known.

Discovering More

Much, much more information about HTML and Web page design is available than we have room for in this chapter. We haven't even touched on forms, frames, VRML, or any of the other advanced Web features.

The Web is one of the best places to find out more about HTML. The following address takes you to a good Web page from which to start your quest — the HTML home page at the World Wide Web Consortium:

```
http://www.w3.org/pub/WWW/MarkUp
```

Webreference, the Webmaster's reference library, has all kinds of Web-page-authoring information for beginners through experienced Web-page creators:

```
http://www.webreference.com
```

The following page is an excellent reference on HTML usage and low-level Web page design:

```
http://www.sandia.gov/sci_compute/html_ref.html
```

The address that follows is that of the HTML Version 3.2 Specification page at the Web Consortium, which is far more readable than you may expect:

```
http://www.w3.org/pub/WWW/TR/REC-html32.html
```

Many books also are devoted to the topic of Web page design, such as *Creating Web Pages For Dummies,* by Bud Smith and Arthur Bebak, and *Creating Cool Web Pages with HTML,* by Dave Taylor (both published by IDG Books Worldwide, Inc.).

Nothing can substitute for direct hand-to-hand combat, though —
building Web pages, looking at them, and throwing them away. Whenever
you discover a Web page that you think looks particularly nice, instruct
your browser to show you the source for the page so that you can examine
the HTML that created the page. In Netscape 3.0, for example, choose
View⇨Document Source to see the HTML. In Netscape 4.0, choose
View⇨Page Source, or press Ctrl+U.

Part V
Online Odds and Ends

The 5th Wave   By Rich Tennant

"WHAT CONCERNS ME ABOUT THE INFORMATION SUPERHIGHWAY IS THAT IT APPEARS TO BE ENTERING THROUGH BRENT'S BEDROOM."

In this part . . .

This part of the book houses the odds and ends that didn't fit anywhere else (we admit it). These topics are too important to leave out, though. You can read about Internet privacy or a lack thereof, how to use the Internet for business, and how to register your own Internet domain name (such as dummies.net or greattapes.com).

Chapter 18

Using the Net for Business

(Contributed by Carol Baroudi)

In This Chapter

▶ How businesses can use the Net effectively

▶ Better business with e-mail

▶ Finding strategic information on the Net

▶ Opening a virtual office on the Web

Many people wish that they had known about the Internet and online services 15 years ago. But, in fact, few people did. And few people watched the commercial and sociological trends associated with the Net for the past 15 years. Philippe Le Roux, an entrepreneur and Internet expert of the first order, is among those few who watched online developments with a close eye. He shared his insight and expertise with us in a personal interview. The remainder of this chapter conveys to you those insights, as well as the expertise of Mr. Le Roux, on using the Net for business purposes.

Presence of Mind — and Minding Your Presence

You may be tempted to spend lots of money setting up a "Net presence," invest big bucks on fancy graphics to create the spiffiest home page on the Web, and then expect to sit back and wait for the money to roll in. Before you do so, however, read on!

Where the money is

For many people and companies, using the Net for business means having a great Web site. But limiting your Net use to publishing Web information is like using paper and printing only to publish press releases! A strategic Web site can have lots of benefits, but you can get other benefits from the Net easier and cheaper.

First, use the most universal tool of the Internet — e-mail — effectively. E-mail lets you communicate in minutes worldwide for free. E-mail is not as universal as the phone or the fax, but its use is growing quickly in companies around the world. (The number of companies using Internet e-mail grew by 717 percent in 1996!) E-mail is perfect for *asynchronous* communication (when you need to send information to somebody or ask for information without needing to be available at the same time). E-mail is perfect too for small-group communication: a project team, a list of partners, a group of clients, and so on. You can send an e-mail message to an entire group with just one mouse click. E-mail lets you send spreadsheets, images, audio files — even video — as easily as you send text.

In dealing with multimedia projects for companies on three continents, my e-mail use has (at least) doubled my productivity and cut my costs by two-thirds. In fact, if you learn how to effectively use your e-mail address and software, using the power of filters, aliases, and other tools, you can save enough money to pay for your Internet connection and all future development.

Where the info is

The second profitable use of the Internet is to look for strategic information. You can't imagine how much and how many kinds of information you can find on the Internet. Are you looking for data about a new market? You'll find a great deal. Are you looking for information about your competition? They're spending a great deal of money to give you this information on their Web site. Even better, using Web directories and search sites (refer to Chapter 5 in this book and Chapter 7 in *The Internet for Dummies,* 4th Edition), you can find other information about your competitors, such as press releases, articles from newspapers, comments from employees or clients, and more. Are you looking to develop a new line of products or services? Take a look at the technical information on the comparable and competing products available around the Net. Investing a few days in a Net search or hiring a specialist in "digital competitive intelligence" can find more pertinent information than any traditional marketing study for a fraction of the cost. Are you looking for a specific employee with a hard-to-find profile? Between the scientific Web pages and Usenet newsgroups, you can find many specialists you can contact directly and discreetly by e-mail. The tens of thousands of dollars you can save by investing in training yourself to search for strategic information gives you more return on your investment than any Web site. That's mostly because, in proportion, Web sites often do not meet their financial goals, and the cost of managing a Web site often surpasses the initial estimates by a factor of 3 to 10.

Building a Web site — not

The Web is often seen as a multimedia brochure, and companies launch Web projects considering only the graphical and editing costs, sometimes planning a simple interactive application. Then, after the project begins, a Web consultant working with all parts of the organization shows that there's a great deal of other content and interaction to add to the Web site, so the "brochure" grows and the budget explodes. (If that's not the case, you have either read this chapter or you must find another consultant.) The problem is caused, in fact, by a basic ambiguity: Publishers think that they're creating multimedia contents, but users are visiting places. As the experience ranging from the early French Minitel, the Web, bulletin boards, AOL, CompuServe, and online services shows, users of online systems approach sites as places, not just as documents. They say, "Did you go to the IBM Web site?" not "Did you read the new IBM Web site?" People talk about a place, not about media or a brochure.

Your Web site is not a document — it's a virtual part of your organization. Can you imagine opening an information desk or a telephone help line for your customers or prospects and just putting some brochures there? Never! It's the same thing on the Web. You must develop a virtual place where people can reach you, look for information, ask for more material, and give feedback — in other words, a place where the people you want to reach can interact with your company. That's not a design or writing project; it's a business project, like opening a new division on a sixth continent — the virtual one.

This ambiguity has cost many companies a large amount of cash and disillusionment. According to one study from Forrester Research, 20 percent of companies with a Web presence in 1995 were expected to dismantle their sites in 1996.

This ambiguity explains the growing numbers of *dead sites* — Web sites still online but with obsolete information (such as TechKnowlogy Services, at `http://www.fyitech.com/avail.html`, with an interactive schedule for booking an appointment in 1996, or Rhino, at `http://www.rhinonet.com/events/`, an interactive marketing company, with a calendar of events for 1995!). If you plan a Web presence, you must think about those problems before putting yourself and your company in an embarrassing situation. Some problems are easier to prevent than to solve.

Almost every city that calls itself a city hosts at least one Internet conference or forum a week. Self-proclaimed industry experts are ready to take your dollars and sell you a bill of goods. Don't get lost in the hype and hysteria as people flock to the Net as though it's the latest California gold rush. It's important to understand, from a business point of view, that people who understand Net technology should not be confused with people who know how to use the Net to help your business, for the same reason that a printing expert is not often a good editor.

To use the Net to help your business, you have to talk to people who understand Net culture and behavior: Who is on the Net? Why are they there? What relevance — if any — can those on the Net have to your business? If you own a hair styling salon, for example, you're unlikely to find a Web site to generate much new business for you. On the other hand, your business *can* definitely benefit from strategic use of the Net in other ways.

If someone tells you that 50 million Internet users are all waiting to buy your product, he's handing you a line. Many businesses have spent tens, if not hundreds, of thousands of dollars on Web sites but have realized no return on their investments. Other companies have experienced a ten- to twenty-fold increase in sales. Still others say that their sites have saved them between $3 million and $4 million.

What's the difference among these sites? The multimedia presentations, perhaps? Hardly. Some of the most lucrative sites are mainly text-based. Sophisticated software, known as *intelligent agent* software, is already becoming more and more widely available, and these agents are all text-based. Soon, everyone with access to the Net can tell these agents exactly what they want, and the agents will move out across the Web to find it for them. For a long time to come, you can expect this agent software to remain text-dependent — which means that such software, in seeking out your Web site for potential clients, never even "sees" your fancy graphics.

The difference between the success of one Web site over another, in fact, involves how effective the site is at providing what people actually want, *not* what you're trying to sell them. You must begin to think of the Internet as an avenue that provides potential solutions to your business problems, not as an objective itself. If you start by identifying your own business problems, you begin to see how to use the Net to solve those problems.

Saving Time and Money: Better Business with E-Mail

E-mail opens an important new avenue of communication inside and outside an organization. Inside a company, e-mail is a powerful tool for communication and project management. Using e-mail, people communicate more easily with all levels of an organization so that information flows more freely.

Those responsible for projects involving many people find that using e-mail facilitates group communications and heightens accountability. Because e-mail is almost free, sending a message to 245 people costs no more than sending a message to 3. Because people can read e-mail at their own convenience, using e-mail to communicate project information saves time otherwise spent in meetings and lessens the need to interrupt someone with phone or office chatting. I don't think that e-mail replaces talking to people — I just know that it's difficult to get much work done with numerous interruptions, and e-mail can go a long way toward reducing those interruptions.

The cheapest words around

E-mail is probably *the* cheapest way to communicate and is absolutely the cheapest way to reach a number of people around the world. E-mail often reaches its destination in a matter of seconds, and sending e-mail to Hong Kong, Lima, or New York City costs no more than sending it down the hall.

People who use e-mail find that the technology itself changes how they work. Compared to a phone call, for example, e-mail communication is highly structured. Compared to traditional written communication, e-mail is quite versatile and easy to use. Every e-mail system includes a reply feature that enables the responder to include the original message in the text of the new, setting off the original text from the new by using special characters. Therefore, most people generally respond to e-mail point by point. This process enables e-mail recipients to clarify misunderstandings rapidly without retyping or countless rounds of phone tag.

Simply compare the cost of e-mail with the cost of any other type of express mail delivery — or even with the cost of overseas phone calls — and you begin to grasp the effect it can have. Suddenly, enjoying good communications with foreign offices and customers doesn't cost a great deal of money. Suddenly, collaborative work is possible: People can easily and cheaply share files, pictures, and even video and sound. We know — we've been creating entire books for years by using e-mail. (See our *Internet E-Mail For Dummies,* 2nd Edition, published by IDG Books Worldwide, Inc., for more suggestions about using e-mail effectively.)

Bulk e-mail

E-mail is so efficient and cheap that many companies are building e-mail mailing-list servers in place of postal mailing lists or group fax systems. For example, I once helped analyze how an international company could best use the Net. I installed a news release system, publishing the release on the company's Web site and sending it automatically to 400 people around the world as an e-mail message. Because some of the company's contacts don't yet have e-mail, the system is connected to a fax server that sends the release by fax. The cost of the system was recovered in two months, and the investors are happy to receive their messages by e-mail and to be able to use the data directly in their own applications.

Take care when you're sending e-mail unsolicited by the recipients, however, which is traditionally completely unacceptable. One impact of the current democratization of the Internet is the slight softening of those rules, but you must take care. Now it is accepted to send an unsolicited e-mail if you send it to only a few people who are directly interested (for example, using e-mail addresses given by the users of your Web site). Some companies sell large e-mailing lists or send your message to hundreds of thousands of users. They claim that those large mailings can return 2 or 3 percent results, but this number is probably exaggerated.

Moreover, the other 97 percent of the recipients will hate your company for sending them junk e-mail, and most junk e-mailers operate on the fringes of the law, using "throwaway" dial-up accounts to avoid the wave of complaints that junk e-mail always produces and often wreaking technical havoc on the systems of unwilling recipients. Seeing your promotional message quoted in *The Wall Street Journal* as the cause of an Internet shutdown on America Online or hack to the White House e-mail server should not be the kind of coverage you want for your company.

Competitive Intelligence in the Age of Information Overload

If you use the Net or, at least, have seen a demonstration of it, you know the "search agent syndrome." It's the syndrome of the guy looking for information about fish, for example, for his schoolwork. He sends a request to AltaVista (at `http://altavista.digital.com`) and finds hundreds of thousands of documents with the word *fish* in it. Reading through all those documents — which include fishing stories, recipes, and even jokes — would take ten times longer than walking to the library and asking for a good book, even if the library were on the other side of town.

The other form of this syndrome is when your boss talks about buying another company and you — as a new, excited user of the Net — tell him, "No problem, boss — I'll find a bunch of information about the company before you finish your coffee." Then you go to Yahoo, the marvelous directory of the Web, and discover that the company doesn't have a Web site. Is this possible? Of course — many companies don't have Web sites yet.

Clever searching

Does that mean that finding information on the Net works only for engineers and university researchers? No, it just means that effectively searching the Internet is a skill that's learned like anything else. Although I would need at least an entire book to teach you all the techniques, this section gives you some tips.

First, because the search systems available on the Internet are based on *Boolean* (logical) techniques, you should learn the basic commands of this powerful technology. In our first example, rather than type *fish* in the AltaVista search box, you could type *sea fish.* You get more responses rather than fewer, however, because AltaVista lists all the documents with the word *sea* as well as all the documents with the word *fish.* Typing *sea AND fish* gives you the result you're looking for — all the documents that include both words. Better yet, typing *tropical NEAR fish AND NOT recipe* gives you a very good response. You're interested in river fish too, though, so you try *(sea OR ocean OR river) NEAR fish AND NOT recipe.*

That's how Boolean searching works. Boolean operators such as AND, OR, and NEAR look difficult to manage but are easy to learn step-by-step. The AltaVista help page has many good examples; just visit http:// altavista.digital.com and click the Help icon at the top of the page. Each Internet search agent uses its own version of Boolean searching, but the principles and logic stay the same.

Choosing your search page

Next, learn the difference between search agents and directories. *Search agents,* such as AltaVista, Lycos, Web Crawler, and Excite, use robots crawling the Web and trying to index every word on every Web page. Search agents are powerful, and some of them index more than 30 million pages; with this power, however, comes the problem that when you're looking for something generic, you have far too many pages to look through. That's where the directories help. *Directories,* such as Yahoo, Magellan, and A2Z, have lists of Web sites described in a few words and classified by specific criteria. They're perfect when you're looking for something generic. For example, you can go through the Yahoo directory until you reach the category Science/Zoology/Animals or Pets/Marine Life/Fish. Directories such as Yahoo are ideal when you're looking for a global resource (a scientific aquarium Web site, for example), and search agents are better for searching for a specific item, such as a paper published one year ago about the recent evolution of whales.

Directories are less exhaustive than the search agents because they need human intervention for classifying the sites and because a great deal of information is on individual pages and not on sites. Even the largest search engines, such as AltaVista and Hotbot (at `http://www.hotbot.com`) index only a part of the Web and are not updated daily.

Searching newsgroups

The Web isn't the only good source of information; be sure to try Usenet newsgroups too. If your question is interesting, you can be sure that someone has already asked it in a newsgroup, and you can be sure that someone else has responded. Because newsgroups are plagued with inappropriate messages, they're often difficult to follow regularly. Rather than wade through newsgroup messages, use AltaVista or Deja News (at `http://www.dejanews.com`), two Web sites that index the newsgroups. I prefer Deja News because it's designed specifically for searching newsgroups and because it indexes newsgroups starting further back in time than AltaVista. (A project to index all the newsgroup archives from their beginnings in the 1970s is in progress by Deja News in collaboration with MIT. This index will be an invaluable mine of information.)

You can use Deja News in other ways too. For example, a large company asked us to screen what employees were saying about their company to outsiders. Making a search for the e-mail address of those employees in Deja News gave us a good report about their comments even in newsgroups not related to the company or its fields of business. In fact, those tools begin to show problems of privacy. What happens if you find that one of your employees is writing regularly in the `alt.sex.bestiality` newsgroup? How about interviewing a potential employee and saying, "You say that you want to join our company, but seven years ago you criticized it severely in the X and Y newsgroups"?

There are hundreds of other ways to find information on the Net. Using the Net, I can write in three days of work a research report that is more thorough than reports built by experienced analysts in three weeks of Netless work. Small- and medium-size companies can now access the world of competitive intelligence (reserved until now for big corporations), such as an exhaustive study on the strategies of your competitors or specifications of your competitor's products.

Value-Added Web Sites

Now that you've analyzed your competition and its strategy, you have developed your new killer product. It's time to use the Web to promote it and sell it and give your customers support for a fraction of the traditional cost. It's time to open your virtual office on the World Wide Web.

The Web is not a broadcast medium like television or radio. The Web involves *access on demand,* which means that people see your Web site only if they choose to visit it. You may have the coolest Web site on the planet, but without a reason to go there, no one will know about it. In determining how to make your Web site a must-visit kind of place, you have to distinguish between these three categories for your information or service:

- Is it cool, fascinating, scintillating, enthralling, or otherwise unbelievable?
- Can it really improve people's lives and do they really *need* it?
- Do people really *want* it?

Make sure that your Web site contains a healthy dose of the last category. Doing so is the *only* way to ensure that people visit your site.

Actively interactive

Just because your Web site links to other pages doesn't make your site interactive. *Interactive* means that people using the site get to *do* something — for example, buy train tickets, check the weather in Buenos Aires, or determine whether they qualify for a mortgage.

You may have something spectacular to tell everybody about, but at this point, no one even dreams of its existence. How do you get people to look at you, or *for* you, if they don't yet know that they want what you have to offer? One solution is to give them something they *do* want. When they arrive at your site, you have a golden opportunity to show them even more than they're shopping for.

Giving for getting

If you give away something that people want, shouldn't you get something from the deal as well? (Sure, you can *sell* your information, but that's an entirely separate business.) You need to know, for example, exactly *who's* visiting your site. This information can be invaluable to you: It may be the basis of your next prospect list. It may also give you vital demographic information about the people visiting your site. Knowing who's looking at your Web site may even help you understand what people on the Web want — and how you can provide what they want to them. Before allowing people to download your free demo, ask them to fill out a form. Get the data you need. Providing this type of information is a small price that most people are usually willing to pay.

Soliciting required

Ask for feedback on every page. Don't just think that you can put it on the last page — many people never get there. People need a way to communicate with you, and you need their input. Make it easy for people to give you feedback, and acknowledge their feedback in a timely fashion.

Lovely Rita, meter maid

Measuring the success of your Web site is extremely important. Does your site solve the problem you set out to solve? Determine *how* you can measure the success of your site *before* you implement it. This type of success matrix may well guide the design of your site. The number of hits a Web site gets is never a good matrix of success. If you want to increase your sales, for example, you have to determine how you can measure sales as related to your Web site. If you want to reduce calls to customer support, you must make sure that you have a way to track the data on how many people visit your Web site instead.

Steps for developing a successful Web presence

Because no two situations are the same, your best strategy will be unique. Here's an overview of the main steps in developing a strategic Web presence:

1. **Define the purpose of your Web site.** Many objectives can be reached by developing a Web site, but what is your objective? Those objectives must be specific. The more precisely you shoot, the better your chance to put your arrow in the center of the target.

2. **Define the people you want to interact with on your Web site.** Be sure to verify that those people use the Web.

3. **Look at what your competitors are doing on the Web.** They may have spent a great deal of money letting you see how they're dealing with the Web.

4. **Determine why those people will come to your site.** Never think that they will come because you have nice people in your company and because you have good products at low prices. ("Did you visit my home site yet? I can assure you that we're very smart and efficient and charge less than our competition.")

5. **Think about what kind of interaction you will give to your users.** Clicking an underlined word to access a new page is exciting, but it's not interactive. Interaction means that some software deals with the data the users provide, such as searching in a database or simulating a situation. That's the added value for users.

6. **Plan to update your Web site.** If a site doesn't change, users won't need to come back to see the same thing. Your site must be updated frequently, and you must add up-to-date information and new kinds of content to it. The rhythm of updating directly affects many things: how frequently users come back and the work and cost involved in updating and managing the information. Consider installing tools that let you automate the process without having to rewrite everything in HTML codes. The cost of those tools can be quickly amortized.

7. **Think about the promotion of the site.** How will you make your site known to the people you're looking for? Just being listed in AltaVista and Yahoo and other search engines is not sufficient. You can think about ads on the Web, but check carefully first. Because those commercials are very expensive, try to target exactly the people you want to reach. Promote your Web site in your traditional means of communication. In fact, the URL of your site should be present everywhere that the name of your company appears.

8. **Analyze and respond to the feedback from the users of your Web site.** Even if the messages are negative, users are showing interest in your site. They took the time to visit your site and to write to you — capitalize on it. They're telling you freely what you could pay a large amount of money to find out from some market study — what they want.

How much will it cost? That's the one-billion-dollar question. I have another for you: How much does a house cost? It depends on whether you're talking about the White House or some apartments in Harlem or a little farm in Georgia. The costs of a Web site are between $300 for a Web business card and a few million for Web sites like the ones for IBM and Disney. A good budget for starters is between $10,000 and $100,000, depending on the size of your company, the level of competition you have on the Net, and the results you want. Remember that Forrester Research showed that managing

_____

a Web site costs two times more per year than developing it and that opening your Web site is not the end of the process but the beginning of your troubles — the management and the evolution of your site.

French-born Philippe Le Roux is a founder of the Canadian Internet and online services consulting company VDL2, which develops Internet strategies for corporations including the Montreal Stock Exchange, VIA Rail Canada (Canada's rail system), TV5 (International French-speaking television), and Hydro-Quebec (a Quebec utility). He is on the national board for Technology Watch and is editor of Benefice.Net, a Canadian magazine dedicated to business use of Internet technologies. His article "Virtual Intimacy" can be found in Internet SECRETS *(IDG Books Worldwide, Inc., 1995). You can send him e-mail at* `leroux@vdl2.ca.`

Chapter 19

Have I Got a Secret?

● ●

(Contributed by Arnold Reinhold)

In This Chapter

▶ Protecting your e-mail

▶ Responding to security problems

● ●

The Internet is big enough to have both good guys and bad guys, and what bad guys on the Net like to do is to spy on unsuspecting victims. Fortunately, in recent years, cryptographers have found surprisingly effective ways to let you send your messages in code so that even if a bad guy does intercept your messages, he can't figure them out.

Keeping Those Love Letters Private

As your e-mail message travels through the Internet, it goes through many different computers. Someone can intercept and read your message anywhere along the way without too much trouble. Some people on the Internet, however, think that they have solved this security problem.

Public-key cryptography

The basic idea of encryption has been around for thousands of years — Julius Caesar used one of the earliest encryption schemes. You take the message you want to keep secret and scramble (*encode*) it using a *key,* a secret password that tells exactly how the scrambling takes place. You send the scrambled version to the recipient, who then unscrambles (*decodes*) the message. Traditional codes use the same key for encryption and decryption, which causes two problems. One problem is the *key distribution,* which arranges for the sender and recipient of a secret message — but no one else — to have the secret key. The other problem is *key management,* which means having the right key to use for every message you want to send. To keep everything private, you would need a separate key for each possible pair of users — with 1,000 users, you would need 1,000,000 different keys and some mighty big key chains.

The solution to both problems is *public-key cryptography*. Invented in the mid-1970s, this technology simplifies encrypted communication by enabling the general public to exchange keys used to encode messages. Each user has two keys — a secret one (your private key) and a not-at-all-secret one (your public key).

Here's how public-key cryptography works:

If John and Arnold, for example, want to exchange encrypted e-mail, each must first have the other's public key in his computer:

- ✔ John encodes messages to Arnold by using Arnold's public key.
- ✔ Arnold decodes John's messages by using Arnold's secret key.
- ✔ Arnold encodes his reply to John by using John's public key.
- ✔ John decodes Arnold's reply by using John's secret key.

No one ever needs to give anyone else a secret code, yet everyone can communicate with privacy. Anyone can send you a secret message using your public key, but only you can decode those secret messages with your private key. You can tell anyone your public key without giving him or her the ability to read your mail.

You can also use public-key cryptography in reverse to sign your messages in a way that cannot be forged — unless, of course, someone somehow manages to discover your secret key. For signing, you use your private key to encode a message that anyone can then decode using your public key. Because only *your* public key decodes that message, people can be sure that it's from you.

Public-key cryptography has been mired in hot political and legal controversy since its invention. Many governments around the world, including the U.S. government, wish that this technology had never been invented, because it makes it much more difficult for them to listen in on the electronic messages of individuals and companies. Governments are trying their best to control the use of encryption, as illustrated in these examples:

- ✔ Export of strong cryptographic software is illegal in the United States unless it allows government access to your key. See the section "What is key escrow?" later in this chapter.
- ✔ The United States has appointed an Ambassador for Cryptography to coordinate cryptographic policy with other countries.

- ✔ The European Union is considering restrictions on cryptography.
- ✔ France and Russia have banned cryptography outright.

Internet Explorer and Netscape Navigator use public-key cryptography to let you send and receive encrypted information to and from special sites called secure servers. This feature is particularly useful when you want to send your credit card number over the Net. PGP, which we discuss in the next section, uses public-key cryptography to let you send, receive, and sign secure e-mail.

Public-key infrastructure

Before all of us are encrypting all our e-mail, folks on the Internet will need an easy way to obtain and verify someone's public key. One proposed method involves the creation of an international *public-key infrastructure* — a large hierarchy of organizations, sort of like the post office, that would issue keys to people. The infrastructure works like this:

- ✔ Your key is signed by the office that issues it.
- ✔ That office's key is signed by a higher office and so on.
- ✔ The top-level key is no doubt kept in a vault at the United Nations.

A number of companies are in the key-certifying business. In fact, the U.S. Postal Service is even considering offering key certification.

One company that provides this service now is VeriSign, at `http://www.verisign.com`. VeriSign likes to call its certified keys "Internet driver's licenses." It offers these electronic key certificates to the general public at three levels:

- ✔ **Class 1:** Low level of assurance. VeriSign only makes sure that your name and electronic address are unique. You don't have to prove who you are. Sometimes offered free with other software, a Class 1 certificate normally costs $6 per year.
- ✔ **Class 2:** Next level of assurance. Your identity is checked using consumer databases, but without requiring your physical presence. Cost is $12 per year.
- ✔ **Class 3:** A higher level of assurance. If you need additional verification, you have to appear before an agent, such as a notary public. Cost is $24 per year.

Carefully read all the material VeriSign or any other key certifier asks you to accept before signing its subscription agreement.

Internet Programs That Use Encryption

Several widely available Internet applications let you use encryption to send and receive messages more securely.

PGP

PGP, which stands for Pretty Good Privacy, is a freeware encryption program with a strong following on the Internet. If you want electronic privacy, PGP is the program to get. Although others talk about e-mail security, PGP has been providing it for years. Here are some things you should know about PGP:

- It's free only for noncommercial use.

- A commercial version of PGP is available in North America from PGP, Inc. Call the company at 602-944-0773 or visit its Web site at `http://www.pgp.com`.

- The current freeware version of PGP, 2.6.2, is somewhat hard to use. Easier-to-use commercial versions, including a plug-in for Eudora, are being developed by PGP, Inc.

- PGP lets you make your own public and private key pairs at no charge.

- PGP public keys are distributed and certified via an informal network called "the web of trust," which is sort of like the letters of introduction popular in the pre-electronic era. This method raises fewer civil liberties concerns than the public-key infrastructure other systems need. See the section "Public-key infrastructure," earlier in this chapter.

- Most experts consider PGP to be very secure if it's used correctly.

The U.S. government threatened Philip Zimmermann, the developer of PGP, with federal prosecution because PGP had been exported from the United States (but not by him), before dropping the case in January 1996. For the moment, there's no legal challenge to PGP in the United States.

The free version of PGP is distributed in the United States and Canada via the Massachusetts Institute of Technology PGP site:

`http://web.mit.edu/network/pgp.html`

If you're in other parts of the world, you should visit the International PGP home page:

`http://www.ifi.uio.no/pgp`

Programs are available on the Internet that make PGP easier to use. For more information about PGP and related privacy issues, visit Francis Litterio's Cryptography, PGP, and Your Privacy page:

```
http://world.std.com/~franl/crypto.html
```

You may also want to follow the Usenet newsgroups alt.security.pgp and comp.security.pgp.discuss.

To read more about PGP, see Chapter 23 of *Internet E-Mail For Dummies* (IDG Books Worldwide, Inc.).

Netscape Navigator and Internet Explorer

Netscape Navigator and Microsoft Internet Explorer support encrypted transactions — for stuff like submitting filled-out forms and supplying your credit card number over the Net — through a version of public-key cryptography called *SSL*.

Netscape Navigator shows a key icon in the bottom left corner of the screen. If the key is depicted as broken, the connection is not secure.

Only the versions of Netscape Navigator and Internet Explorer offered in North America offer full security. The export and regular free versions have been deliberately weakened to comply with U.S. export regulations. (U.S. residents can download a full-security version of Netscape, but only after affirming U.S. resident status.)

Eudora

Although Eudora — one of the most popular e-mail programs — does not encrypt mail for you, the latest versions let you add plug-in programs that do. Plug-ins are under development for PGP and other encryption schemes, including the National Security Agency's Clipper chip.

Other Hot Topics

While we're on the topic of security, here are some areas that people often ask us about.

Should you give out your credit card number over the Internet?

This question always comes up. Several views on this practice exist.

One camp says that crooks can get credit card numbers in lots of other ways, so why worry about sending yours over the Net? Fishing a discarded paper receipt from a trash can in a back alley is much easier than intercepting messages on the Net. In the United States, a credit-cardholder's liability is limited in cases of fraud to $50 per card.

The other camp says that computer use enables fraud to take place on a much more massive scale than in the past. Therefore, the best available technology should be used to make cyberspace as safe as possible, and we should all insist on secure links before using the Internet for credit-card and other financial transactions.

We think that, in general, the integrity of the outfit to whom you send your card number is more important than any possible theft en route. Indeed, to date, we have *never* heard of a credit card number being stolen while in transit over the Net. (We have heard of people breaking into files on computers connected to the Net, but that problem is a separate issue — in one case, an Internet provider's entire user file, including credit card numbers that had been supplied over the phone and by paper mail, got swiped.)

How secure is public-key cryptography?

Pretty darned secure, we think, with a few ifs:

- ✔ If the program you're using is carefully written. In late 1995, for example, some students discovered several ways to break the encryption then used by Netscape, thanks to errors in the Netscape code. Those errors have been fixed, and we hope that others don't exist. Encryption programs have to be scrutinized by cryptographic experts for a long time (months or years) before anyone will believe that they're secure.

- ✔ If your key is long enough — see the next section.

- ✔ If no breakthroughs in the mathematical knowledge needed to crack public keys occur — progress to date has been slow but steady.

- ✔ If you can keep your private key secret. A bad guy who has the right tools, who knows how to use them, and who can get physical access to your computer can steal your private key without your knowing it.

What are tokens?

Some encryption schemes use *tokens,* credit-card-size modules that plug in to your computer. You store your secret key on a tiny, tamper-resistant encryption computer inside the token. Tokens make it much more difficult for someone to steal your private key.

Although public-key technology is good, you cannot rely on cryptology to keep your messages secret forever.

How should you pick your pass phrase?

A first line of defense against someone stealing your private key is to use software, such as PGP, that encrypts your private key before storing it. You choose a password or phrase that's used as the key for this encryption. If you pick a pass phrase that's too easy to guess (a single word will never do), the encryption can be broken. For advice about picking a secure pass phrase, see the Diceware home page:

```
http://world.std.com/~reinhold/diceware.html
```

How big should your key be?

Public-key encryption depends on arithmetic — lots of arithmetic. Your public key is the product of two large *prime numbers,* which are numbers that cannot be divided evenly by any other number. Your private key is one of those primes.

What makes public-key cryptography work is that, although multiplying two prime numbers is easy — if you're a computer, at least — figuring out which two primes create a particular product is hard. The larger the primes (or, in computerese, the more bits the primes contain), the harder this task.

RSA, the company that owns the patents on this type of public-key cryptography, recommends that your public key be at least this long:

- ✔ For short-term security, 768 bits
- ✔ For medium-term security, 1,024 bits
- ✔ For long-term security, 2,048 bits

The largest public key that can be legally exported from the United States is a 512-bit key, which today's technology can break, albeit with a great deal of work. Most PGP users choose at least 1,024-bit keys.

What is key escrow?

Key escrow is a type of encryption technology in which a master key that can read all your messages is split into pieces. The pieces are stored for safekeeping at two different *escrow agents* — special organizations that promise not to give out your key information without proper authorization. Key escrow appeals to

- ✔ Large organizations which fear that an employee may abscond with the keys needed to decode vital data
- ✔ Law-enforcement and intelligence agencies that want to be able to read the messages of people they consider a threat to society

The U.S. government wants all encryption approved for export to include provisions for government access to keys. The European Union is working on a similar proposal of its own. Civil-liberties groups and many people on the Net are horrified by the idea, likening the concept to that of the police demanding a key to your home in case they ever need to search it.

You can follow this debate on `talk.politics.crypto`, a Usenet newsgroup.

The U.S. government's first attempt to push key escrow, the *Clipper chip,* has not caught on with the public but is being used by the government. If you don't mind the U.S. government having access to your keys, this technology offers well-tested, very strong security. For more information about Clipper-based security solutions, contact the National Security Agency at 800-688-6115.

For more information about security and cryptography, see Chapter 5 in our book *Internet SECRETS* (IDG Books Worldwide, Inc.).

Chapter 20

How to Register Your Own Domain Name

Domain names have class, cachet, and style — having your own domain name shows the world that you're a classy dude (or dudette). Gee, IBM has `ibm.com`, Microsoft has `microsoft.com`, and Procter & Gamble has `diarrhea.com`. Wouldn't it be cool to have your own name as the domain name of your e-mail address, something like `elvis@presley.com`? We thought so too, and John registered a bunch of domains, including `dummies.com` and `dummies.net`, years ago. Margy registered a few too, including `greattapes.com` for her Great Tapes for Kids Web site (check it out at `http://www.greattapes.com`).

Registering a domain name for just yourself doesn't make a great deal of sense — registering takes time and costs about $50 a year. If you have a business, club, or other organization, however, a domain name may be just the thing. If you registered `dummies.net`, for example, you can have a Web server named `www.dummies.net` and an FTP server named `ftp.dummies.net`, and you can receive e-mail addressed to `info@dummies.net` or `sales@dummies.net`. (Our Web server is named `net.dummies.net`, `www.dummies.net`, and `dummies.net` — any one works. We don't have info or sales addresses. Yet.)

What's a domain, anyway?

A *domain* is a name given to a computer or group of computers on the Internet. In the smallest domains, the domain itself is used as a computer name; in most cases, however, other names are assigned within the group. All the computers at the White House, for example, are in the domain whitehouse.gov, such as www.whitehouse.gov and ftp.whitehouse.gov. All the computers on our home network are in the domain iecc.com, such as ivan.iecc.com and caetano.iecc.com.

The last part of a domain name is the *zone*. The three-letter zones, known as *generic* zones, are used mostly for U.S. domains, although most of them accept registrations from around the world.

The com zone is for commercial sites, gov for the U.S. government, edu for educational institutions, net for network organizations, int for international bodies, mil for the U.S. military, and org for other groups, such as nonprofits.

Two-letter zones are used for geographically organized domains: A two-letter zone exists for each country in the world. For example, ca is the Canada zone, and us is the United States zone.

Domains and zones are described in more detail in Chapter 21, and you can find a list of two-letter zones from around the world at http://net.dummies.net/countries.

A way around registering new domains

If your organization already has a domain name, consider using subdomain names rather than registering additional domains. Suppose that you work at The Plebney Group and have registered plebney.com. If you open a new waxed-fruit division, rather than register waxedfruit.com, you can create a second-level domain name as part of plebney.com — waxedfruit.plebney.com. The computers in this new division can have names such as these:

www.waxedfruit.plebney.com

ftp.waxedfruit.plebney.com

sales.waxedfruit.plebney.com.

Setting up subdomains is much easier than getting a new domain name; your organization's system manager can usually create a new subdomain in a few minutes, and you save 50 bucks a year.

What Kind of Domain Do You Want?

The Internet, as a fairly big place, has several different kinds of domains. You can have a full-fledged domain, which can contain lots of different computers, or you can have a simple domain that works only for e-mail. You also have choices about where to register your domain.

Do you have what it takes?

When you register a domain, you're asking to have your domain *delegated* to you. That is, when someone asks for a name in your domain, the name system passes the request to you so that you can answer the request yourself. For this process to work, you need a *domain server,* a computer permanently attached to the Net that can respond to name requests. To make things work reliably, you need at least two separate servers, a main server and at least one backup server, in case the main server or its network link fails. (This two-server requirement is nonnegotiable. Name registries do not accept a registration request without verifying that the two servers for the new domain are working.)

Unless you have at least two separate machines with permanent Net connections, you have to get someone else to be your domain server. In most cases, your Internet provider will, for a modest fee, be your domain server.

If you ask your provider to be your domain server, you may as well ask your provider to handle the entire registration. Provider registration usually doesn't cost much and can save you a great deal of work.

What do you offer?

What do you plan to do with your domain? E-mail? Web pages? FTP archives? If you plan to do anything more than e-mail, you need a server permanently attached to the Net to provide the Web pages, FTP server, and so on. Again, if you don't have a machine permanently connected to the Net, your provider can host your Web pages and other services for you as well.

If you want to use your domain only for an e-mail address, you can use a dial-up machine. You can use a special Domain Name System feature called *mail exchange* (MX) to route all the mail for your domain to your provider's computer, where it can be stored until you call in to pick it up.

Where do you live?

Two kinds of domains are on the Net — geographic domains, which end with a two-letter country code, such as us for the United States, and generic domains, which end with a three-letter code for the type of organization, such as com for companies. People in the United States most often register a generic domain, and people in other countries most often register in their countries' domains. No matter where you live, you can register either way.

Registration is a multistep process: First, pick a name; second, set up domain servers; and third, send an application to the registry that handles the domain you want. The InterNIC is the organization that registers generic domains which end with com, edu, gov, org, or net. For com, org, and net names, InterNIC charges $100 for the first two years and $50 a year thereafter for each domain you register. Table 20-1 lists the country registration contacts for the United States and most English-speaking countries. Drop a short e-mail note to your country's contact to find out your country's registration rules.

If you're in the United States, names in the us domain are structured geographically. Because I.E.C.C. is in Trumansburg, New York, for example, it has a geographic domain name of iecc.trumansburg.ny.us. If you want to register only a single machine or a name simply for e-mail, registering in the us domain is sometimes much easier than registering in any generic domain. For one thing, you don't sometimes have to provide your own domain servers (they just add your entry to their master servers); for another, most of the U.S. domain registries still don't charge anything. We recommend using the us domain, unless you expect to have many different computers in your domain. For more info about the us domain, aim your Web browser at http://www.isi.edu/innotes/usdnr/.

Starting in 1996, "domain speculators" such as nametamer.com, family-domains.com, and southern-domains.com, scooped up a number of cities in the us domain and charge for registrations in them (about $10 per year) while usually providing inferior service. Although this situation is lamentable, it's still cheaper than the $50 per year for the InterNIC domains.

Table 20-1	Country Registration Contacts	
Country	*Contact*	*Address*
Australia	Elz, Robert	kre@munnari.oz.au
Bahamas	Ambrister, Barbara	ambri@cob.edu.bs
Bermuda	DeZoysa, Gamini	gamini@bercol.bm
Canada	Demco, John	demco@cs.ubc.ca
Cayman Islands	Mole, Clint	clint@infogate.ky
Cook Islands	Nordqvist, Jorgen	jnord@gatepoly.co.ck
Fiji	Kumar, Sunil	postmaster@usp.ac.fj
Guam	Nguyen, Luan, Dr.	admin@ns.edu.gu
India	Ramani, Srinivasan	ramani@saathi.ncst.ernet.in
Ireland	Hostmaster Team	hostmaster@ucd.ie
Hong Kong	Ng, Nam	nng@cc.hku.hk
Jamaica	Manison, Keith	manison@uwimona.edu.jm
New Zealand	Houlker, John Charles	j.houlker@waikato.ac.nz
Norfolk Island	Ryan, Robert	rryan@real.com.au
Papua New Guinea	Khademazad, Kamrooz	root@unitech.ac.pg
Puerto Rico	Moreno, Oscar	moreno@uprr.pr
St. Lucia	Daniels, Albert	adaniels@isis.org.lc
Singapore	Tan, Marc	marctan@ncb.gov.sg
South Africa	Lawrie, Mike	mlawrie@frd.ac.za
Trinidad	Hosein, Patrick	hosein@ldc.uwi.tt
United States	Cooper, Ann Westine	us-domain@isi.edu
United Kingdom	Black, Dr. Willie	W.Black@nominet.org.uk
Vanuatu	Audebeau, Jacky	jacky@tvl.net.vu
Zambia	Bennett, Mark	mbennett@unza.zm
Zimbabwe	Sheppard, John	postmaster@zimbix.uz.zw

The seven new domains

In early 1997, an ad hoc committee of Internet powers-that-be known as the International Ad Hoc Committee (IAHC) decided to create seven new domains called firm, store, web, arts, rec, info, and nom. (See Table 21-3 in Chapter 21 for a list of what they're supposed to mean.) At the time this book was printed, the details of registering in these domains hadn't been settled, other than that the InterNIC would *not* be the registrar and a group of 28 registrars around the world would jointly accept registrations. For updated details about registering in these new domains, check our domain update page, at http://net.dummies.net/domains.

"Somebody Took My Name!"

Before you try to register, use the whois service to make sure that the domain name you want isn't already taken. Here's how:

1. **Use your World Wide Web browser to see this Web page:**

   http://www.internic.net/

2. **Choose Registration Services and then Whois Query Form on the page that appears.**

   Alternatively, go directly to this URL:

   http://rs.internic.net/cgi-bin/whois

   You see a Web page that looks something like Figure 20-1.

3. **Type a domain name in the blank and press Enter.**

   If you want to register caviar.com, for example, type that name. (By the way, it's already taken.) When you press Enter, your request flies over the Internet back to InterNIC. You see a response like the one shown in Figure 20-2.

   If whois can't find the domain name, the name is not registered. You're in luck! If some lout has already taken the domain name you had set your heart on, click the Back button on your Web browser and try another name.

Figure 20-1:
Who
registered
this
dandruff
site
anyway?

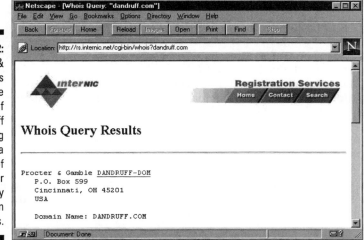

Figure 20-2:
Procter &
Gamble is
listed as the
owner of
the dandruff
site along
with a
bunch of
other
savory
domain
names.

If your computer has a whois program (nearly all UNIX shell systems have one, as do many Windows Internet packages, such as Chameleon), use that program, which is faster.

When you find a domain name that you like and that isn't already taken — bingo! You're ready to move along to the next step.

When you're choosing a domain name, if you decide to use a generic do-main, remember to use the right zone for your domain name (the last part of the name). If you're a commercial organization, use com. If you're a nonprofit organization, use org. If you're a four-year educational institution, use edu.

Where Will Your Domain Live?

A domain name has to be connected to a computer on the Internet. In fact, a domain can be used for one, two, or hundreds of Internet hosts — just imagine how many computers with names ending in microsoft.com or digital.com must be on the Net! No matter what, you need at least one Internet host computer to which your new domain name can apply or that at least can receive mail for your domain.

You can arrange to have at least one Internet host computer in two ways: Do so yourself, or get your Internet provider to do so.

Do it yourself

If your organization has its own permanently connected Internet hosts, talk to the system administrator to find out whether the new domain name can apply to an existing computer in your organization. One computer can have lots of domain names. For example, John has one computer named dummies.net, ivan.iecc.com, www.dummies.net, ftp.dummies.net, iecc.com, jclt.com, gurus.com, creamery.com, www.creamery.com, services.net, abuse.net, greattapes.com, www.greattapes.com, and a few other miscellaneous names.

You also need two permanently connected Internet hosts that agree to be domain name servers for your domain. Your system administrator can probably help you with this process too.

Get your Internet provider to do it

Your commercial Internet provider can list your new domain on its domain name servers. Simply ask your provider to register your domain name (see the next section), and the provider handles the domain name server business.

Registering Your Name

After you have chosen a domain name that no one else has registered, found a computer on which to use the name, and enlisted two domain name servers to list your new domain name, you're ready to register your name. Again, you can either register your name yourself or get your Internet provider to do so. One of our Internet providers (TIAC, in Bedford, Massachusetts) charges about $20 to do the job.

To register a generic domain yourself, send a form by e-mail to InterNIC. If you want to register within your country's domain, the process is similar, but you have to ask your country's registration contact (refer to Table 20-1) for the details.

Here's how to register a name at InterNIC:

1. **Use your Web browser to visit the form-creation pages at the InterNIC. (A partial example is shown in Figure 20-3.) The form is available on the Web at this URL:**

   `http://rs.internic.net/cgi-bin/itts/domain`

Figure 20-3:
The domain registration form from InterNIC.

2. **Enter your e-mail address and the name of the domain you want to register on the first screen, click the New button, and then click the bar at the bottom of the page to continue to the next screen.**

3. **Fill out each page, following the instructions that are given.**

   You have to give the name and address of the organization registering the domain (which can just be you); a one-sentence purpose of the domain; name, phone, and e-mail addresses of the administrative, technical, zone, and billing contacts (which can also all be you); and the names and numerical addresses of at least two domain servers for the domain. You also have to give some security rules about who's allowed to make changes to the domain; the default "mail from" is okay.

4. **When you have completed the form, InterNIC e-mails it to you.**

   This process seems strange, but there's a good reason: It wants to make sure that it's you who was creating that domain and not some prankster elsewhere on the Web.

5. **Remail the form by e-mail to** hostmaster@internic.net.

   You will receive a reply from the InterNIC mail robot, including a tracking number. If you need to send any e-mail asking about your registration, be sure to include the tracking number in the subject line of the e-mail. InterNIC can take anywhere from ten minutes to several months to process a domain registration, depending on its workload and the whim of its registration software.

   Sooner or later, you get a response from InterNIC, confirming that your domain is registered. InterNIC may also reject the registration if, for example, someone else registered the same name minutes before you did or if your two domain name servers didn't list your new domain properly.

6. **Pay your bill.**

   After a while, you get an invoice from InterNIC for the domain. As of 1997, registering a domain name costs $100, which includes the first two years' fees. After that time, you're charged $50 per year.

Remember that InterNIC accepts these forms *only* by e-mail. Don't print the forms to complete by hand. Only e-mail will do. Be sure to check the InterNIC home page (at http://www.internic.net/) for any changes in the registration instructions since the time this book was printed.

Now What?

After your domain is set up, you have to connect it to something. Again, your system administrator or your Internet provider is the first place to ask about setting up e-mail, a Web server, and other services in your new domain.

First, get your Internet provider or system administrator to set up the mail system so that you can get e-mail at your new domain. You have to specify what should happen to mail addressed to users with names such as `info`, `postmaster`, `sales`, `help`, and the like at your domain because people wanting to know about your domain are likely to send mail to those addresses. You must be able to handle mail to `postmaster`. All other mail addresses are optional.

Our Internet provider charges about $20 per month to maintain a Web address such as `http://www.whatever.com/` for Web pages. Your Internet provider may also be willing to provide space on its FTP server for your files so that you can offer files with a domain name of `ftp.whatever.com`.

Part VI
Hideous
Technical Details

The 5th Wave   By Rich Tennant

"IT HAPPENED AROUND THE TIME WE SUBSCRIBED TO AN ON-LINE SERVICE."

In this part . . .

John is addicted to knowing exactly what's going on under the hood, and we know that lots of our readers are too. Well, some of our readers. A few of our readers. Actually, we got two e-mail messages requesting this stuff, only one of which we wrote ourselves. Anyway, if you want to know about protocols, ports, packets, links, networks, and circuits, this part of the book is for you.

Chapter 21
A Look under the Hood

This chapter contains gruesome details about how the Internet sends data from one place to another. You can skip this entire part of the book, if you want. We don't advise that you do, however, because we think that this stuff is interesting. The first few pages of this chapter even contain stuff that mortals may use in day-to-day Net work. (Hmmm, guess that means if you read the rest of this chapter, you must be an immortal.)

First, Get Organized

When you send an e-mail message or ask to see a Web page, the address includes the name of the host computer, the part that looks like `www.yahoo.com` or `net.dummies.net`. Okay, so more than three million computers are attached to the Internet, and you're looking for information on a particular host computer. How do you find the host computer you want? You have two options. (Nobody said that this was going to be simple.) Each machine on the Net can be identified by a number and by a name. First, we look at the numbers and then at the names.

Executive summary

The way the numbers and names are assigned on the Internet is, unavoidably, fairly technical. Here's the short version, in case you would rather save the full version for later:

✔ Each machine on the Net (called a *host* in Internet-ese) has a number assigned to identify it to other hosts, sort of like a phone number. The numbers are in four parts, such as 123.45.67.89. You should know the host number of the computer you use most; otherwise, you can forget about the numbers. If you use a dial-up connection that lets you use Internet applications such as Netscape or Eudora, your computer has a host number while it's connected to the Net. (It may also have a host number while it's not connected to the Net, but we get to that in a moment.)

✔ Most hosts also have names, which are much easier to remember than numbers. Dots separate the names' multiple parts (for example, `chico.iecc.com`, the name of one of our computers). Although hosts can have more than one name, which name you use doesn't matter.

✔ Complicated rules control how names and numbers are assigned. Because you're not likely to be doing any of the assigning, however, you don't really have to know these rules.

✔ Each network on the Internet has rules about which types of network traffic (e-mail, terminal sessions, and other connections) it allows. You should know the rules that apply to the network or networks you use to avoid getting the network managers mad at you.

What's in a number?

Any computer of any kind, from the smallest to the largest, that's attached to the Internet is called a *host* (which must make us users parasites — yuck). Some hosts are giant mainframes or supercomputers providing services to thousands of users. Some are little workstations or PCs with one user. Some are specialized computers, such as routers, which connect one network to another, or terminal servers, which let dumb terminals and PCs dial in and connect to other hosts. From the Internet point of view, all these things are hosts.

Each machine is assigned a host number, which is sort of like a phone number. Hosts, because they're computers, like 32-bit binary numbers. For example, the number of one of our computers is

```
11001101111011101100111101011100
```

Hmmm. That number is not very memorable. To make the number slightly easier to remember, it's broken up into four 8-bit groups. Each group is then translated into a decimal equivalent, so our computer's number turns into

```
205.238.207.92
```

Although that number isn't a whole lot better, at least it's possible for humans to remember for a minute or two.

How much should I care about these numbers?

By and large, you can get by without knowing any host numbers because you use, in most cases, the much more memorable host names described in the section "What's in a Name?," later in this chapter. Occasionally, though, the naming scheme breaks down. In this type of case, writing down the following two numbers is helpful:

✔ The number of the computer you use, if you use a SLIP, PPP, or shell connection (If you use a provider such as AOL or CompuServe, you don't get a number.)

✔ The number of a nearby computer to which you have access

If you can contact a nearby computer by number but not by name, you can reasonably conclude that your connection to the naming system has failed. If you can't contact a nearby computer either way, it's more likely that the network, or at least your network connection, has failed, quite possibly because you inadvertently kicked a cable loose. Oops.

Networks have numbers too?

We're afraid so. Consider, for a moment, your phone number, which is something like 202-653-1800. In the phone number, the first six digits designate where the phone exchange is located — in this case, Washington, D.C. The last four digits are a particular phone in that exchange. (Call it for a good time, by the way).

Internet host numbers are also divided into two parts: the network number and the local part. (Remember that many different but interconnected networks comprise the Internet.) The local part is a host number on that particular network. In the case of the computer we mentioned, host number 205.238.207.92 means network number 205.238.207 and local host number (on that network) 92. Sometimes, for added confusion, people write out network numbers in four parts by adding zeros, such as 205.238.207.0.

Because some networks have more hosts than others, networks are divided into three sizes: large, medium, and small. In large networks (Class A), the first of the four numbers is the network number, and the last three numbers are the local part. In medium networks (Class B), the first two numbers are the network number, and the last two are the local part. In small networks (Class C), the first three numbers are the network number, and the last is the local part.

The first of the four numbers tells you the network's class. Table 21-1 summarizes classes and sizes.

Table 21-1		Network Numbers and Sizes	
Class	First Number	Length of Net Number	Maximum Number of Hosts
A	1–126	1	16,387,064
B	128–191	2	64,516
C	192–223	3	254

Great big organizations (or at least organizations that have a huge number of computers) tend to have Class A networks. Because IBM has network 9 and AT&T has network 12, for example, host number 9.12.34.56 is at IBM, and 12.98.76.54 is at AT&T. Medium-size organizations, including most universities, have Class B networks. Rutgers University has network 128.6, and Goldman-Sachs (an investment broker that must use a number of computers to keep track of all the money it handles) has network 138.8. Class C networks are used by small organizations and sometimes small parts of large organizations. Network 192.65.175, for example, is used by a single IBM research lab. (Why don't they use the general IBM network number? Who knows?)

Rules of conduct

Parts of the Internet have fairly firm rules of conduct. Depending on which part of the Net you're attached to, the rules may be more or less strict. The most restrictive rules were for the NSFNET, which in its day prohibited all commercial activity. Regional networks have less restrictive policies, and commercial networks are less restrictive still. All reserve the right to boot you off for malicious or destructive conduct. Be aware of the rules that apply to your site, and be prepared to honor them.

If you're on a less restrictive network and decide to use a more restrictive one — for example, you log on to a machine at an educational institution that uses the NSFNET rules — you're subject to the most restrictive rules of any net you use.

Most networks require that users act in a way that doesn't adversely and unnecessarily affect other network users or users of other networks to which they're connected. Networks at educational institutions usually require, because of their tax-exempt status, that users of their network refrain from using the network for direct commercial advantage. This limitation typically means that ordering something over the Net or posting short "for sale" messages about used stuff you want to get rid of is okay, but advertising or taking orders for a business with which you're affiliated is not. Don't take our word for it, though — check out your network's rules before, rather than after, someone gets mad at you for breaking them.

Some host and network numbers are reserved for special purposes. In particular, any number with a component of 0 or 255, two numbers with great mystical significance to computers, is special and can't be used as an actual host number. (Although this statement is a slight exaggeration, it's close enough for most purposes.)

Networking on the cheap

Early on, all the networks on the Internet were big, industrial-strength networks that had permanent, expensive adapters to connect their computers. In the 1980s, a researcher at M.I.T. was working on connecting then-new IBM PCs to the M.I.T. network, and the thought occurred to him that you didn't have to use those expensive network adapters. PCs have cheap *serial ports,* originally designed to connect to printers and modems but quite capable of carrying network data, so in about two minutes, he invented a *Serial Line Internet Protocol,* also known as *SLIP.* We have been stuck with SLIP ever since. SLIP makes a network from two computers connected through a serial line. (The M.I.T. guy didn't think that SLIP was that great — the note he wrote describing SLIP calls it a "nonstandard" — but that didn't stop him from starting a rather successful company to develop and sell PC Internet software.)

SLIP connections originally were *hardwired* — a wire went directly from the serial port on one computer to the serial port on another computer, and the only way to change the network setup was to change the plugs. Serial ports connect just fine to dial-up modems, however, so with only a little extra twiddling, setting up a SLIP connection between two computers connected by modems and a phone line, even computers thousands of miles apart, became possible. This trick became wildly popular, and these days the standard way you connect your PC to your Internet provider is with a SLIP or SLIP-like connection. Because a SLIP connection is considered to be a network, it has a network number, and each of the serial ports on the end has a host number, at least while the connection is active.

What's the point!

After people realized that SLIP was here to stay, its shortcomings became impressively apparent. (On a dial-up connection, for example, SLIP doesn't offer any way for one end to check who the other end is, a security hole roughly the size of the Grand Canyon, which in practice has to be addressed with a variety of software Band-Aids.) The Internet powers-that-be went to work to figure out what a SLIP-like scheme should really do. They came up with the *Point to Point Protocol,* or *PPP.*

Subnets, supernets, super-duper nets. . . .

This discussion is extremely technoid. Don't say that we didn't warn you.

Frequently, an organization that has a single network number wants to set up its computers internally on multiple networks. All the computers in a single department, for example, are usually attached on a single network, with some sort of connection linking department networks. (Although both administrative and technical reasons exist for this arrangement, we don't bore you with those details.) Adhering to the way the Internet was originally set up means that an outfit with 25 internal networks would have to get 25 different network numbers.

This need for multiple network numbers was bad news for several reasons. Every time a company wanted to set up a new internal network, it had to apply for a new network number. Even worse, the rest of the Internet world had to put that network number in their tables so that they knew how to route messages to it.

Clearly, something had to be done. That something is *subnets*. One network can be divided into pieces called subnets. On a subnet, part of what would normally be the host number now becomes part of the network number. For example, we used to be attached to network 140.186. In addresses on that network, the third number in the host number is the subnet number. For machine 140.186.83.1, therefore, the subnet number is 140.186.83, and the host number is 1. Subnets enable plenty of local networks to be installed. (They currently use only 80 of the 254 possible subnets in that network.) As far as the outside world is concerned, they still have only the single network 140.186 to worry about.

In practice, all except the smallest networks are subnetted, and you almost never have to worry about subnets. When your computer is first attached to the Net, the guru who installs it has to set its *subnet mask* to reflect the local subnet setup. If the mask is wrong, you may have strange problems, such as being able to communicate with half your company's departments (such as the even-numbered ones and not the odd-numbered ones).

Many organizations have an opposite problem. They have too many computers for a Class C network (more than 254) but nowhere near enough to justify a Class B. (These days, the demand for network numbers is so great that getting anything bigger than a Class C is practically impossible.) In this case, the organization can get a block of adjacent network numbers and treat part of the network number as a host number, in a process called *supernetting*.

The supernetted number is then invariably subnetted, an extra wart we don't even start to consider. Supernetting is uncommon now but will become more widely used as more companies put a large number of computers on the Internet. As with subnetting, you don't have to worry about the supernetted number unless someone screws up your system's configuration.

The final straw in this load of camel, er, whatever, is *Classless Internet Domain Routing*, invariably abbreviated *CIDR*, which is pronounced "cider." CIDR lets network managers treat groups of networks and subnets of whatever class as a single network. Again, you don't have to worry about CIDR unless someone screws up your system's configuration.

From a user's point of view, there isn't much difference between SLIP and PPP. They both do the same thing — transfer data over a serial line — and they both do so at about the same speed. PPP is a zillion times easier to set up, however. If you have a SLIP connection, all the SLIP options have to be set up by hand before the SLIP connection starts. If you get anything wrong, the usual symptom is that the connection mysteriously hangs. PPP does *protocol negotiation,* in which the two computers have a little chat when they're first connected and automatically come up with the best usable set of options. Because the two computers set the options automatically, you don't have to, and much less can go wrong at setup time.

We return to the gory details of SLIP and PPP in Chapter 22, but what we have told you is already more than you need to know to be able to use them.

Multiple multiple numbers numbers

A final added confusion in host and network numbering is that some hosts have more than one number. The reason is quite simple: Because some hosts are on more than one network, they need a host number on each of the networks to which they're attached. If you need to contact a machine with multiple host numbers, which number you use doesn't matter.

What's in a Name?

Because normal people use names, not numbers, Internet hosts — in a rare bow to normality — are usually referred to by name, not by number. For example, the machine we have heretofore referred to as 205.238.207.92 is named chico. In the earliest days of the ARPANET, machines had simple one-part names, and a master list of names existed. The machine at Harvard was called HARVARD, for example. Although simple names worked fine on a net with only 100 hosts, with a million machines on the Net, coming up with different names for all strains the creativity of even the most dedicated literary nerd.

To avoid a crisis of naming creativity, the solution was to go to multipart names, in a scheme grandly known as the *Domain Name System,* or DNS. Host names are a string of words (or at least wordlike things) separated by dots. In the multipart regime, chico's real name is CHICO.IECC.COM. (The naming scheme was evidently invented by people WHO LIKE TO SHOUT EVERYTHING IN CAPITAL LETTERS. Lowercase in host names is, fortunately, taken to be equivalent to uppercase, and henceforth we avoid shouting and put the names in lowercase.)

Zones, domains, and all that

You decode an Internet name from right to left, which may seem perverse. Reading a name backward, however, turns out in practice to be more convenient than the other way around, for the same reason we put surnames after first names. (In England, where they drive on the left side of the road, they used to write host names from left to right. Typical.)

The rightmost part of a name is called its *zone*. If we examine chico's full name, the rightmost part is com, which means that this address is a commercial site (in the com zone), as opposed to educational, military, or some other types of zones we mention in the next section.

The next part of chico's name, iecc, is the name of John's company, the Invincible Electric Calculator Company. (Yes, it's sometimes pronounced "yecch" — John should have picked a better abbreviation.) The part to the left of the company name is the particular machine within the company. Because this address happens to be a rather small company with only six computers, chico's friends milton, tom, ivan, astrud, and xuxa are known as milton.iecc.com, tom.iecc.com, astrud.iecc.com, ivan.iecc.com, and xuxa.iecc.com.

Logic actually exists for the naming of chico and friends. They're named after our favorite Brazilian singers. Chico (pronounced "SHEE-ku") is Chico Buarque, who's quite political. Tom (pronounced "tome") is the late Antonio Carlos "Tom" Jobim, who wrote *Girl from Ipanema,* best known in the United States from a soda pop ad 25 years ago. Milton is Milton Nasciemento, who's more lyrical and melodic. Ivan is Ivan Lins, who, after an early embarrassing "soul man" period, has found his niche with solid, popular, melodic pieces. (He even shows up on the Net for the occasional online chat.) Xuxa is sort of a cross between Madonna and Mr. Rogers. Astrud is Astrud Gilberto, known in the United States for singing the original pre-soda-pop version of *Girl from Ipanema.*

The host naming system is quite egalitarian. In it, iecc.com, a company with one and two-thirds employees, is right up there with ibm.com, a company with several hundred thousand employees. Larger organizations usually further subdivide machine names by site or department; a typical machine in the computer science department at Yale University is called bulldog.cs.yale.edu. Each organization can set up its names any way it wants, though in practice names with more than five components are rare, not to mention hard to remember and type.

If you type a simple host name with no dots, your local computer assumes that the rest of the name is the same as the computer you're using. If we're logged in to milton and want to contact chico, for example, we can simply refer to chico, and our local computer assumes that we mean chico.iecc.com.

Are you on the Internet, or aren't you?

The most popular Internet service is still electronic mail, and many mail systems not directly attached to the Internet have indirect connections, using an intermediate system on the Net to pass messages back and forth. Originally, to send mail to these indirectly connected mail systems, you had to use strange and ugly mail addresses that involved lots of illegible and incomprehensible punctuation. The Internet powers-that-be eventually arranged a special feature, *mail exchange,* or *MX,* host names to handle all this mail. For the purposes of sending mail, an MX name works like any other name; for any other service, however, the host doesn't exist. Because MCI Mail has a mail connection to the Internet, for example, you can send mail to users at `mcimail.com`. Because that's an MX address, however, you can't use the World Wide Web, FTP, finger, or other Internet services to contact `mcimail.com`. (It does have a Web page now, at `www.mcimail.com`.)

The Twilight Zone?

Zones (the rightmost part of the host name) are divided into three general categories: the three-letter kind and the two-letter kind. The three-letter and longer zones are sort of set up by organization. You have seen `com` for commercial. Table 21-2 lists the rest of the traditional three-letter zone names, and Table 21-3 lists the new general-purpose zones created in early 1997.

Table 21-2	Traditional Three-Letter Zone Names
Zone	*What It Means*
com	Commercial organizations
edu	Educational institutions
gov	U.S. government bodies and departments
int	International organizations
mil	Military sites
net	Networking organizations
org	Anything else that doesn't fit elsewhere, such as professional societies

Table 21-3	New General-Purpose Zone Names
Zone	**What It Means**
firm	Businesses or firms
store	Businesses offering goods to purchase
web	Activities related to the Web
arts	Cultural and entertainment activities
rec	Recreation and entertainment activities
info	Information services
nom	Individual or personal names (*nom* is French for "name")

In the United States, most Internet sites have names in one of the three-letter zones. Elsewhere, other countries usually use geographic names, which are discussed in the next section.

Where's Vanuatu?

Two-letter zone names are geographically organized. Each zone corresponds to a country or Other Recognized Political Entity. An official international standards list of two-letter country codes exists and is used almost but not quite unmodified as the list of two-letter zones. Because the country code for Canada is CA, a host at York University in Canada is called nexus.yorku.ca. Each country's network administrators can assign names as they see fit. Some countries have organization-level subdivisions; a site at an Australian university, for example, is called sait.edu.au. Other countries assign names more haphazardly. Because a two-letter code exists for every country in the world, a host whose name ends in vu, for example, is in Vanuatu.

Is there a complete list of host names anywhere?

No. In principle, you should be able to go through all the systems where names are registered and enumerate them all. People used to try to do that, partly out of nosiness and partly out of an interest in collecting network statistics. They gave up after the Net had grown to the point that the collection program ran for more than a week and still hadn't finished.

In the United States, few computers have names in the geographic U.S. zone, which is organized by city and state. Because I.E.C.C. was in Cambridge, Massachusetts, `chico.iecc.com` used to be known as `iecc.cambridge.ma.us`. (John hadn't named it chico yet because at the time it was the only computer he had.) In the United States, the choice of geographic or organizational names is somewhat arbitrary. If you have one or two machines, getting a geographic name is easier. If you have more computers, getting an organizational name, which lets you administer names within your organization yourself, is easier. (Chapter 20 has the gruesome details of how names are registered.)

Table 21-4 lists common geographic zone names. You can find a complete list at our Web site:

```
http://net.dummies.net/countries
```

Incidentally, Vanuatu, an island in the South Pacific, was formerly known as the Condominium of the New Hebrides. France and Britain jointly administered the island; when you arrived, you had to state whether you wanted to be subject to French or British law. Now Vanuatu has a limited dial-up Internet connection, and we have gotten e-mail from there.

Table 21-4	Common Two-Letter Zone Names
Zone	**Country**
AU	Australia
AT	Austria (Republic of)
BE	Belgium (Kingdom of)
CA	Canada
CZ	Czech Republic
DK	Denmark (Kingdom of)
FI	Finland (Republic of)
FR	France (French Republic)
DE	Germany (Federal Republic of)
IN	India (Republic of)
IE	Ireland
IL	Israel (State of)
IT	Italy (Italian Republic)

(continued)

Table 21-4 *(continued)*

Zone	Country
JP	Japan
NL	Netherlands (Kingdom of the)
NO	Norway (Kingdom of)
RU	Russian Federation
SU	Former Soviet Union (officially obsolete but still in use)
ES	Spain (Kingdom of)
SE	Sweden (Kingdom of)
CH	Switzerland (Swiss Confederation)
TW	Taiwan, Province of China
UK	United Kingdom (official code is GB)
US	United States (United States of America)

Other random zones

You may run into a few other zones and pseudozones. Even though the ARPANET, the Internet's predecessor, has been officially dead for years, a few sites still, for historical reasons, have names ending in arpa. As for machines on the UUCP and BITNET networks, you occasionally see names ending in uucp and bitnet. These zones aren't real, and hence names using them aren't really valid host names, but many systems treat these names as special cases and route mail to them anyway. Because any BITNET or UUCP site can arrange to get itself a real host name, bitnet and uucp names are heading for well-deserved oblivion.

Why the Post Office Isn't Like the Phone Company

Gruesome detail alert: The details of what goes on in the Net get much more gruesome from here on. Although you don't *have* to know any of the stuff in the rest of this chapter to be able to use this book, we still think that these little details are interesting.

Enough of this administrative nonsense. We get back to the grotty details. What the Internet does, basically, is transmit data from one computer to another. How hard could that be? Although it's not that hard, it is fairly complicated.

The most familiar examples of information transfer in real life are the post office and the phone company. If you want to contact someone by telephone, you pick up the phone and dial the number. The phone company then arranges an electrical circuit from your phone to the phone you're calling. You and the other person gossip until you're done, or, if you're calling on a modem, your computer and the other computer gossip until they're done, and then you hang up, at which point the phone company releases the circuit. Then you can call someone else. At any particular moment, you can have only one call in progress over a particular phone line. (Yeah, you can use three-way calling, but that doesn't count.) This scheme is called *circuit switching* because a circuit is set up for the duration of the conversation. Well, the Internet doesn't work this way, so forget this nice little scenario. (Don't entirely forget it; we come back to simulated circuit switching later.)

The other model is the post office. If you want to mail a package to someone, you write the recipient's address and your return address and mail your goodies. The United States Postal Service doesn't have dedicated trucks from every post office to every other post office. (The post office may be inefficient, but it's not *that* inefficient.) Instead, the package is routed from your local post office to a central post office, where it's then loaded on a truck or a train headed in the general direction and repeatedly passed from office to office until it gets to the recipient's post office, at which point a letter carrier delivers it to the door along with the rest of the day's mail.

The Internet works more like this second scenario. Each time a host wants to send a message to another host, either the recipient is on a network to which the first host is directly connected, in which case it can send the message directly, or else it's not. In that case, the sender sends the message to a host that can forward it. The forwarding host, which presumably is attached to at least one other network, in turn delivers the message directly if it can or passes it to yet another forwarding host. A message passing through a dozen or more forwarders on its way from one part of the Net to another is quite common.

You're probably wondering, "What kind of cretin would think that the post office is a better model than the phone company?"

Don't be led astray by the analogy. The main complaints that people have about the post office are that it's slow and it loses stuff. Although the Internet occasionally has both these problems, they're not as much of an issue as they are with paper mail. In the middle of a busy day, the Net can indeed slow down, though the time a message takes to be delivered is still measured in seconds. Losing stuff turns out not to be a problem in practice, for reasons discussed later in this chapter, in the section, "TCP: The Rocket-Powered Mailman."

All the world's a packet

Let's take the postal analogy a step further. Suppose that you want to send a copy of the manuscript for your new and very long book to a close friend in the island nation of Papua New Guinea. (Papua New Guinea, a country so primitive it can't even afford any punctuation in its name, doesn't have many bookstores.) Unfortunately, the manuscript weighs 15 pounds, and the limit on packages to Papua New Guinea is 1 pound. So you divide the manuscript into 15 pieces, and on each package you write something like "Part 3 of 15" and send them off. When the packages eventually arrive, probably not in the right order, your friend takes all the pieces, puts them back in order, and reads them.

The various networks on the Internet work in pretty much the same way: They pass data around in chunks called *packets,* each of which carries the addresses of its sender and its receiver (those host numbers we talk about earlier in this chapter). The maximum size of a packet varies from network to network, but is generally between 100 and 2,000 *octets* (Internet-speak for *bytes* or *characters*). A typical size is 1,536 octets, which, for some long-forgotten reason, is the limit on an Ethernet network, the most popular type of local network. Messages too large for a single packet have to be sent as several packets.

One advantage the Internet has over the post office is that when Internet software breaks a large package of data into smaller pieces, putting the pieces back together is no problem. When the post office delivers something in small pieces, you're generally out of luck.

Defining the Internet protocols

The set of conventions used to pass packets from one host to another is known as the *Internet Protocol,* or *IP.* (Catchy, huh? The network is named after the protocol, not the other way around.) The Internet is, quite simply, the collection of networks that pass packets to each other using IP.

You can set up a network that uses IP but that isn't really connected to the Internet. Many networks are set up that way in companies that want to take advantage of IP (which comes free with every UNIX workstation and now also with Mac System 7 and Windows 95). These inside networks are often called *intranets* and are often used to distribute information inside the company using e-mail, Net news, and particularly the World Wide Web (Netscape, Explorer, and all that) the same way they're used to send information around outside.

In the past, many intranets weren't connected at all to the outside world or were connected by only a funky mail connection. In the past year or two, many of these disconnected networks have gotten hooked to the Internet. That's partly because the advantages of being on the Net have increased and mostly because new commercial Internet vendors have made the cost of connection about a tenth of what it used to be. In many cases, a *firewall* computer monitors and controls the connections between the internal and external networks, but don't worry, it's a detail. (Oh, wait, this whole chapter is about details. Well, a firewall is a particularly detailed detail.)

Many protocols are used in connection with IP. The two best known are *Transmission Control Protocol* (*TCP*) and *User Datagram Protocol* (*UDP*). TCP is so widely used that many people refer to it as *TCP/IP,* the combination of TCP and IP used by most Internet applications.

I'll build a gateway to paradise

To work, the Internet has to be able to pass packets from one network to the next so that packets can get routed from the network where they originate to the network of their destination. Three kinds of things (for lack of a better term) pass packets from one Internet network to another: bridges, routers, and gateways. Here's a quick rundown of the differences so that you can hold your own at nerd cocktail parties.

Bridges

A *bridge* connects two networks in a way that makes them appear to be a single, larger network. Bridges most commonly are used to connect two Ethernet local-area networks. (An Ethernet physically consists of a long cable connecting all the machines on a network, and a single cable's length is limited.) The bridge looks at all the packets flying by on each network, and, when it sees a packet on one network destined for a host on the other, the bridge copies it over.

Ethernet host numbers (which, of course, are different from Internet host numbers) are assigned by the serial number of the Ethernet card rather than by network number. The only way the bridge can tell what hosts are on which network is to build a big table listing all the hosts on each network, based on the return addresses of all the packets flying by on each network. It's a miracle that it works at all.

The good thing about bridges is that they work *transparently* — the hosts whose packets are being bridged do not have to be aware that a bridge is involved, and a single bridge can handle a bunch of different kinds of network traffic (such as Novell Netware as well as IP) at the same time. The disadvantages of bridges are that they can connect only two networks of the same type and that bridging fast networks that are not physically next to each other is expensive.

Routers

A *router* connects two or more IP (that's the Internet Protocol) networks. Although the hosts on the networks have to be aware that a router is involved, that's no problem for IP networks because one IP rule is that all hosts have to be able to talk to routers.

- ✔ A good thing about routers is that they can attach physically different networks, such as a fast, local Ethernet to a slower, long-haul phone line.

- ✔ A bad thing about routers is that they move packets slower than bridges do. Figuring out how to route packets requires more calculation than it does to bridge them, particularly when the networks are of different speeds.

Because a fast network can deliver packets much faster than a slow network can take them away, causing network constipation, the router has be capable of telling a sending host to talk more slowly.

Another problem is that routers are *protocol-specific:* The way a host talks to an IP router is different from the way it talks to, for example, a Novell router. This problem is now addressed by the router equivalent of a Ginsu knife that slices and dices every which way and knows about routing every type of network known to humankind. These days, all commercial routers can handle multiple protocols, usually at extra cost for each added protocol. Incidentally, this type of router is usually pronounced "ROO-ter," (except in Australia) because a "ROW-ter" is something you use in a woodworking shop.

Gateways

A *gateway* splices together two different kinds of protocols. If your network talks IP, for example, and someone else's network talks Novell or DECnet or SNA or one of the other dozen Leading Brands of Network, a gateway converts traffic from one set of protocols to another. Gateways are specific not only to particular protocols but also to particular applications. The way you convert, for example, electronic mail from one network to the other is quite different from the way you convert a remote terminal session. Gateways are difficult to do correctly, which is why Internet mail to or from a cc:Mail or other office mail system often arrives smashed — the gateway did it.

Routers: the good, the bad, and the really bad

A hot topic among Internet weenies these days is Routing Policy. The Internet is, for the most part, *redundantly connected:* You can get from one network to another in several ways. In the good old days, finding a route was relatively easy because the main goal was to find the shortest route to each known network. Because only a handful of networks were around, the routers (hosts that pass packets from one network to another) simply compared notes to figure out which one had the shortest route to where. If you wanted to be really fancy and if you had two equally fast routes to somewhere, you could monitor the amount of traffic on each route and send packets by the less busy route.

Things are no longer so simple. For starters, the number of networks of which a router has to be aware is no longer a handful (unless you have extraordinarily large hands). More than 100,000 different networks are attached to the Internet, and more are added weekly. Furthermore, the speeds of communication lines have increased much more quickly than have the speeds of computers used for routing, enough so that special hardware is needed to keep up with the networks that will be installed in the next few years.

Another issue is that political as well as technical distinctions exist among networks. The Commercial Internet Exchange (CIX), for example, has a router that handles traffic for only CIX members and their immediate customers. This means that some traffic can't be routed the most direct way, if the traffic isn't appropriate for one of the networks on that route.

Another wart on the face of routing is that many organizations have *firewall* routers that pass only certain kinds of traffic. Typically, firewall routers allow incoming electronic mail but not incoming remote terminal sessions or file transfers, in an effort to keep out ill-mannered users looking for security holes (if you have a large enough internal network, a hole will certainly be found somewhere).

Lots of technical papers are published about advanced new routing schemes, policies, or whatever, each with a new three- or four-letter acronym. (OSPF and BGP are currently trendy, and RIP and EGP are passé. What they stand for doesn't matter.) You as a user can, fortunately, ignore the issue because as long as routers eventually get your packets to the right place, how they do so doesn't really matter.

Mix-and-match terms

These terms are not cast in stone. The term *gateway* has often been used for what we here call a *router,* and things called *brouters* act like something halfway between a bridge and a router. Also, keep in mind that because all the differences among bridges, routers, and gateways are based on software, in some cases it's quite possible to make the same pieces of hardware into a bridge, router, or gateway by loading in software from different floppy disks.

TCP: The Rocket-Powered Mailman

We have established that the Internet works just like the post office, in that it delivers hunks of data (packets) one at a time. So what do you do if you want to "have a conversation," such as logging in to a remote computer? Back to the postal analogy. Suppose that you're a chess player. Normal chess is played face-to-face with each player immediately responding to the other. Abnormal chess is sometimes played by mail with each player mailing moves to the other. These types of games can take months to complete. What if your mail were delivered by someone with rocket shoes who zipped each move to the other player within a fraction of a second? That would be much more like normal chess.

TCP (Transmission Control Protocol) is that rocket-powered mailman. TCP provides what looks like a dedicated connection from one computer to another. Any data you send to the other computer is guaranteed to be delivered, in the same order it was sent, as though a dedicated circuit were connected from one end to the other (the details of this process are explained in the next section). What TCP provides isn't really a circuit, in fact, but rather a number of IP packets. What TCP provides is a *virtual circuit*. A virtual circuit is real enough for most purposes, which is why nearly every Internet application uses it.

TCP has to add quite a bit of glop to each packet to do its magic, which makes TCP somewhat slower than the underlying IP. A simpler protocol called *UDP (User Datagram Protocol)* doesn't make any promises about reliability. UDP uses much less glop, making do with whatever reliability IP gives it, for the benefit of applications that want to roll their own reliability features or that can live with the flakiness. (In local networks, IP usually delivers upward of 99 percent of all packets correctly, even without the help of TCP.)

Certify That Packet!

Make no mistake, the Internet shares with the United States Postal Service some inherent unreliability. The postal service has two schemes for ensuring that something is delivered: registered mail and return receipts. If you're mailing something of great intrinsic value, such as an original 45 RPM record of Bill Haley and the Comets' "Rock Around the Clock," you send the package registered. When you mail something registered, the clerk at the post office immediately puts it in a locked drawer. Every time the package is moved from one place to another, it's carefully logged and signed for all the way until the recipient signs for it. Registered mail is quite reliable but slow because of all the logging and signing. (Yeah, these days any sane person uses overnight express, but it turns out to be handled much like registered mail: Electronically scanning the bar code on the package label logs the package's progress. But we digress.)

The other scheme is used for certified letters that don't have any intrinsic physical value but contain an important message, typically a letter from your insurance company saying that it has canceled your insurance again. These letters are sorted and handled normally until they're delivered, at which point the recipient signs a card that's mailed back to the sender. If the sender doesn't get the card back in a reasonable amount of time, it sends the letter again.

Different computer networks use either scheme. A network scheme called *X.25,* used in commercial networks such as Tymnet and Sprintnet, uses the registered model, with each packet carefully accounted for. A protocol called X.75 is even used to hand packets from one network to another very reliably. Although X.25 works okay, it's slow for the same reason that registered mail is slow: all that logging and checking at each stage.

TCP/IP is much more like certified mail. As IP routes each packet through the network, it does what it can to deliver it; if some problem arises or if the packet is garbled on a communication line, however, tough luck — IP simply throws the packet away. TCP numbers each packet, and the TCP software on the two communicating hosts (but not on any intermediate hosts) tracks the packet numbers: Each tells the other what it has received and what it hasn't and resends anything that got lost.

This approach has two advantages over the X.25 approach. The end-to-end approach is faster and fundamentally more reliable because it doesn't depend on all the intermediate hosts, between the sender and the recipients, doing everything correctly. (We can report from considerable experience with X.25 networks that intermediate hosts often *don't* do everything correctly, causing annoying *connection resets.*) TCP/IP also enables networks to be built much more cheaply because routers can be much dumber. A router for TCP/IP needs to understand only IP, not TCP or any other higher-level protocol.

On a small network, you can build a perfectly adequate router from a small computer and a few network cards. All the Internet traffic to and from the network at I.E.C.C., for example, used to pass through a router built from an old clone 286 PC, which cost only $300. Worked fine.

Any Port in a Storm

The final topic in this survey of Internet geekspeak is *ports*. In postal terms, port numbers are similar to apartment numbers. Suppose that you want to communicate with a particular host. Okay, you look up its host number, and you send the host packets. You have two problems, however. One is that because a typical host has lots of programs running that can be having simultaneous conversations with lots of other hosts, you have to find a way to keep the different conversations separate. The other problem is that in contacting a host, you have to tell it what sort of conversation you want to have. Do you want to send electronic mail? Transfer files? Fetch Web pages?

Ports solve both problems. Every program on a host that's engaged in a TCP or UDP conversation is assigned a *port number* to identify that conversation. Furthermore, a large set of low port numbers is reserved (sort of like low-numbered license plates) for particular well-known services. For example, if you want to fetch pages from a host using the Web's standard HTTP service, you contact port 80 because that's where the HTTP server is.

ISO protocols: Trust us — they'll be great

The *International Organization for Standardization* (inexplicably known as *ISO*) has for many years been developing a set of communication protocols that was supposed to replace TCP/IP. Because ISO is an enormous international consortium of standardization groups, it probably will not come as a big surprise to hear that it moves ahead at a rate which suggests that it is stapled to a rather arthritic snail.

Although a bunch of ISO standards are supposed to define various network protocols (we mentioned X.25 already), they are in most cases slow, complex, and not well debugged (much like the group that's defining them), so nobody uses even the ones that exist unless they're forced to for political reasons. If someone tells you to forget all this unofficial and unsanctioned TCP/IP nonsense because ISO protocols will replace them all, nod politely and pay no attention. People who build actual networks use TCP/IP.

In fairness, the ISO electronic-mail protocols have achieved moderate success. The mail-transfer standard is called X.400 and is used in many places as a gateway protocol between mail systems. (You can find out about sending mail to X.400 addresses in Chapter 8 of *The Internet For Dummies,* 4th Edition, published by IDG Books Worldwide, Inc.) X.400 is in some ways better than Internet mail because you can use addresses similar to those you would use for real postal mail rather than often arbitrary login names, as is more common with Internet mail. The standard for name-lookup service, X.500 is late and slow but looks to be widely adopted because the Internet has nothing like it. Mail is the *only* place, however, where ISO is getting much attention — its standards for file transfer and other applications were dead on arrival.

Connections to *client programs* — programs that use remote services — are assigned arbitrary port numbers used only to distinguish one connection from another. Servers, on the other hand, use well-known port numbers so that the clients can find them. Several hundred well-known (well-known to Internet programming geeks, at least) port numbers are assigned. Hosts are under no obligation to support them all, just to use the correct number for those they support. Some well-known numbers are pretty silly, such as port 1025 for network blackjack games; others are very specialized, such as port 188 for an implementation of the MUMPS database language. They're there if you need them, though.

Although you usually don't have to worry about port numbers, in a few cases it's handy to know about them. When you want to use a conversational service on another computer, the usual technique is to use the telnet program to connect to port 23 on the remote computer and log in as a normal user. (Chapter 12 has all the gory details.)

Other ports provide some services, however. For example, a computer in Michigan offers a geography server, at `martini.eecs.umich.edu`, that lets you look up any place name or zip code in the United States. If you telnet to that computer on the standard port 23, you get an invitation to log in as a regular user. This invitation isn't very useful because you don't have any passwords for that computer. (If it makes you feel better, neither do we.) If you telnet to port 3000 on the same computer, however, you're connected directly to the geography server. When you need to use a port other than the standard one to contact any service, that's noted in the service's description.

Two separate sets of port numbers exist: one for TCP and one for UDP. All the well-known port numbers, however, are assigned identically for both. Because TCP port 23 is telnet, for example, UDP port 23 is also telnet for inattentive users who don't mind whether some data gets lost.

Chapter 22

You Made Us Do This — More Gory Details

In This Chapter

▶ Lots of technoid details about the innards of the Net

▶ Deep, dark secrets about TCP, IP, and other unspeakable acronyms

*T*he original edition of *The Internet For Dummies* had two chapters with fairly detailed descriptions of how computers communicate on the Internet. We figured that the information should be in there, but that nobody would read it. One reviewer even complained that those chapters were a waste of paper that otherwise would have been healthy living trees.

Well, our original conclusion was wrong. "More, more!" people demanded in their e-mail messages. Okay, your wish is our command. In this chapter, we look "under the hood" at some of the lower-level operations of the Net.

See that little guy with the glasses there? You see him frequently in this chapter — it's the most technical icon in this book. If you're not sure that you want to read all this tech stuff, check the following Executive Summary sidebar, and you will *know* that you don't want to read it.

An Executive Summary of this chapter

A bunch of detailed glop is going on at the lower levels of the Internet. Big deal.

Feel particularly free to skip this chapter unless you have a morbid need to know what's going in the bowels of the Internet or perhaps if you have a particularly stubborn case of insomnia.

Packets and All That

As we allege in an earlier chapter, the Internet, stripped down to its skivvies, is two things:

- ✔ A way to move data from one computer to another
- ✔ A whole bunch of conventions, known in networkese as *protocols,* about how programs use that capability to communicate with each other

When you send electronic mail to someone over the Internet, for example, your mail program and the mail program at the other end communicate using a convention called SMTP (the optimistically named Simple Mail Transfer Protocol) to transfer the message from your computer to the recipient's. SMTP, in turn, uses other protocols (TCP and IP, in particular, which we discuss in detail in Chapter 21) to handle some of the details of message transfer.

On the level

The workings of the Internet are complicated enough that nobody, not even the world-class network geeks who designed it, can keep the whole business in mind at one time. To make things understandable (at least by geek standards), it's traditional to divide up the design into *levels* (sometimes also called layers, just to keep us all confused). At each level, you sort of take all the lower levels for granted and worry only about what happens at your own level.

To take a somewhat strained example, imagine that you're making a tuna salad sandwich. The recipe says that you take bread, tuna salad, and mayo and make a sandwich out of them. At that level, the sandwich-construction level, you assume that you have the ingredients on hand. At the next level down, however, the sandwich-making level, you need a recipe for making bread, a recipe for tuna salad, and a recipe for mayonnaise. More likely, you would buy the bread and the mayo, but at the sandwich-construction level that's a detail we can ignore. Enough of this example — we're getting hungry.

Exactly what the levels are in the Internet is a religious issue among network types, but here's a typical list, from highest to lowest:

- ✔ **Application level:** Two useful programs talking to each other; for example, the mail client program talking to the mail server program. Typical message: "Deliver mail item to `moreint3@dummies.net`." Each different type of program (mail, file transfer, remote login, and so on) has its own protocol. The application-level protocol assumes that the next level down will take care of passing the messages reliably between the programs.

- ✔ **Transport level:** A program on one computer connected to another program on another computer, carefully making sure that everything the first program sends is received by the second program and vice versa. Typical message: "We just received 14,576 characters of data from your program number 42. Urrp." The usual transport-level protocol used on the Internet is called *Transmission Control Protocol,* or *TCP.* (Pretty creative naming, eh?) The transport-level protocol assumes that the next level down will take care of moving chunks of data from one computer to the other.

- ✔ **Internet level:** One computer sending a chunk (known as a *packet*) of data to another computer, which may or may not be on the same network. Typical message: "Send this packet to computer number 205.238.207.92, by way of computer number 199.224.103.214, which is on the same network I am." The usual Internet-level protocol is called (this is *really* creative naming) *Internet Protocol,* or *IP.* The Internet-level protocol assumes that the next level down will take care of moving packets on the local network.

- ✔ **Link level:** Actually transferring data between two computers physically located on the same network. The connection may be an Ethernet, for computers connected in an office, or a phone line, for computers connected across town. Typical message: "Send this packet to computer number 127.45.22.81, which I can see across the hall."

Some people put another level below the link level to deal with the different physical ways two computers can be connected, but enough is enough.

One way to think of the flow of information is that it starts at the highest level, percolates down to the lowest level on the sending computer, across the actual network wires to the receiving computer, and then percolates back up from the lowest level to the highest.

Now we take a quick look (perhaps not quick enough) at the levels the Internet uses, from the bottom to the top.

What's a packet?

The fundamental item the Internet slings around is a *packet.* A packet of what? A packet of, er, stuff. One of the few notably consistent aspects of the Internet is that all data sent through the Internet is sent as packets. If you're logged in to a remote computer and you press the Z key, that Z is packed up in a packet and shipped from your computer to the remote system. Its response is in turn packed into a packet (or several packets, if it's long, because a single packet is limited to about 1,000 characters) and shipped back to your computer, where it's displayed to you.

A single packet contains

- Header bookkeeping stuff
- Even more header bookkeeping stuff
- Actual data (because of network megalomania, the actual data is optional)

Each network level adds its own header information to keep track of what's happening at its level. With the encrustation of headers, a packet can easily end up with more header than actual data, which isn't great (headers do take up space in memory and take time to transmit over network links), but that inconvenience is the price we pay for all the flexibility of the Internet.

Down in the Links

We start in the basement of the Internet, the link level, which passes a packet from one computer to another on the same network. At the link level, two kinds of networks exist — the kind with only two computers and the kind with more than two computers. The kind with two computers is usually some type of phone line with a computer at each end (including some rather exotic phone lines, such as high-speed fiber optic connections that send 155 million bits per second). The kind with more than two computers is usually a local network, such as an Ethernet. The reason for the difference is quite simple: When your computer ships out a packet, if only one other computer is on the network, you don't have to worry about specifying the recipient. If several other computers are on the network, the link level has to make sure that the packet goes to the right one.

Getting to the point

For phone-line-style links (usually called *point-to-point links,* an amazingly normal term for network types to use), you may think that to send a packet from one end to the other, all you have to do is ship it down the wire. After all, how is the packet going to get lost between one end of a phone call and the other? Although the packet won't get lost, plenty of complications are on the way:

🗸 **Framing:** A 25-cent word that merely means that because you can't automatically tell where one packet ends and the next begins, you need a way to mark the boundary between them.

🗸 **Error detection:** It's nice to know when a message gets corrupted by a bird sitting on the phone line or some other problem.

🗸 **Multiprotocol support:** Suppose that you have an expensive high-speed phone line connecting two branches of your company and you have some modern, efficient TCP/IP networks and some other kinds of grungy obsolete networks, such as Novell Netware and DECnet (from Digital). All the various kinds of networks (or, in networkese, *network protocols*) sharing the expensive phone line saves money.

🗸 **Authorization:** If the connection involves one machine dialing up another using a modem and a regular phone line and you have the least interest in security (which, admittedly, many Internet sites don't), you can require passwords or something before you start shipping data to whomever just dialed in.

How we SLIPped up

The least complicated approach to handling these link-level complications is known as *SLIP* (Serial Line Internet Protocol), declared in its defining document to be an official "nonstandard." SLIP deals with most of the preceding issues by ignoring them. Errors in transmission? Tough. Multiprotocol support? Forget it. Authorization? Not our problem. (If you read Chapter 21, you may recall that SLIP was designed in about two minutes on the back of a matchbook.) SLIP does at least handle framing, by defining a special character to put between packets so that you can tell where one packet ends and the other begins.

Despite its, er, technical shortcomings, SLIP has become quite popular, partly because, for a long time, the widely accepted way to connect computers to the Internet has been to use a regular phone line. SLIP actually works pretty well. Transmission errors aren't usually a problem because these days most modems do error correction automatically, so SLIP doesn't have to. Most systems with SLIP handle authentication somehow — usually your computer has to send a login name and a password, and only then does SLIP start. SLIP suffers from a great deal of slightly different versions, however, a topic we mention in Chapters 3, 4, and 5.

As the bits flow by, a packet of data as sent by SLIP looks generally like

```
C0 hexadecimal (that is, a character containing binary 1100
        0000)
packet data, however long it is
C0
```

On the backbone

As we have already mentioned about 400 times, the Internet is a collection of computer networks. Some networks are fast, long-distance ones (across the continent or across the Atlantic Ocean, for example) that have to be managed a little more carefully than your typical dial-up phone line. For one thing, building a modem that works at a million bits per second is tougher than building one that works at 28,000 bits per second. Also, when you have a network link that runs that fast, many people will depend on it, and those people will get really annoyed at you if you're in charge of the link and it fails. You need network-management tools, therefore, so that you can tell, for example, how often a message sent from one end of the link arrives garbled. (Links often go slightly flaky in preparation for dying completely. It's like the cough that may develop into pneumonia.)

Furthermore, these fast links are often set up in groups so that if one fails, its traffic can be shifted to the others and, because they're long-haul links, they tend to be located all over the country. Because you can have dozens, or more, of these links all over the place, having technicians running to each end of each link to check whether it's okay is a mite inconvenient. So PPP supports *remote network monitoring,* an obvious idea that took about 20 years to think up, which uses the network itself to transmit network-management information to a central site where a single set of technicians can manage the entire network. Large networks take management very seriously, and all have people monitoring the network 24 hours a day, 7 days a week, so central management has the important benefit that the network needs only one set of expensive all-night network managers.

PPP has an extremely complete set of network-monitoring facilities, the details of which we spare you because the descriptions read like this:

"If true(2), then the local node attempts to perform Magic Number negotiation with the remote node. If false(1), then this negotiation is not performed. In any event, the local node complies with any Magic Number negotiation attempted by the remote node, per the PPP specification. Changing this object will have an effect when the link is next restarted."

(Magic Number negotiation is a way for a system to check whether a link was wired wrong and the system ends up talking to itself. See? We told you that you didn't care about this stuff.)

PPP solves another problem for fast networks: Until PPP came along, no standard existed for fast Internet links. If a link was faster than SLIP could handle or the link was too important to put up with SLIP's cruddiness, manufacturers invented their own link protocols. If you had at one end of a link a Brand X router, a specialized computer that moves packets from one network to another, and a Brand Y router at the other end, you would have to be sure that they could talk to each other. As you may expect, each router manufacturer would cheerfully point out that the easiest way to avoid compatibility problems was to buy all your routers from them, and each network did indeed tend to have all the same type of routers.

Because PPP provides a standard link protocol that everyone is supposed to support, eventually you should be able to plug in any kind of computer to any network link. To our surprise, this idea works — when Internet For Dummies Central got its fast million bps phone line in late 1995, we plugged in our PC to our end of the line, the people at the phone company plugged in their computer to the other end of the line, we both told our respective ends to speak PPP, and packets started to flow as soon as we got the modem switches set right. Wow!

That is, the packet data is sandwiched between two special C0 characters. But what if a C0 is in the packet? No problem; in that case, you send two characters, hex DB and DC. But what if a DB is in the packet? Still no problem; in that case, you send a DB followed by a DD. But what if a DD is in the packet? Stop bothering us. (In fact, those two substitutions turn out to be all that SLIP needs.)

One major mutant version of SLIP is called *Compressed SLIP,* or *CSLIP.* A smart guy named Van Jacobson was looking at the data sent over a typical SLIP line and noticed that the header data in one packet was usually nearly the same as the header information in the preceding packet. By simply sending the header differences rather than the entire header every time, the link got faster because less data overall was sent. This scheme, give or take a few details that aren't worth going into, is now known as CSLIP. CSLIP uses the same C0 framing as SLIP.

If you have a choice, CSLIP is always preferable to SLIP because it sends less data and, as a result, is faster.

Getting to the point, for real this time

After a while, system managers and a few users began to get tired of dealing with SLIP's flakiness. So the Internet powers-that-be (formally known as the IETF, or Internet Engineering Task Force) came up with a swell new industrial-strength, full-featured, kitchen-sink replacement for the link level, called *Point-to-Point Protocol,* or *PPP.* (In fairness, PPP also solves other problems with high-speed lines. Refer to the preceding sidebar, "On the backbone.")

PPP is a much more complicated protocol than SLIP. The definition of SLIP consists of only 6 pages, 4 of which contain only descriptive examples. The PPP definition takes up 66 pages, not counting the descriptions of all the network-management information, which takes another 60 pages. PPP is built on top of a widely used low-level link-handling scheme known as HDLC (Hierarchical Data Link Control, for what it's worth), which is what most fast modems used already.

A typical packet sent via PPP looks like

```
7E (hex) Here comes a packet
FF (hex) required by HDLC
03 (hex) Also required by HDLC
00 21 (hex) This is an Internet packet
   actual data at last!
xx xx Frame Check Sequence (see below)
7E (hex) There went the packet.
```

The first three characters (7E FF 03) say that this packet is an HDLC message destined for whomever is at the other end of the link. Because computers are fairly stupid, they don't find that to be obvious. The 00 21 says that this packet is Internet data, not Novell, AppleTalk, DECnet, Hairnet, or anything else. Then comes the actual data, followed by a Frame Check Sequence (FCS), and a final end-of-packet flag. The FCS, which is used to see whether the packet was received correctly, is calculated by the sender by scrambling together the binary values of all the bytes in the packet (this description is an oversimplification, but the actual details would fill ten pages even more boring than this one). The receiver makes the same calculation and should come up with the same FCS. If not, the packet got messed up on the way, so the receiver throws it away to avoid using corrupted data.

PPP has all sorts of configuration facilities so that when a PPP link first starts up, the two ends can have a nice chat, introduce each other, and nail down some last-minute details about the link, such as what is the largest packet it is willing to receive from the other. PPP includes optional compression, like CSLIP; during the initial chat, the two ends can agree whether they want to use it.

Even though PPP is more complex than SLIP, it solves many more problems and works much better in the case of errors (phone-line glitches, garbled packets, and the like) than does SLIP. The automatic configuration also makes PPP much easier to set up.

Given a choice among SLIP, CSLIP, PPP, choose PPP.

Through the ether

Compared to sending your packets over a point-to-point link, sending them over an Ethernet is a breeze. Framing and error detection, the first two problems that provoked people to write PPP, are handled automatically by Ethernet hardware. (Sounds too good to be true, doesn't it?)

Multiprotocol support is pretty much automatic as well. The only fly in this otherwise perfect ointment is *addressing*. Your typical Ethernet has 100 computers attached to it, so we need some way to tell which of the 100 computers the packet is intended for. An obvious solution is to put the Internet address of the destination computer at the front of the packet. Then, as each packet flies by, only the computer with the correct address receives it, and the rest ignore it. This idea is indeed almost what they do, except for the minor problem that Ethernet has its own rules for addresses, and they're not the same as the rules on the Internet. Unlike Internet addresses, Ethernet addresses are much longer, 48 bits rather than 32, and they're assigned almost entirely at random. (Well, not quite. No two computers get the same Ethernet address; other than that, however, the addresses may as well be random.) Before your computer can ship a packet over the network, therefore, you must figure out the minor issue of which Ethernet address corresponds to the desired Internet address. If you're smart, you will take our word for it when we say that there's a plan to handle that. Or, if you insist, read the following sidebar, "ARP, ARP, RARP!"

ARP, ARP, RARP!

ARP is the *Address Resolution Protocol* for Ethernet that figures out the hardware Ethernet address that corresponds to a software Internet address. ARP (considering that a network is involved) is amazingly simple — the computer that needs to know the address shouts, "Hey, what's the address for 127.45.32.11?" and the computer with that address shouts back, "I'm 9a374cdf9e32 on the Ethernet."

This process works because on an Ethernet you can *broadcast* a message, which means that the message is received by all the computers on that network rather than just one computer. In this case, the first computer broadcasts the question, and then the one with the right address broadcasts an answer; the rest ignore both the question and the answer.

Adding the inevitable confusion to this pristine situation, we have *Proxy ARP* and *Reverse ARP,* or *RARP.* In Proxy ARP, a computer answers an ARP request with a message saying, "Send messages for that host to me, and I'll take care of it." Proxy ARP mostly helps hosts so dumb that they can't handle ARP themselves. Reverse ARP is for the benefit of diskless workstations (recently rechristened "network computers" in the hope that people will have forgotten how much they disliked

diskless workstations). When a diskless workstation starts up, because it has no disk to load from, it has no software loaded and no idea of what its Internet address is. It loads itself up over the Net using something called BOOTP, the details of which we skip. Then the workstation sends a RARP message saying, "My Ethernet address is 373db49c7e12 — who am I?" A better-informed computer (which presumably does have a disk) looks up the newly hatched machine on a list and sends back an ARP response saying who it is. This scheme makes it easy to have a network of a few dozen diskless computers, which are all physically identical except for their hardware Ethernet addresses, load them up with identical software (BOOTP handles that), and then use RARP to give them separate Internet numbers, which they need in order to work with the rest of the Internet.

Fortunately, ARP and RARP work largely automatically. If you're feeling inquisitive, on a UNIX system there may be a command called `arp` or `/etc/arp` that shows you the table of Ethernet and Internet addresses. On a PC or a Mac that's attached to an Ethernet, you can probably find the ARP table on the Status menu of your network software.

On the Internet Level

Enough of that link-level stuff already. Now step up one more level, to the Internet level. The link level handles the details of getting a packet from one computer to another on the same network. What happens when you need to send a packet of data to a host on *another* network? That's where the Internet level comes in.

The process of passing a packet from network to network until it gets to its final destination is known as *routing*. A packet that passes through 20 or even 30 hosts on its way from your computer to one on a far-flung network is quite common. Suppose that one of the users at Lightlink, an Internet provider in upstate New York, fetched a Web page on a computer here at I.E.C.C. The packet left the Lightlink customer's computer; passed through two routers to the local network provider; through another six routers via Syracuse, New York, and New York City to a network exchange point in New Jersey run by SprintLink (one of the long-haul networks our provider uses); then to our provider's router near Scranton, Pennsylvania; through two more routers to I.E.C.C.; and, finally, through our router here at I.E.C.C. to the computer with the Web page. The total distance the packet traveled was about 1,000 miles, and the trip took about $1/5$-second. Lightlink is physically about ten miles away from IECC, but the network is fast enough that the extra detour doesn't really matter.

Take this packet and . . .

Every time a host on the Internet receives an IP packet, it asks "Is this one for me?" If so, great: The host passes the packet to the next-higher level of software (usually TCP, which we discuss in Chapter 23). If not, the host has to route the packet. Your typical Internet host is attached to only one network, and only one "gateway" machine on that network attaches the host to the outside world, so the host sends all packets for other networks to the gateway. For a host connected to more than one network, the routing is a little (or maybe a lot) more complicated. Indeed, the routing is complicated enough that in the network backbones (the high-speed links that connect the fastest networks), routing is done by dedicated routers, which are specialized computers that do nothing other than fling packets from one network to another.

How many networks would a network network?

Back when the Internet was young and dinosaurs roamed the earth, routing seemed to be a simple problem. Because only a dozen or so networks were in the Internet, each computer could keep a little table listing each network along with the best route to that network. When a packet arrived, the computer could look up the network number of the destination (the network number is the first few digits of a host's address) and send the packet on its way.

Although that system worked fine for a while, now the Internet has become a victim of its own success. For one thing, the communication links have gotten much faster; for another, about 100,000 networks are now in the Internet, with more joining every day. Both these things make routing much more difficult. In the dinosaur days, the fastest network link ran at 56,000 bits per second, which seems fast to people but is a snail's pace for a computer. These days, your typical network link runs at a million bits per second (known in telephone-ese as "T1"), and the backbone links are trading up to 45 or even 155 million bits per second. (That's "T3" and "OC3," respectively. Nobody seems to know what happened to T2.) Because a typical Internet packet is about 1,000 bits long, in the old days a link could transmit only about 50 packets per second. However, T1 can transmit 1,000 packets per second; T3, 45,000 packets per second; and OC3, 155,000. We turn those numbers inside out to see how long the receiving machine has to handle a packet, measured in milliseconds ($1/1,000$-second):

Line Speed	Packets Per Second	Time/Packet
56,000	50	20 milliseconds
T1	1,000	1 millisecond
T3	45,000	.02 milliseconds
OC3	155,000	.006 milliseconds

(Note to the arithmetically inclined: Yes, we rounded these numbers.)

The problem is that, in 1 millisecond, a typical modern computer barely has time to look up a network number in a table with tens of thousands of entries. In .006 milliseconds, it barely has time to notice that a packet has arrived, much less do anything with it. For the hosts in the network backbones, which really have to know where all the networks are and can't punt most messages to a gateway, expensive special hardware is needed that can look up routes quickly and send packets on their way.

Where does routing come from; where does routing go?

The astute reader may have noticed that we haven't said anything about where tables of routes come from. If only a handful of networks existed, skilled network managers could load the routes into the routers, updating the routes on the rare occasions when new network links were added. As we say in the computer biz, though, maintaining tables by hand doesn't scale well. Now that the Internet is composed of 100,000 networks, it probably has 150,000 routers, and an army of administrators of any size can't keep them up to date. Instead, the routes are updated automatically.

Even when the Internet was tiny, in fact, the routes were still updated automatically. A major goal of the projects leading to the Internet was to create networks that would continue to work if the links and routers failed. (Although the military, which funded the work, was worried about enemy attack, the same techniques are just as useful when an errant construction crew cuts a buried cable, known puckishly as "backhoe fade.")

Every few seconds, each router on the Net sends messages to each of its neighbor routers (other routers on the networks to which it is directly connected). By comparing notes, the routers can figure out who's connected to which network and which way to send packets to each of the thousands of networks. Routers originally just tried to minimize the number of hops a packet would have to take to get to its destination. That focus made sense when all network links were about the same speed, but now it's much quicker to take four hops on OC3 links (the superfast 155 million bits per second kind) than one hop on an old 56,000 link. Political issues also exist. Some networks allow general traffic, and others allow only research traffic, and you can't route from one general network to another through a research network, no matter how fast the links are.

Cough, cough — we seem to have congestion

As though routing weren't a severe enough problem (and it's pretty bad — lots of Ph.D. students have gotten theses out of routing problems), there's the related problem of congestion. If you think of network links as roads, imagine two two-lane roads funneling into a third two-lane road. If both the incoming roads are full of traffic, there just isn't room for all those cars on the outgoing road, and traffic backs up. The standard solution to network congestion may surprise you: Throw away the extra packets. The IP level is officially unreliable, which means that if a problem occurs during the delivery of a packet, the heck with it. Although that attitude may seem awfully antisocial, it turns out to be the best solution, mostly because all the schemes to make the network reliable at this level are more trouble than they're worth. (You can make sure that your data gets delivered — we get to those ways in Chapter 23.)

When someone's packets get thrown away, the host that does the throwing away is supposed to send a special "source quench" message back to the sender, which tells it to talk slower. This message helps somewhat. There's no question, though, that at peak hours the Net can get awfully congested and slow, and the only solution is more and faster (and more expensive) network links.

A peek inside a packet

Every packet handled by IP has a *header*, a bunch of information stuck on the front of the packet that IP uses to keep track of the packet's progress through the network:

✔ **IP version number:** Always 4 — evidently Versions 1, 2, and 3 didn't make the grade. (In the next few years, they will be upgrading to Version 6.)

✔ **Header length:** The size of the IP information, as distinct from the actual data that IP is supposed to be sending

✔ **Type of service:** A hint that this packet should be sent faster or more reliably than normal

✔ **Total length:** The total size of the packet, including both the IP stuff and the contents

✔ **Identification:** A sequence number to help tell this packet apart from other packets of similar appearance

✔ **Fragment info:** Described in the nearby sidebar "Aargh! I've been fragmented"

✔ **TTL:** *T*ime *to l*ive, a freshness date saying how much longer this packet can be passed around before it gets stale and should be thrown away

✔ **Protocol:** The higher-level protocol (TCP, most likely) that uses this packet

✔ **Checksum:** Checks for scrambled or corrupted header info

✔ **Source addr:** IP address of the original sender

✔ **Dest addr:** IP address of the ultimate recipient

✔ **Options:** Every general's favorite features, things such as "top secret" or "priority flash override"

Aargh! I've been fragmented

You may occasionally hear network prop-ellerheads complaining about *packet frag-mentation.* Each network in the Internet has a largest-allowed packet size, known as the *maximum transmission unit,* or *MTU.* Although the MTU on an Ethernet is about 1,500 charac-ters, the limit on a dial-up link may be only 500 characters. What happens when a 1,500-char-acter packet needs to be sent over a 500 MTU link? The packet gets broken up into pieces, called *fragments.*

Fragmentation is, from the point of view of network implementers, a pain in the neck. If a sender breaks a packet into three fragments,

the receiver has to wait for all three fragments to arrive before it can reassemble the packet and send it along to the next network. What if the fragments arrive out of order, which can happen for technical reasons? Or if one of the fragments gets lost? How long should the re-ceiver wait before giving up and considering the whole packet to be lost? There's no good answer.

If you use network software that lets you set your own system's MTU (Trumpet Winsock, discussed in Chapter 4, is one), be sure to set it fairly low, like 500 or less, to avoid dreaded fragmentation.

What Next?

Your eyes have probably glazed over by this point, so here's a quick sum-mary of what this chapter says:

✔ The workings of the Internet are best explained as a series of levels.

✔ The lowest *link* level handles the process of passing a packet of data from one host (computer) to another over a single network. There are far too many ways to pass a packet.

✔ The next *Internet* level handles the process of passing a packet of data from one host to another, even though the hosts are on different networks. The way the hosts figure out how to route the packet from network to network is darned complicated.

✔ The Internet level is unreliable, and although it tries to get each packet to its destination, sometimes it can't.

Chapter 23

Even More Grotty Details

● ●

In This Chapter

▶ What's a circuit and why

▶ More about TCP

▶ The innards of packets

▶ A live example: delivering an e-mail message

● ●

You've read Chapter 22 and you're still reading? Are you nuts? There's no accounting for taste, evidently.

In Chapter 22, you read that the Internet, using the creatively named *Internet Protocol (IP)*, is capable of sending packets of data from one computer to another, even when the two computers are on different networks in different parts of the world. A single packet is rarely enough, however, to say anything useful. (It's like saying "Hi" to someone and not waiting around to hear an answer.) This chapter looks at the way the Internet uses packets — lots and lots of packets — to create conversations between two computers. (That's called the *transport* level of the Net.) Finally, to show that you can make all this nonsense do something useful, you use the transport level to deliver an e-mail message.

Executive Summary of this chapter

The lower levels of the Internet have even more detailed glop going on than we discuss in Chapter 22. Big deal.

You don't have to read any of this chapter to follow the rest of the book or to use the Internet. In the unlikely event that you have read Chapter 22 and you're still interested in this stuff or if your insomnia is still a problem, read on.

Controlling Those Transmissions

As you read in Chapter 21, when you have a network connection between two computers, the most convenient kind of connection to have is known as a *circuit*. The most familiar example of a circuit connection is a telephone call. If we call you, after the connection is made, everything we say is transmitted to you, and everything you say is transmitted to us. (If this scenario seems obvious, that's because it is.) A circuit connection between two computers works the same way — everything one computer sends is received by the other and vice versa. When you dial in over the phone to a BBS or a UNIX provider, you have a circuit connection to the BBS or UNIX provider.

The Internet, on the other hand, doesn't have circuits. It has packets. So what's a circuit lover to do? You fake it, that's what you do. You take the stream of data you want to send over a circuit to another computer, slice it into packets, number them, send them to the other computer using IP, and put them back together in numbered order. Although the result isn't a real circuit, it's close enough that you can pretend that it is and call it a *virtual circuit*. The scheme that creates these virtual circuits is known as *Transmission Control Protocol,* or *TCP*. Because TCP depends on IP to do the actual packet delivery, the two together are usually known as TCP/IP.

If Circuits Are So Swell, Why Not Use Them Directly?

In olden days, people did. IBM has its own network scheme, grandly named *Systems Network Architecture* (*SNA*) that, when you make a connection, establishes a circuit through the network for the duration of the connection. It turned out that the TCP/IP approach — with virtual circuits created atop a sea of packets and only the computers at the ends of the connection worrying about the circuit stuff — worked much better.

The reason is that a network connection involves not just the two computers at the ends but also all the computers in between that route the data from one network or piece of a network to another. In an SNA-like scheme, all the routers in the middle have to know about all the circuits that pass through them. (We oversimplify here, somewhat. Don't worry about it.) Having to know about circuits greatly complicates a router's job compared to the TCP/IP approach in which a router merely moves packets from one network to another, without regard to which virtual circuit each packet may be part of. In one of our networks, for example, an ancient 1984-vintage 286 PC was adequate to route data from one network to another, even though hundreds of virtual circuits can be active at any time. If a 286 PC had to track each circuit, it probably wouldn't be up to the task.

Living in duplex

A connection between two computers can be one-way, two-way, or, sometimes, both. (Strange but true.) In the interest of avoiding excess clarity, these possibilities are referred to as *simplex, full duplex,* and *half duplex.*

Suppose that you're retrieving a Web page from another computer. After you click the link for the page, your Web browser makes a connection for the Web page's data, the data comes streaming across from the remote computer to your computer, and, when it's done, that connection is closed. That's a simplex connection because the data flows only one way.

On the other hand, suppose that you're using telnet to connect to a remote computer. (Chapter 12 tells you about telnet.) Everything you type is immediately sent to the other computer, and everything it says is immediately sent back to you, with no particular synchronization between the two directions. You can, for example, type ahead of what the remote computer is reading, and it catches up with your typing when it gets around to it. That's a full duplex connection.

On the third hand (this lecture is evidently being given by a Hindu deity), in some cases the data flows in one direction for a while and then in the other direction for a while, flip-flopping back and forth. The classic example is if you're talking to someone (actually talking — no computers here) via a radio phone. One person talks and says "over" when finished, and the other person talks and says

"over," and so on. (Incidentally, the terms simplex and duplex originally come from radiotelephony, the first place in which the issue of one- versus two-way conversation arose, probably in the 1920s.)

When computers are talking to each other without pesky humans directly involved, for example, in transferring news or e-mail, half duplex connections are the norm because they're easier for computers to keep straight than are full duplex. Simplex isn't usually adequate because you need a way to get errors and acknowledgments back in response to a message. (If you're wondering about FTP, it uses two connections: a half-duplex one for commands and messages — the ones you see when you type commands to FTP — and a separate simplex one for file data.)

For an excellent example of half-duplex communication, we recommend the old British World War II romantic comedy *I Know Where I'm Going,* in which Wendy Hiller plays a gold-digging young English woman who's heading for a remote Scottish isle to marry a rich old industrialist. While waiting for a storm to clear so that she can take a boat to the island, Wendy instead falls in love with the impoverished but raffishly charming local nobleman. Several scenes show Wendy at the post office, saying via the half-duplex radio telephone to her industrialist, "I miss you, darling, over" and so on. The non-half-duplex parts of the movie aren't bad either.

The TCP/IP approach is also much more robust in the face of enemy attack (see the description of backhoe fade in Chapter 22). If a TCP/IP network link fails but alternative links can get packets to the same place as the failed link did, a router only has to send packets via the alternative links. The computers on the end don't even notice. When a number of alternative links are available, sending different packets in the same virtual circuit via different links, depending on which is busier at the moment each packet arrives, is quite common. Even if one router fails, taking down all its links, the network still operates as long as alternative routes are available.

In a network system with real circuits, on the other hand, each circuit that used a failing link has to be identified and rerouted individually. This process is slow and error-prone and is an administrative nightmare.

By the way, for more than a century, telephone calls have all been circuit switched, with the facilities for each call set up when the call is established and dedicated to that call until you hang up. In recent years, even staid phone companies are climbing aboard the packet-switching bandwagon, turning your phone calls into lots of little packets of data, whipping them through the network at high speed, and turning them back into voice at the other end. The current telephone buzzword is ATM (an unhelpful acronym for *a*synchronous *t*ransfer *m*ode), which is actually high-speed packet switching for both voice and computer data.

TCP Takes Control

Now you know (still awake? — just checking) that the job of TCP is to deliver data from one computer to another. TCP's job can be broken down into several parts:

- **Reliability:** Everything sent has to be received. The sender has to be prepared to send everything over and over again until the receiving end confirms that the message got there.

- **Sequencing:** Everything sent has to be received in the correct order. The sending computer's TCP slices the data into packets, and by the time the packets are routed through the network, they may be out of order. The receiver has to put them back into the correct order to avoid having the message be received like this (message this like received be). TCP assigns a sequence number for each data byte sent, and each packet identifies the sequence numbers of the data in that packet.

- **Flow control:** A fast computer sending to a slow computer can easily send data faster than the receiver can process it. To avoid network congestion (known in the extreme case as network constipation — ouch), the receiver sets a *receive window* that limits how fast the sender can send.

TIP

What does the "Transmission" in Transmission Control Protocol have to do with the transmission in my car?

Nothing whatsoever. What did you expect?

Marching in sequence

The operation of TCP is, in principle, simple. (In practice, it's utterly baroque, but most of the barocity comes from being prepared to handle errors and exceptional conditions.) Each byte of data sent over a connection has a sequence number. Suppose, for the moment, that the sequence number of the last data handled was 1000 and our computer is sending 100 data bytes per packet. A packet therefore contains data 1001–1100. When the receiver gets that packet, the receiver sends back an acknowledgment (ACK, for short) saying, "I've received up through 1100; now send starting at 1101." The sender then can send 1101–1200.

If the sender waited for an ACK after each and every packet, it would spend more time waiting than sending, so it's allowed to send several packets beyond what's been ACKed. The number of data bytes it's allowed to get ahead of what's ACKed is called the *window* — and yes, people really do say "ACKed," even though they sound like Bill the Cat. If the window were 300 bytes wide, the sender would actually send 1001–1100, 1101–1200, and 1201–1300 before waiting for an acknowledgment. If the sender then receives an acknowledgment up through 1200, it can go 300 bytes beyond that, so it can now send 1301–1400 and 1401–1500. When the network is working smoothly (which, surprisingly, it does most of the time), the data and acknowledgment messages arrive at roughly the same rate, so the data keeps flowing at a constant speed.

Could you repeat that, please?

What happens if the sender sends a packet but never gets an ACK? Or, more commonly, what if it has sent up through 1300, but it keeps getting back ACKs only though 1100? It means that a packet has gotten lost. (Remember that IP is allowed to throw away packets in case of a transmission error or lack of network link capacity.) What happens now? Simple. It resends the lost data. Because the sender has ACKs through 1100, it resends 1101–1200 and 1201–1300. Eventually the sender gets ACKs for the resent data (if not, it has to send the data again until it does), and it can resume passing more data to the other end. An essential rule for TCP is that the sender must hang on to a copy of everything sent until the receiver ACKs it, because the data may have to be retransmitted.

Stereo networking

Adding a little more complication to this scenario (that's "a little," as in when your dentist says, "This may cause a little discomfort") is the full-duplex-itude of a TCP connection. For a connection between Boston and Geneva, data can be flowing both eastbound and westbound at the same time, so a separate set of sequence numbers and a separate window exist for each direction. In the interest of packet economy, each TCP packet can include both data and a sequence number for one direction and an acknowledgment and window for the other direction. A packet might say, "Here are bytes 5001–5100 of my data; I'm ACKing up through byte 97,000 of your data, and my window is 600 bytes." Even though the packets are shared, each direction is logically separate, so you can think of them separately, sharing packets only to save network overhead.

I feel congested — can you close the window?

To keep the network working well, each receiver has to set a reasonable window. If windows are too large, senders may send packets so fast that the network becomes overloaded. If windows are too small, however, senders spend most of their time waiting for ACKs, needlessly slowing down communication.

The traditional rule of thumb is that the window for a connection should be the amount of data that can be sent in the time it takes to make a round trip on the network. For example, assume that you have a fast network that can transmit 100,000 bytes per second and that the time to send a packet to a distant host is $1/4$-second. (These numbers are fairly typical.) The round-trip time is twice $1/4$-second, or $1/2$-second. In $1/2$-second, you can send 50,000 bytes, and a reasonable window is 50,000 bytes.

Now the black magic begins. If the network isn't congested and no packets are ever lost to errors, that is the perfect window size. In real life, however, the network is always congested when you want to use it, and errors do happen. Detecting network congestion is fairly easy — the sender may receive "source quench" packets from a router that had to throw away packets, and the receiver may notice packets arriving less often than they would if the network were flowing freely. So the sender should shrink the window to slow down and alleviate the congestion. How much should it shrink the window? Well, er, some. Lots of theories but no accepted rules of thumb exist, so there are no doubt lots of Ph.D. theses yet to be written on congestion control.

A related question is how long after you send a packet do you wait for an ACK before you conclude that you have to send it again? If the time is too short, you needlessly transmit data twice, wasting network capacity. (Because the recipient can tell from the sequence numbers that the second copy of the data is redundant, the situation is handled correctly, but it's still a waste.) If the amount of time is too long, you can end up waiting a long time until the sender finally gets around to retransmitting a lost packet. The traditional rule of thumb is that you should wait about twice the round-trip time, but there are lots of theories and upcoming Ph.D. theses here too.

Socket to Me

So far, we have considered how to handle one TCP connection (or virtual circuit) at a time. On a real networked computer, however, you don't have just one connection — you have a whole bunch, potentially thousands on a large server system. TCP keeps connections separate by using *ports*.

If you think of a computer's Internet address as a phone number, the port represents an extension number. Any particular TCP connection runs from a particular port on one host to a particular port on the other host. A single port on a particular host can have multiple connections active as long as they are to separate ports on other hosts.

By convention, standard server programs use agreed-on low-numbered ports. For telnet, you connect to port 23; for FTP, to port 21; for HTTP (Web pages), to port 80; and so on. On a UNIX system, the list of port numbers is in a file called /etc/services. On PCs, the list is usually in a file called services or services.txt in your network software directory.

When a client program wants to establish a network connection, it asks its system for an unused port, usually in the 1200 range, and then connects to the low-numbered port for the service it wants. When the connection is done, the client program gives its high-numbered port back to the system for later use.

Grotty Packet Details

For the masochists among you, here are the details of the header info that TCP puts on each and every packet it sends. Remember that because TCP packets are sent inside IP packets, the sender and receiver host addresses are already handled by IP.

- **Source port:** The port number on the sender's machine

- **Destination port:** The port number on the recipient's machine

- **Sequence number:** The number of the first data byte in this packet

- **Acknowledgment number (optional):** The sequence number of the next data byte this sender is expecting to receive

- **Data offset:** The size of the TCP header so that the recipient can figure out where the actual data starts

- **Control flags:** Special indicators, such as "reset this connection," "ACK number is present," and "end of data"

- **Window:** The size of the receive window, in bytes

- **Checksum:** A control total of all the data in the header, to be recalculated and compared by the recipient to detect scrambled packets

- **Urgent pointer:** A marker indicating that the packet contains "urgent" data that's delivered immediately to the recipient's program (in a telnet session, Ctrl-C may be considered an urgent message because it usually tells the server to interrupt what it's doing)

- **Options:** Miscellaneous junk that can include a hint to the recipient about a good maximum number of data bytes to send per packet

Isn't there an awful lot of header glop on each and every packet?

You bet. TCP is what's known as a *heavyweight* protocol. A typical packet has 40 bytes of TCP header and 20 or more bytes of IP header, which seems a wee bit top-heavy for a packet that may contain a single data byte representing a keystroke you have typed on a telnet connection.

The design of TCP/IP is cast in stone (ten million computers will have to have their software updated when it's changed), but some gross hacks, er, advanced techniques, can cut down the header bloat. The most notable technique is Compressed SLIP, or CSLIP. Because this technique takes advantage of the fact that the headers in one packet tend to be much like the headers in the packet that preceded it, CSLIP usually just sends a single byte with a code for "same as last time." The original bloated headers are reconstructed by the recipient, which saves time over slow links (by not sending the bloat) but remains compatible with the rest of the TCP/IP world. PPP, the industrial-strength successor to SLIP, offers similar header compression.

By the way, when we said that TCP/IP is cast in stone, we were lying. The Internet is running out of IP addresses, partly due to profligate handing out of addresses in the early 1980s to people who didn't end up using them and partly due to the Net's growing much more than anyone expected. A new version of IP has been introduced that has much bigger addresses — 128 rather than 32 bits —

enough addresses to assign a separate one to every electron in the universe, which we presume will be enough. Fortunately, the old and new address schemes will be able to coexist for several years as everyone's host software is upgraded. This new addressing scheme will make the header bloat problems even worse, however, because the IP header will grow from a minimum of 20 bytes to more like 30 or 40 bytes. We presume that yet more header compression will allow people on slow PPP links to avoid having all their packets become larger and take longer to send, but the details of that aren't even under discussion yet.

An opposing view: Keep it simple

For some purposes, TCP is severe overkill. There is, for example, a simple time service, where the sender sends a request asking, "What time is it?" and the recipient sends back a response with the time and date. Each message can fit in a single packet, so using TCP, which needs a minimum of five packets to start and stop a connection, to send one packet each way seems silly.

For those lean, mean, network applications, the *User Datagram Protocol* (*UDP*) is an alternative to TCP. UDP has ports like TCP does, to handle multiple programs on a single host, and an optional checksum for error detection; other than that, however, it doesn't do you any favors. If a program sends a UDP message, that message turns into one packet. UDP can be much faster than TCP because it sends fewer packets and the packets it does send are smaller.

Because UDP is used for very simple applications, such as time of day, and also for applications that do their own error-checking, the applications don't need TCP to do it for them. The most important of these applications is the *Network File System* (*NFS*). Each NFS operation involves a client's sending a request and the server's sending back a response. Whether the responses arrive in the same order the requests were sent (they often don't because NFS operations can take much longer than others) doesn't matter because NFS takes care of matching up a response with the corresponding pending request. NFS performance is extremely important (for many workstations, most or all of their disk operations are handled over a network via NFS), so small, fast UDP is just the ticket.

Let's Play Postman

For the grand denouement of this chapter, consider the operation of an actual Internet application, the euphemistically named *Simple Mail Transfer Protocol* (*SMTP*). Mail programs use SMTP when they're sending e-mail messages on the Internet. In this section, you watch as SMTP delivers an e-mail message.

In an SMTP operation, the receiving machine is considered to be the server, and the sending machine the client. To deliver a piece of mail, the sending machine opens a TCP connection to the server on port 25, where the receiving machine's SMTP server should be waiting to receive something. The communication between the two machines uses plain old lines of text.

The sender sends a sequence of commands, each of which is a four-letter word (usually spelled wrong, unless the word really has four letters), perhaps followed by some parameters. The recipient sends back status messages. Each message starts with a three-digit number identifying the message so that dumb computers can use the numbers to figure out what's going on without having to try to read the text that follows.

Note: The following examples use S: and R: to identify lines from the sender and the recipient, respectively. Putting commands and responses in upper-case is historically conventional, although today the commands can be uppercase, lowercase, or mixed.

Suppose that `aaron@aardvark.com` is sending a message to `zeppo@zebra.org`. The sender, `aardvark.com`, makes a connection to the recipient's server at `zebra.org`. The first computer to speak after the connection is made is the recipient:

```
R: 220 ZEBRA.ORG Mail server version 123.4A ready
```

Then the sender sends a HELO (we already said these commands aren't spelled very well) to identify itself, and the recipient acknowledges it:

```
S: HELO AARDVARK.COM
R: 250 Hi, AARDVARK.COM, pleased to meet you
```

(Mail programmers have a sense of humor too, sort of.) Then the sender announces that a piece of mail is coming and who it's from, followed by a recipient (spelled RCPT) line, identifying who the mail is for:

```
S: MAIL FROM:<aaron@aardvark.com>
```

```
R: 250 OK
S: RCPT TO:<zeppo@zebra.org>
R: 250 OK
```

If more than one recipient exists, more than one RCPT command can be used. Here's a command for an invalid address:

```
S: RCPT TO:<elvis@zebra.org>
R: 550 No such user here
```

The recipients having been named, the sender prepares to send the text of the message:

```
S: DATA
R: 354 Start mail input; end with <CRLF>.<CRLF>
```

Then the sender sends the literal text of the message, ending with a line consisting of a single dot:

```
S: From: aaron@aardvark.com
S: To: zeppo@zebra.com
S: Subject: lunch
S: Date: 14 Sep 1997 11:30:00 EDT
S:
S: How about lunch at the Glenwood?
S: .
R: 250 OK
```

The OK response means that the message has been accepted. That's it; a QUIT command wraps up the session:

```
S: QUIT
R: 221 Sayonara
```

You can actually send mail this way by using a telnet program to connect to a host and typing very carefully. (No provision for correcting typing errors exists because SMTP is intended for computers, not for humans.) As is common in computer-to-computer communications, this exchange is a half-duplex conversation. One side talks, then the other side, and then the first, alternately, until they're done.

Had Enough?

That wraps up our tour of the bowels of the Internet. Please remember to leave your hard hats at the exit and to wipe your feet on the way out.

If you're a glutton for punishment, the documents that define all these protocols and many, many others, are available online. They are, as standard computer documents go, fairly readable, which means that they sort of make sense if you stare at them for a long time. The Internet documents are known, for some ancient reason, as Request For Comment documents, or RFCs. (You can comment all you want about TCP, IP, UDP, and SMTP, but it's about 12 years too late now.) Some RFCs define standards, some comment on problems with standards or propose changes, and many propose possible standards that never went anywhere. You can find RFCs at the InterNIC. The Web page is `http://www.internic.net/ds/dspg0intdoc.html`. Each RFC is numbered, and more than 2,000 of them exist. A few RFCs you may, maybe, want to look at are

- **rfc768:** User Datagram Protocol (UDP)
- **rfc791:** Internet Protocol (IP)
- **rfc792:** Internet Control Message Protocol (source quench and all that)
- **rfc793:** Transport Control Protocol (TCP)
- **rfc821:** Simple Mail Transfer Protocol (SMTP)
- **rfc822:** Format of Mail Messages

Web pages and downloadable files with an index of all the RFCs and the RFCs that define actual Internet standards also are available.

Appendix

Internet Country Codes

● ●

*T*his appendix contains a list of the two-letter country codes found at the end of Internet e-mail addresses and in World Wide Web domain names.

New countries join the Net every month. For the latest version of this table, visit http://net.dummies.net/countries/.

In this table, *I* means that the country is connected to the Internet, and *M* means that it has an e-mail-only connection.

Country Code	Connection Type	Country
AF		Afghanistan
AL	I	Albania
DZ	I	Algeria
AS		American Samoa
AD	I	Andorra
AO	M	Angola
AI	M	Anguilla
AQ	I	Antarctica
AG	I	Antigua and Barbuda
AR	I	Argentina
AM	I	Armenia
AW	I	Aruba
AU	I	Australia
AT	I	Austria
AZ	I	Azerbaijan
BS	M	Bahamas
BH	I	Bahrain
BD	M	Bangladesh

(continued)

(continued)

Country Code	Connection Type	Country
BB	I	Barbados
BY	I	Belarus
BE	I	Belgium
BZ	I	Belize
BJ	I	Benin
BM	I	Bermuda
BT		Bhutan
BO	I	Bolivia
BA	M	Bosnia-Herzegovina
BW	M	Botswana
BV		Bouvet Island
BR	I	Brazil
IO		British Indian Ocean Territory
BN	I	Brunei Darussalam
BG	I	Bulgaria
BF	M	Burkina Faso (formerly Upper Volta)
BI		Burundi
KH	M	Cambodia
CM	M	Cameroon
CA	I	Canada
CV		Cape Verde
KY	I	Cayman Islands
CF	I	Central African Republic
TD	M	Chad
CL	I	Chile
CN	I	China
CX		Christmas Island (Indian Ocean)
CC		Cocos (Keeling) Islands
CO	I	Colombia
KM		Comoros
CG		Congo
CK	M	Cook Islands

Country Code	Connection Type	Country
CR	I	Costa Rica
CI	M	Cote d'Ivoire
HR	I	Croatia
CU	M	Cuba
CY	I	Cyprus
CZ	I	Czech Republic
DK	I	Denmark
DJ	I	Djibouti
DM		Dominica
DO	I	Dominican Republic
TP		East Timor
EC	I	Ecuador
EG	I	Egypt
SV	I	El Salvador
GQ		Equatorial Guinea
ER	M	Eritrea
EE	I	Estonia
ET	M	Ethiopia
FK		Falkland Islands (Malvinas)
FO	I	Faroe Islands
FJ	I	Fiji
FI	I	Finland
FR	I	France
GF	M	French Guiana
PF	M	French Polynesia
TF		French Southern Territories
GA		Gabon
GM	M	Gambia
GE	I	Georgia
DE	I	Germany
GH	I	Ghana
GI	I	Gibraltar

(continued)

(continued)

Country Code	Connection Type	Country
GR	I	Greece
GL	I	Greenland
GD	M	Grenada
GP	M	Guadeloupe
GU	I	Guam
GT	I	Guatemala
GN	M	Guinea
GW		Guinea-Bissau
GY	M	Guyana
HT	M	Haiti
HM		Heard and McDonald Islands
HN	I	Honduras
HK	I	Hong Kong
HU	I	Hungary
IS	I	Iceland
IN	I	India
ID	I	Indonesia
IR	I	Iran
IQ		Iraq
IE	I	Ireland
IL	I	Israel
IT	I	Italy
JM	I	Jamaica
JP	I	Japan
JO	I	Jordan
KZ	I	Kazakhstan
KE	I	Kenya
KI	M	Kiribati
KP		Korea (North)
KR	I	Korea (South)
KW	I	Kuwait
KG	I	Kyrgyz Republic

Country Code	Connection Type	Country
LA	M	Laos
LV	I	Latvia
LB	I	Lebanon
LS	M	Lesotho
LR		Liberia
LY		Libyan Arab Jamahiriya
LI	I	Liechtenstein
LT	I	Lithuania
LU	I	Luxembourg
MO	I	Macau (Ao-me'n)
MK	I	Macedonia
MG	I	Madagascar
MW	M	Malawi
MY	I	Malaysia
MV		Maldives
ML	M	Mali
MT	I	Malta
MH	M	Marshall Islands
MQ		Martinique
MR		Mauritania
MU	I	Mauritius
YT		Mayotte
MX	I	Mexico
FM		Micronesia
MD	I	Moldova
MC	I	Monaco
MN	I	Mongolia
MS		Montserrat
MA	I	Morocco
MZ	I	Mozambique
MM		Myanmar
NA	I	Namibia

(continued)

(continued)

Country Code	Connection Type	Country
NR	M	Nauru
NP	I	Nepal
NL	I	Netherlands
AN	M	Netherlands Antilles
NC	M	New Caledonia
NZ	I	New Zealand
NI	I	Nicaragua
NE	M	Niger
NG	M	Nigeria
NU	M	Niue
NF	I	Norfolk Island
MP		Northern Mariana Islands
NO	I	Norway
OM		Oman
PK	I	Pakistan
PW		Palau
PA	I	Panama
PG	M	Papua New Guinea
PY	I	Paraguay
PE	I	Peru
PH	I	Philippines
PN		Pitcairn
PL	I	Poland
PT	I	Portugal
PR	I	Puerto Rico
QA		Qatar
RE	I	Réunion
RO	I	Romania
RU	I	Russian Federation
RW		Rwanda
SH		Saint Helena
KN		Saint Kitts and Nevis

Country Code	Connection Type	Country
LC	I	Saint Lucia
PM		Saint Pierre and Miquelon
VC	M	Saint Vincent and the Grenadines
WS	M	Samoa
SM	I	San Marino
ST		São Tome and Principe
SA	I	Saudi Arabia
SN	I	Senegal
SC	M	Seychelles
SL	M	Sierra Leone
SG	I	Singapore
SK	I	Slovakia
SI	I	Slovenia
SB	M	Solomon Islands
SO		Somalia
ZA	I	South Africa
ES	I	Spain
LK	I	Sri Lanka
SD	M	Sudan
SR	I	Suriname
SJ	I	Svalbard and Jan Mayen Islands
SZ	M	Swaziland
SE	I	Sweden
CH	I	Switzerland
SY		Syria
TW	I	Taiwan, Province of China
TJ	M	Tajikistan
TZ	M	Tanzania
TH	I	Thailand
TG	M	Togo
TK		Tokelau
TO	M	Tonga

(continued)

(continued)

Country Code	Connection Type	Country
TT	I	Trinidad and Tobago
TN	I	Tunisia
TR	I	Turkey
TM	M	Turkmenistan
TC		Turks and Caicos Islands
TV	M	Tuvalu
UG	I	Uganda
UA	I	Ukraine
AE	I	United Arab Emirates
GB	I	United Kingdom
US	I	United States
UM		United States Minor Outlying Islands
UY	I	Uruguay
UZ	I	Uzbekistan
VU	M	Vanuatu (formerly New Hebrides)
VA	I	Vatican City State
VE	I	Venezuela
VN	M	Vietnam
VG		Virgin Islands (British)
VII		Virgin Islands (U.S.)
WF		Wallis and Futuna Islands
EH		Western Sahara
YE		Yemen
YU	M	Yugoslavia
ZR		Zaire
ZM	I	Zambia
ZW	I	Zimbabwe

Index

IDG BOOKS WORLDWIDE REGISTRATION CARD

RETURN THIS REGISTRATION CARD FOR FREE CATALOG

Title of this book: **MORE Internet For Dummies®, 3E**

My overall rating of this book: ❏ Very good [1] ❏ Good [2] ❏ Satisfactory [3] ❏ Fair [4] ❏ Poor [5]

How I first heard about this book:

❏ Found in bookstore; name: [6]

❏ Advertisement: [8]

❏ Word of mouth; heard about book from friend, co-worker, etc.: [10]

❏ Book review: [7]

❏ Catalog: [9]

❏ Other: [11]

What I liked most about this book:

What I would change, add, delete, etc., in future editions of this book:

Other comments:

Number of computer books I purchase in a year: ❏ 1 [12] ❏ 2-5 [13] ❏ 6-10 [14] ❏ More than 10 [15]

I would characterize my computer skills as: ❏ Beginner [16] ❏ Intermediate [17] ❏ Advanced [18] ❏ Professional [19]

I use ❏ DOS [20] ❏ Windows [21] ❏ OS/2 [22] ❏ Unix [23] ❏ Macintosh [24] ❏ Other: [25]_____

(please specify)

I would be interested in new books on the following subjects:

(please check all that apply, and use the spaces provided to identify specific software)

❏ Word processing: [26]

❏ Data bases: [28]

❏ File Utilities: [30]

❏ Networking: [32]

❏ Other: [34]

❏ Spreadsheets: [27]

❏ Desktop publishing: [29]

❏ Money management: [31]

❏ Programming languages: [33]

I use a PC at (please check all that apply): ❏ home [35] ❏ work [36] ❏ school [37] ❏ other: [38] _____

The disks I prefer to use are ❏ 5.25 [39] ❏ 3.5 [40] ❏ other: [41]_____

I have a CD ROM: ❏ yes [42] ❏ no [43]

I plan to buy or upgrade computer hardware this year: ❏ yes [44] ❏ no [45]

I plan to buy or upgrade computer software this year: ❏ yes [46] ❏ no [47]

Name: _____ Business title: [48] _____ Type of Business: [49]

Address (❏ home [50] ❏ work [51]/Company name: _____)

Street/Suite# _____

City [52]/State [53]/Zipcode [54]: _____ Country [55]

❏ **I liked this book!** You may quote me by name in future IDG Books Worldwide promotional materials.

My daytime phone number is _____

IDG BOOKS

®

THE WORLD OF COMPUTER KNOWLEDGE

YES!

Please keep me informed about IDG's World of Computer Knowledge.
Send me the latest IDG Books catalog.

NO POSTAGE
NECESSARY
IF MAILED
IN THE
UNITED STATES

BUSINESS REPLY MAIL

FIRST CLASS MAIL   PERMIT NO. 2605   FOSTER CITY, CALIFORNIA

IDG Books Worldwide
919 E Hillsdale Blvd, STE 400
Foster City, CA 94404-9691